W9-AVA-710

Baseball Bafflers

Quizzes, Trivia, Other Ballpark Challenges for the Hardball Know-It-All

EDITED BY FASTBALL MAKOV

Baseball Bafflers

Compilation copyright © 2001 by Sterling Publishing Company, Inc.
This edition contains the texts of the following original editions. They have been
reorganized and reset for this volume. This edition was originally published in
separate volumes under the titles:
Baseball Trivia Quiz Book © 2000 by David Brown and Mitch Williams
Baseball Brain Teasers © 1986 by Sterling Publishing Co., Inc.
Baseball's Strangest Moments ©1988 by Robert Oboski
Baseball's Zaniest Moments ©1988 by Robert Oboski
Baseball Oddities © 1998 by Wayne Stewart
Baseball Bafflers © 1999 by Wayne Stewart
Baseball's Funniest People © 1997 by Michael J. Pellowski
Test Your Baseball IQ © 1993 by Dom Forker

Baseball Bafflers 2

Compilation copyright © 2002 by Sterling Publishing Company, Inc.
This edition contains the texts of the following original editions. They have been
reorganized and reset for this volume. This edition was originally published in
separate volumes under the titles:
Baseball Trivia Quiz Book © 2000 by David Brown and Mitch Williams
Baseball Bafflers © 1999 by Wayne Stewart
Baseball's Zaniest Moments © 1999 by Robert Obojski
Baseball Oddities © 1998 by Wayne Stewart
Baseball's Funniest People © 1997 by Michael J. Pellowski
Test Your Baseball IQ © 1993 by Dom Forker
Baseball's Strangest Moments © 1988 by Robert Obojski
Baseball Brain Teasers © 1986 by Sterling Publishing Co., Inc.

All rights reserved. No part of this book may be reproduced in any form or by any
electronic or mechanical means including information storage and retrieval systems,
without written permission from the publisher.

Published by:
Tess Press, an imprint of
Black Dog & Leventhal Publishers, Inc.
151 West 19th Street
New York, New York 10011

Cover design Paige Rosenberg
Book design by Martin Lubin Graphic Design
Printed in the United States of America
h g f e d c b a
ISBN-10: 1-57912-605-7
ISBN-13: 978-1-57912-605-6

CONTENTS

Introduction
7

Baseball's Strangest Moments
9

Baseball's Funny Moments
57

You're the Manager
99

You're the Umpire
129

Baseball Trivia
165

Baseball Bloopers
189

Baseball Oddities
209

More Baseball Trivia
221

Outrageous Episodes
229

Baseball's Funniest People
307

You Make the Call
333

The Last Pitch
353

Roster
361

INTRODUCTION

Baseball, on the surface, is a very simple game. Beneath the surface, however, it is a very complex sport. The National Pastime has been played for 101 years—since 1900—in the modern era. Every play that has ever taken place on a major league diamond is covered in the rule book and its amendments. The umpires know the official rule book from cover to cover. Yet, new and unusual plays are constantly taking place, before they can be covered in the rule book, and umpires are still huddling with each other to interpret these new situations. If the official interpreters of the game can be stumped, it is not surprising that we, fans, reporters and followers of the sport, can be confused, too.

Some of the new twists that have come up include the following:
1) A non-pitcher who committed a balk without touching the ball
2) Four stolen bases on one pitch 3) A runner stealing first base, and
4) A batter-runner circling the bases in reverse order after a home run!

Would you anticipate such plays? Of course not. Does the umpire anticipate such plays? Again, the answer is no. But he has to be ready to react to them. He has to be informed. So should you. This book will teach you to be in the right position—as an umpire or a manager—to call these tricky plays.

Baseball, on the surface, is a very structured sport. Beneath the surface, however, as sports announcer Joe Garagiola has said, it can be a funny game.

It's a game which has more than its share of oddities—of wild and interesting characters, of unusual plays, of crazy coincidences and witty quotes. You will find some of these humorous, sometimes bizarre, incidents in the following pages

Finally, the hardball trivia chapter will truly test your baseball I.Q. with everything from entertaining "Who said it?" match-ups to challenging "Who Am I?" quizzes.

Baseball Bafflers offers a look at the other side of the sport, the fun part that made us fall in love with this wonderful game in the first place. So, sit back, relax, and enjoy.

Baseball's Strangest Moments

MULHOLLAND'S MITT MAGIC

After watching baseball for decades, many fans come to believe that they've seen it all. In reality, the nature of baseball is such that just about the time you start to become blase, something odd will come along to make you shout, "Wow!"

One such play occurred on September 3, 1986, when a San Francisco Giants rookie pitcher named Terry Mulholland made an amazing fielding play. He was facing the New York Mets in the third inning when he stabbed a hard grounder off the bat of Keith Hernandez. It turned out the Mets All Star had drilled the ball so hard, it became lodged in Mulholland's glove. The southpaw hurler tried to pull the ball loose, but he also realized time was running out, and Hernandez would soon reach base safely. So, he trotted a few strides towards first base, gave up on freeing the ball, removed his glove (the ball still nestled inside), and tossed the glove to the first baseman, Bob Brenly. The umpire didn't miss a beat as he correctly ruled that Hernandez was out—in a truly bizarre play.

OPTICAL ILLUSION

During a 1969 game between the Atlanta Braves and the Houston Astros, a Houston base runner committed a terrible base running blunder. His mistake wasn't due to disobeying a coach, being outwitted by an opponent, or being unaware of the game situation. Instead, it was his own faulty eyesight that that duped him.

It began with the runner taking a normal lead off third base. As the pitcher began his delivery, the runner danced down the base paths a few steps. Then, upon seeing the ball bounce wildly off the mitt of Atlanta catcher Bob Didier, the daring runner darted home. It's hard to say who was more astonished a few seconds later, the runner or the catcher. But both men were clearly perplexed. The runner couldn't believe his eyes because there was Didier, still squatting at the plate with the ball in his mitt. Didier had certainly not missed the ball and was wondering why the runner would dash for a well-guarded home plate. Didier, however, was not so baffled that he didn't easily apply the tag for a ridiculously easy out.

MORE HUMILIATION

Max West was playing for the Boston Red Sox when he perpetrated a strange faux pas. It started innocently enough when West was retired at first base on a routine groundout. On the play, a teammate advanced to third base. West trudged back to his dugout, and he apparently was extremely slow in doing so. As he was about to descend the steps and make his way to the bench, he spied a baseball.

He probably assumed the ball had been fouled off by the next batter. So, as a friendly gesture, West stooped over, picked up the ball, and tossed it to the enemy catcher to save him a few steps.

But the ball had not been fouled off! It was in play, having escaped from the catcher after a pitch. In other words, it was a passed ball that would permit the runner off third to score. And, normally he would have scored with ease, but not when a teammate throws a perfect strike to the opposing catcher.

Needless to say, the runner was nailed at the plate. An official scorekeeper might even be tempted to teasingly give West an assist on the play. It's not quite certain what West's manager wanted to give him. But we can only imagine.

LOOPHOLE

Don Hoak of the Pittsburgh Pirates is said to have searched for, and actually found, a gaping loophole in baseball's record book. During a game in the 1960s, he reached second base. The next batter hit a long foul ball down the left-field line. Since Hoak couldn't be certain at first if the ball might drop in fair territory, he ran full speed for third base.

When the third base coach told him to hold up, that the ball was indeed foul, Hoak slowed down. He did not, however, retrace his steps back to second base, as is the normal procedure. Instead, he stayed in his tracks just a few steps away from third.

The umpire was puzzled and asked Hoak what he was doing. Hoak replied, "I'm taking my lead." There was no rule saying he had to return to second, and there certainly was no rule limiting the lead a runner could take off a base.

Therefore, the pitcher was given the ball and told to resume play. When the pitcher toed the rubber to get his sign for the next pitch, Hoak simply took a large stride and reached third base. Officially he was awarded a stolen base. Unofficially, he could joke with teammates about the great jump he got. Finally, a rule was devised to prohibit such tactics ever again.

Hoak's ingenuity was reminiscent of a Bill Veeck line.

Famous for taking advantage of any weakness in the rulebook, Veeck once proclaimed, "I try not to break the rules, but merely to test their elasticity."

BIZARRE BASE BURGLARY

Contrary to a widely held belief, Herman "Germany" Schaefer was not the first man to "steal" first base. Still, his story is such a classic it's worth repeating as a sort of Ripley's Believe-It-or-Not play. In 1911, while playing for the Washington Senators, Schaefer was on first base while a teammate, Clyde Milan, was taking his lead off third. On the next pitch, Schaefer took off for second, hoping to draw a throw from the catcher that might allow the runner from third to score. Instead of succeeding on this double steal, Schaefer was able to take second unimpeded, since the catcher offered no throw.

Undaunted, on the next pitch Schaefer scampered back to first base, and was again ignored by the catcher. That was fine with Schaefer, known to be the "clown prince" of baseball. In this case, however, he had more in mind that just foolery.

His plan was to retreat to that base in order to set up the double steal again. Of course, he wasn't officially credited with a steal of first, but it's said that he did rattle the pitcher.

So, on the very next pitch, Schaefer again streaked for second. For the second time in a matter of moments he stole that base. It's almost enough to lead to a facetious search of the record books for an entry; "Most times stealing the same base during one at bat, twice by Schaefer, 1911."

What's more, the runner from third finally did cross home in one of the game's most peculiar plays ever. Needless to say, nowadays there is a rule forbidding such an event. The rulebook bans such tactics, as it makes a "travesty of the game."

THE CASE OF THE DISAPPEARING BASEBALL

In 1958, Leon Wagner was a raw rookie for the San Francisco Giants. During a July game, the opposing Chicago Cubs took advantage of his inexperience. Cubs' batter Tony Taylor hit a shot to left field, where Wagner was positioned.

The ball bounded into the Cubs' bullpen before Wagner could track it down. He did notice, though, that the relief pitchers, who were viewing the game from that location, scattered. When those relievers stared under their bench, Wagner knew the ball had come to rest there.

He was wrong. He had been fooled by the enemy, who realized the ball had actually gone beyond the bullpen. In truth, the ball had come to a stop about 45 feet further down the foul line. It was nestled in a rain gutter. By the time Wagner understood he had been faked out, Taylor had breezed around the bases for one of the oddest inside-the-park homers ever.

DON'T ROLL THAT TARPAULIN COLEMAN MIGHT BE INSIDE!

Back in the old days, tarpaulins were spread out to cover baseball fields overnight and then rolled back manually by groundskeepers. Today, electrically operated tarps have become vogue. Push a button and it can be spread over the infield in a jiffy—push another button and it can be rolled back just as quickly.

One of the classiest of all powered retractable tarps is operated at St. Louis' Busch Stadium, and by sheer accident it became a cause célèbre during the 1985 League Championship Series between the Cardinals and Los Angeles Dodgers. Vince Coleman, the Cards' star outfielder and base stealing king, happened to be standing on the tarp along the first base side, casually warming up before the series fifth game, when a ground-crew member, not realizing anyone was still on the tarp, activated the rollup button. Within a second or two,

Coleman found himself trapped inside, being swallowed up as if a giant boa constrictor had wrapped its coils around him.

Coleman's screams brought out a rescue team, but not before some damage was done. His legs were so badly bruised that he could neither play in that fifth game, nor in the ensuing World Series that saw the Cardinals matched against the Kansas City Royals.

"The Coleman-tarpaulin episode certainly ranks as one of the strangest on-field accidents in baseball history," a St. Louis sportswriter commented.

"That tarp was a real man-eater," Coleman himself commented.

Sometimes when Busch Stadium is very quiet, one can almost hear faint murmuring from deep inside the tarpaulin machine, below the green artificial turf near first base. "Vince," the machine seems to gurgle, like the crocodile seeking the rest of Captain Hook in *Peter Pan*. "Vince, come a little closer to me, Vince."

Coleman, sensing that the tarp machine's appetite still may not be satiated since it tried to ingest him, runs faster than ever now—away from that "monster" machine.

TWO BALLS IN PLAY AT SAME TIME AN UMPIRE'S MENTAL LAPSE

A college professor can be excused for being absent-minded, but not a big league umpire during the course of a ball game. Because Vic Delmore became absent-minded at a St. Louis Cardinals—Chicago Cubs game played at Wrigley Field on June 30, 1959, he caused one of the strangest and most bizarre plays in baseball history.

The Cards' top hitter Stan Musial was at bat with a 3-1 count when the next pitch got away from Cub catcher Sammy Taylor and skidded toward the backstop.

Umpire Delmore called "Ball four" and Musial trotted toward first. But Taylor and pitcher Bob Anderson argued vehemently with the ump that it was a foul tip.

Since the ball was still in play, and Taylor had not chased it, Musial ran toward second. Fast-thinking third baseman Alvin Dark then raced to the backstop and retrieved the ball. Meanwhile, Delmore was still involved in the argument with the Cubs' battery mates when he unthinkingly pulled a second ball out of his pocket and handed it to catcher Taylor. Suddenly noticing Musial dashing for second, pitcher Anderson grabbed the new ball and threw to second—at the same time that Dark threw to shortstop Ernie Banks with the original ball!

Anderson's throw sailed over second base into center field. Musial saw the ball fly past his head, so—not realizing there were two balls in play—he took off for third only to run smack into Banks who tagged him out with the original ball.

After a lengthy conference, the umpires ruled that Musial was out since he was tagged with the original ball.

Also called "out" was Vic Delmore himself. Citing a "lack of confidence" in Vic, National League President Warren Giles fired him at season's end.

HIT A HOMER IN JAPAN AND WIN A SWORD

Earl Averill, the Cleveland Indians hard-hitting center fielder, was a part of the delegation of American League All-Stars who traveled to the Orient in the fall of 1934 to play a series of 16 exhibition games against a team of Japan's top amateur and semi-professional players called the "All-Nippon Stars."

Averill's teammates included stars Babe Ruth and Lou Gehrig, sluggers Bing Miller, Charlie Gehringer and Jimmie Foxx, and pitchers Lefty Gomez and Earl Whitehill. The exhibitions were staged in cities throughout Japan, and by the time the series ended in late November the Americans had made a clean sweep by winning all 16 games.

One particular game between the Japanese and the Americans, played at Itatsu Stadium in Kokura, an industrial city on the island of Kyushu,

"May I honor you with this sword?"

revealed quite graphically the almost limitless enthusiasm the Japanese have for baseball. Rain fell the night before the game, which was scheduled for 2 p.m. on November 26, and the precipitation continued steadily as game time approached. The fans, however, didn't allow bad weather to prevent them from seeing a contest they had been eagerly anticipating, particularly since this was the only appearance the two teams would make in Kokura.

Hard-core baseball aficionados began lining up at the gates outside the park at 5 A.M. and when the gates opened around noon, some 11,000 persons had "bleacher" tickets. The catch was that there were no seats in the bleachers, which consisted only of the bare outfield turf. Unfortunately, the outfield was by then ankle deep in water, so the hardy bleacherites had to stand, kneel, or squat in the shallow lake for the entire game. (The total crowd reached 20,000 that day. Itatsu Stadium had only 9,000 permanent seats in addition to its "bleacher" capacity.) The fans in the outfield did not permit this minor inconvenience to dampen their enthusiasm for the big game, nor were they too disappointed when the All-Nippon Stars lost 8-1. They saw a well-played contest and, for the first time, got a chance to view close up the big American stars Babe Ruth and Lou Gehrig, about whom they'd read and heard so much.

One spectator, a middle-aged shopkeeper, walked 80 miles to see the game at Kokura, and he carried a sword which he vowed to give to the first American smashing a home run against the All-Nippon Stars. This valuable trophy was won by Earl Averill, who drove a long homer into the right field seats. It was the highest possible honor he could have received:

Among the Japanese, a sword was not only a weapon, but also the warrior's badge of honor—it was thought to be his very soul.

When we spoke with Averill at Cooperstown's Hotel Otesaga in July 1981, just two years before his death, he recalled the 1934 Japanese tour and the game in Kokura. "That Japanese sword is the most unusual and prized trophy I ever received in baseball, and I've kept it in a glass case at my home in Snahomish [Washington] all these years," Averill said.

Averill hit 8 home runs on the 1934 exhibition series, while Babe Ruth paced the long ball parade with 13 homers. That trip to Japan marked Babe Ruth's last appearance in a New York Yankees uniform, incidentally, since in February 1935 he was handed his unconditional release.

GET THE X-RAY MACHINES READY!
NO CORK IN THE BATS, PLEASE!

In a mid-August 1987 game against the San Francisco Giants, New York Mets third baseman Howard Johnson poled a mighty home run at Shea Stadium, that allegedly measured about 480 feet. Roger Craig, the Giants manager, charged out of the dugout and told the umpires the bat should be impounded and turned over to league officials for examination.

"There's no way Howard Johnson could hit a ball that far without the bat being corked," Craig fumed.

"Check that one again."

Johnson's bat was taken to National League President A. Bartlett Giamatti's office, and from that point it was sent out to a nearby hospital where it was X-rayed for cork. The X-rays proved negative. No cork was found in the barrel.

According to newly established major league rules, the manager of each team is allowed to challenge one bat during the course of a game. Since challenges are being registered in so many games, both the National and American League offices are considering buying their own X-ray machines in order to cut down on fees being paid to hospitals!

When cork is placed in the barrel of a bat, the batter is able to speed up his swing and hit for greater distances. Bats are supposed to be constructed of wood—and no other substance.

When manager Craig registered his protest, he noted that Johnson had never hit more than 12 homers in one season during his big league career before 1986 but he slammed more than 36 in 1987. He believed equipment tampering caused this phenomenon.

Ah, but Craig didn't realize that Johnson has been on well-planned weight and strength programs and had no need for corked bats in order to sock baseballs into orbit.

HIT ON HEAD BY BAT
WHILE IN ON-DECK CIRCLE

In 1945, Mobile catcher Harry Chozen had hit safely in 33 consecutive games and was on his way to setting a new Southern Association record of hitting safely in 49 consecutive games. Then, while kneeling in the on-deck circle, he was hit on the head and knocked unconscious by a flying bat that slipped from the hands of teammate Pete Thomassie as he followed through on a vicious swing. Chozen was forced to retire from the game.

After this episode, Chozen proceeded to hit safely in 16 additional games before being stopped. Southern Association President Billy Evans was called upon to rule, and decided that Chozen's failure to get a hit in that July 6 game, where he had walked in his only time at bat before being knocked out, did not break the hitting streak. The record Chozen broke stood for 20 years.

Chozen's record is interesting in several other ways. Twice during the streak he was used as a pinch hitter and delivered. On two other occasions, he entered the game in late innings, batting only once in each game, but he still managed to get his base hit. He broke the previous record of 46 in a truly dramatic manner by smashing a long home run in his first at bat in his forty-seventh game. (Chozen's only big league experience came in 1937 at the age of 22, when he caught one game for the Cincinnati Reds. He had a single in four trips to the plate.)

However, during an August 1978 game, Los Angeles Dodgers catcher Steve Yeager wasn't quite as lucky as Chozen in a batting circle accident. A Dodgers hitter broke his bat on a pitch causing a jagged piece of ash to sail straight for Yeager's throat. The team's trainer and doctor worked with lightning speed to remove the splintered wood from the jugular vein area. Yeager might otherwise have choked and bled to death. But after a couple of weeks on the disabled list, Yeager was back in action.

CENTER FIELDER CARLISLE MAKES UNASSISTED TRIPLE PLAY

The unassisted triple play is one of the rarest plays in baseball, with only 8 having occurred in the major leagues, and only a handful in the minors.

But Walter Carlisle, a center fielder for the L.A.-based Vernon team, on July 19, 1911, in a game against the Los Angeles Angels, executed perhaps the most spectacular unassisted triple play in professional baseball history.

With the score tied in the ninth inning, Charles Moore and George Metzger of the Angels walked. Pitcher Al Carson of Vernon was replaced by Harry Stewart. The Angels' third baseman, Roy Akin, connected on Stewart's first pitch for a low line drive over second base for what appeared to be a clean single. Moore from second and Metzger from first were off running on a hit-and-run signal. Carlisle, playing in close behind second, lunged forward and caught the liner just off the turf, ending with a somersault, landing on his feet (he had been a circus acrobat). He raced to second base and touched the bag, while Moore was well on his way to the plate. Then he trotted to first, touching the bag to retire Metzger, who was still well past second.

Carlisle's name is secure in the record books, since he is the only outfielder to have pulled off the unassisted triple play. (Tris Speaker, the Hall of Fame center fielder active in the majors 1907–28, mostly with the Boston Red Sox and Cleveland, usually played in close and made several unassisted double plays. But Speaker never came close to running off the solo triple play.)

In recognition of Carlisle's singular achievement, the Vernon and Los Angeles fans presented him with a diamond-studded gold medal.

CRAMER AND WILLIAMS: A CLASSIC COLLISION IN THE OUTFIELD

When this writer was still in primary school, he saw one of his first big league games ever at Cleveland's Municipal Stadium on Sunday, June 23, 1940, as the Indians faced the Boston Red Sox.

In the eighth inning, Cleveland second baseman Ray Mack lined a drive deep into the left center field gap, with center fielder Doc Cramer and left fielder Ted Williams converging on the ball. In their mad dash they didn't see each other, collided head-on, and were both knocked unconscious as the ball rolled to the gate at the 463-foot sign. Mack got an easy inside-the-park homer.

Cramer was the first to get up, and after getting a whiff of smelling salts from the trainer, he was able to continue on in the game. But poor Ted Williams was carried off the field on a stretcher, and taken to a local hospital to have his fractured jaw repaired. "Ted the Kid" remained hospitalized for a couple of days and missed more than a week's worth of action.

It was always my impression that the collision was Cramer's fault because he was a 12-year big league veteran and should have directed the play on Mack's drive, while Williams was only a 22-year-old sophomore in the league.

We finally got our chance to question Williams about the play 47 years after it happened, at the 1987 Hall of Fame Induction Ceremonies at Cooperstown. Williams said: "Hell no, don't blame that collision on Cramer, it was my fault. I took off like crazy after Mack's liner and ran into Doc ... if I left him alone, he would have had a good chance to flag it down. From that day on, I tried to look where I was going in the outfield."

PIERSALL CLUBS 100TH HOMER, RUNS THE BASES BACKWARDS

When Jimmy Piersall, one of the most uninhibited spirits in baseball history, slammed out his 100th major league homer while playing for the Washington Senators in 1963, he celebrated the occasion by running the bases backwards and sliding into home plate. Piersall probably thought at the time that this was going to be his last big home run—actually he managed to hit four more before he retired in 1967. Anyway, the league ruled that running the wrong way was illegal thereafter.

THE STRANGE CASE OF PETE GRAY, ONE-ARMED OUTFIELDER

Good ballplayers were extremely scarce during World War II, and the public, as well as the government, wanted baseball to carry on. The result was that many of the big leaguers of the 1942–45 period were those who were too young for the draft, or were classified 4-F (not physically fit for military duty).

The most famous 4-F of them all was one-armed outfielder Pete Gray, who had batted a solid .333 and had 68 stolen bases for the Memphis Chicks in 1944, achievements that won him election as the Southern Association's Most Valuable Player. Gray became the talk of the big league world because his play in the S.A. was so impressive. The lowliest team, the St. Louis Browns, eagerly signed him for the 1945 campaign.

Gray had lost his right arm at the bicep in a boyhood accident, but he developed his left arm to such a degree and compensated for his handicap with such quickness that he became a really solid ballplayer. Gray had started out as a sandlot player in the Nanticoke, Pennsylvania, area as a teenager, and landed his first professional contract with Three Rivers, Ontario, of the Canadian-American League in 1942, at the age of 25. From that point, he moved up the minor league ladder rapidly.

This writer saw Gray in action several times with the Browns in 1945, and vividly recalls his performance against the Indians at Cleveland's Municipal Stadium in one particular four-game series in early June. Gray cracked out 7 hits, including a triple and a double—both hard-hit line drives to deep leftcenter—in 17 at-bats. Moreover, he fielded his leftfield post flawlessly. After catching a fly ball, he would flip his glove under the stump of his right arm in a rapid-fire motion so that he could throw the ball with his bare left hand.

Gray batted only .218 in the tough American League competition. Amazingly enough, however, he struck out only 11 times in 234 official at-bats. When Gray took the field either in a minor league or major league park, no one ever did him any favors—he got along on his own grit. As a result, he became an inspiration, during and after the war, to the multitude of disabled U.S. war veterans.

Gray unfortunately found himself back in the minors once the war was over. He retired from active play after a season with Dallas of the Texas League in 1949.

"GOOFY" GOMEZ
STOPS PITCHING IN WORLD SERIES
TO WATCH PASSING AIRPLANE

Vernon "Lefty" Gomez, one of the most colorful players in big league history, anchored the New York Yankees pitching staff during the 1930s. He became a 20-game winner four times, and wound up with an imposing 189-102 career record. Moreover, he won six World Series games without a loss (a record), and went 3-1 in 1930s All-Star competition. He was elected to the Hall of Fame in 1972.

No matter how critical the situation became on the baseball field, Lefty never lost his sharp sense of humor, and because of his constant practical joking he became known as "El Goofo" or just plain "Goofy" Gomez.

Gomez's most memorable goof occurred during the second game of the 1936 World Series against the hard-hitting New York Giants at the Polo Grounds.

More than 50 years after this episode, Gomez remembered it well as he related:

"It was early in the game, I was a little wild and before I knew it, there were two runners on base. Suddenly I heard a plane flying over the ballpark—it was a big airliner—and I just stepped off the mound, forgot about the runners, the batter, the game and everything else. I stood there watching calmly, until the plane completely disappeared from sight.

"Sure, I kept 45,000 fans (as well as the players) waiting and everyone wondered why I stopped the game this way ... some people thought I was just plain crazy. Well, I was a little tense and I wanted to ease the tension a bit. As I recall, I came out of that inning pretty well unscathed."

The Yankees went on to whip the Giants 18-4 as Gomez went the distance, walking 7 and striking out 8.

The mists of antiquity may have settled a bit on the details of that game, but Lefty Gomez will always be remembered as the player who stopped the World Series dead in its tracks to watch an airplane in flight.

YOGI BERRA STRIKES OUT THREE TIMES, "NOT NOWHERE" WILL HE PLAY LIKE THAT

Yogi Berra is one of the power hitters of yesteryear who almost always seemed to get his bat on the ball, and managed to keep his strikeouts down to an extremely low level.

When he came up with the Yankees at the tail end of the 1946 season, Berra indicated quite clearly through his performance in the seven games he played in that he wasn't going to let too many third strikes slip by him. During those games, he bashed 2 homers and struck out only once. From that point on, Berra, a lefthanded pull hitter who was built like a fireplug (he stood 5-feet-8 inches high and weighed a solid 190 pounds), enjoyed five full seasons where his homers exceeded his K's: 1950–28, 12; 1951–27, 20; 1952–30, 24; 1955–27, 20; and 1956–30, 29.

In nearly two decades of big league play (1946–65), covering 2,120 games, Yogi hit 358 homers against only 415 strikeouts. Moreover, in 14 World Series from 1947 to 1963, covering 75 games, Berra hammered 12 homers against only 17 strikeouts.

Berra didn't play at all in 1964 when he managed the pennant-winning Yankees. And, after he was fired for losing the World Series, he landed on his feet as a coach for the New York Mets in 1965.

The struggling Mets needed an extra catcher badly, and so, Berra, then 40, was pressed into service. Berra saw action in only four games before he threw in the towel. In one game, he struck out three times. Afterward he told reporters : "I never struck out three times in one game before: not in the big leagues, not in the minor leagues, not in the little leagues, not nowhere. Now it's time to quit for good."

If everyone in the big leagues today who struck out three times in one game would voluntarily retire himself, the playing ranks would be surely decimated.

GAME BORES MANAGER— LEAVES BENCH FOR HOT DOG

When Luke Appling was managing the Kansas City Athletics on an interim basis late in the 1967 season, he became so bored with the game that he went up behind the grandstand and ordered a hot dog and beer from a refreshment stand. He didn't come back down into the dugout until he had finished his repast. As a result, Appling, an easy-going

Southerner, was not invited to manage the Athletics for the 1968 season.

Appling, Hall of Fame shortstop, who played 20 years for the Chicago White Sox (1930–50), remained in various coaching capacities, even after his Kansas City experience. He made baseball headlines in 1985, when at the age of 78, he slammed a home run into the leftfield stands at Washington, D.C.'s Robert F. Kennedy Stadium during an Old-Timers' Game.

In 1987, Appling was still listed as batting coach for the Atlanta Braves.

TURNER MANAGES HIS BRAVES FOR ONE DAY

There had been eccentric team owners before. But when the flamboyant advertising billboard and television tycoon, Robert Edward "Ted" Turner III, bought the Atlanta Braves in 1975, little did the world of baseball realize how strange the diamond game could become with a completely uninhibited owner running a major league franchise.

Turner was at his outrageous best during a special "Field Day" staged at Atlanta Stadium shortly after he took charge of the Braves. He got down on his hands and knees, and pushed a baseball with his nose from third base to home plate.

Also, in his earlier days as team owner, he was often the star attraction at home games, where his rooting from his private box became so boisterous that fans often paid their way into the park just to see Turner

Ted Turner on Field Day

in action. In typical Turner fashion, he would settle into his seat, doff his jacket, stuff a plug of chewing tobacco into his face, and bellow "Awwriiight!" every time one of his players batted in a run or made an outstanding play in the field. Or after a foul ball sailed into the seats, his celebrated frugal streak became activated as he sighed, "There goes four dollars," and, after three more fouls followed, he groaned "Sixteen dollars!"

Once his Braves became so deeply mired in the second division, that Turner threatened to call up his entire Savannah farm team to replace all of his Atlanta regulars.

Early in the 1977 season, Atlanta, under manager Dave Bristol, began floundering badly, and on May 10, the situation reached a climax when the Braves lost their 16th straight game. Turner could stand it no longer, so he ordered Bristol to go off on a 10-day "scouting trip" and appointed himself manager. On May 11, tempestuous Ted donned a uniform, ensconced himself in the dugout between two of his most trusted coaches (Eddie Haas and Vic Correll), and formally took over the reins as Braves pilot.

His players cringed at the sight of Turner in uniform because they knew his knowledge of the game's techniques was severely limited. For example, in his first days as owner, as his deputies explained the rudiments of baseball to him, Turner blurted, "What the hell is a bunt?" Despite the cringing and grumbling of his players, Turner called the shots for the entire game—with the assistance of his coaches—but he could do no better than Bristol as the Braves proceeded to lose their 17th straight game (to Pittsburgh) 2-1.

Most of the nation's baseball fans merely laughed off this moment of comic relief, and Turner felt himself ready to manage for a while longer. However, National League President Charles S. Feeney was not amused, and advised Turner that he was in violation of Major League Rule 20, which states in part: "No manager or player on a club shall directly or indirectly own stock or have any financial interest in the club by which he is employed except under an agreement approved by the commissioner..."

Commissioner Bowie Kuhn refused to give such approval, and Ted Turner's managerial career ended after a single game in the dugout.

In that 1977 season, Atlanta finished dead last in the National League's West Division with a dismal 61-101 record. However Turner is still officially listed in all the standard baseball record books as being manager for a day with an 0-1 record.

PITCHES FOR 23 TEAMS IN 13 LEAGUES DURING A 27-YEAR CAREER

In an active baseball career that spanned 27 years (1924–50), Walter "Boom-Boom" Beck, a native of Decatur, Illinois, spent a good deal of his time traveling as he pitched for a total of 23 teams in 13 different leagues, including both major leagues. In addition to his American and National League experience, Beck toiled in the following circuits that are obscure to many fans: Three-I League, Texas Association, Western League, American Association, International League, Southern Association, Pacific Coast League, Inter-State League, Southeast League, Central League and Middle Atlantic League. (In the latter three leagues, he was a player-manager.)

As a major leaguer, the righthanded-throwing Beck saw action with the St. Louis Browns, Brooklyn Dodgers, Philadelphia Phillies, Detroit Tigers, Cincinnati Reds and Pittsburgh Pirates, and posted a 38-69 record in 265 games. In the minors, he went 199-167, making his total pro regular season record come to just one victory over .500, or 237-236.

Beck enjoyed his finest season in the minors with the Memphis Chicks in 1932, when he rolled up an impressive 27-6 mark to rank as the leading pitcher in the Southern Association. That earned him a return trip to the big leagues in 1933, this time with Brooklyn, and it was in Flatbush that Beck earned his unusual nickname.

While pitching against the Phillies on a sweltering 1934 afternoon in Philadelphia's Baker Bowl, Beck was removed from the game by manager Casey Stengel while still holding a slim lead. Losing his cool, Beck wound up and threw the ball with all his strength toward rightfield where it made a resounding "boom" as it struck the tin fence. Outfielder Hack Wilson, who had not been paying attention during the pitching change, heard the boom and, thinking the ball was in play, fielded it and made a perfect line throw to second base. This unusual episode caused all the fans and players, except for Beck, to laugh heartily. From that time on, Beck was known as "Boom-Boom." Wilson, a Hall of Famer, who had his best season in the majors with the Chicago Cubs when he hit 56 homers and knocked in 190 runs (the all-time major league record), was then in the twilight of his career and found himself released by the Dodgers. He signed with the Phillies later in the 1934 season.

After his playing days were over, "Boom-Boom" Beck remained in baseball for another two decades as a coach and scout at both the major and minor league levels. He died in Champaign, Illinois, on May 7, 1987, at the age of 82.

TY COBB: LONG BALL HITTER AND TIGER ON THE BASE PATHS

"Ty Cobb is absolutely the greatest ballplayer I've ever seen on the diamond, and that includes everyone I've either played with or against," declared Hall of Fame infielder, Joe Sewell, in an interview conducted in 1987 at Cooperstown's Hotel Otesaga.

Sewell went on to say:

"When not in uniform, Ty Cobb personified the true Southern gentleman, but once he put on the Detroit flannels, he seemed to change character, almost like a Jekyll and Hyde. He played every inning of every game as if it were the critical point of a World Series …. Even when he took his position in the outfield, he appeared like a tiger ready to spring.

"When he came roaring into second base on a close play, or to break up a double play, he reminded me of a runaway locomotive. He loudly proclaimed that the base line belonged to him, and felt justified in running over any infielder who got in his way. But anyone who saw me play knows I didn't bail out when Cobb barreled into second base. I gave him as much as he gave me."

No question about that because Sewell, who stood only 5 feet 7 inches and weighed 160 pounds, had the reputation of being a very scrappy and aggressive shortstop (later in his career he switched over to third base). He made up for his lack of size with his own special brand of ferocity.

In continuing to recall Cobb's exploits on the baseball diamond, Sewell said:

"When I played against Cobb in the 1920s, he was getting well on into his 30s, but age didn't stop him a bit from being a demon on the base paths. Remember that Cobb was never the fastest runner in baseball, not even when he came up to the Tigers as a kid in 1905. But he knew how to run because he studied how to stride properly … he learned to cut yards off the distance between bases by knowing how to make sharp turns and how to tag the bag on the inside. He ran in straight lines. How many times do you see players today making wide turns and running any number of unnecessary yards in circling the bases?

"Sure, I pick Ty Cobb as the greatest ballplayer of all time, even ahead of Babe Ruth," Sewell pontificated without a noticeable trace of doubt in his voice. "Remember that I played against Ruth during his peak years ... and I was his teammate on the Yankees in the early 1930s when he was still going good. Ruth hit all those home runs, but Cobb could whack the ball as hard as anyone. I know firsthand because I caught lots of his drives that nearly broke my hand.

"The sportswriters began getting on Cobb in the mid-1920s because he was still content to hit singles and doubles when the home run was just coming into vogue. So he decided to show everyone he could match Ruth or anyone else for power. If I remember correctly, it was at St. Louis' Sportsman's Park in early May 1925 that Cobb decided to take a full swing and put on a real power exhibition. In the first game of the series, he went six for six and clubbed three homers, and on the next, he hammered two more homers—that was five in two days and enough to tie the major league record. As I recall, he got two doubles in those two games that nearly cleared the wall. He just missed seven homers in two days.

"Then Cobb went back to his natural snap swing batting style, but he proved his point that hitting home runs was no great trick," Sewell added.

JOE SEWELL: "IRON MAN A TOUGH BATTER TO STRIKE OUT"

Joe Sewell broke into the big leagues under both tragic and dramatic circumstances. He was called up by the Cleveland Indians from the New Orleans Pelicans of the Southern Association on August 18, 1920. This was the day after their regular shortstop, Ray Chapman, was killed by a pitch thrown by the New York Yankees submarine artist Carl Mays at the Polo Grounds, New York. Chapman is the only player in major league history to have been killed during the course of a game.

Sewell stepped right into the shortstop slot and, with his timely hitting and good fielding, helped the Indians capture both the American League pennant and a World Series victory over the Brooklyn Dodgers.

Sewell remained with the Indians through 1930, playing mostly at shortstop, and then spent the final three years of his career with the New York Yankees as a third baseman. In 14 years of big league action, Sewell, a lefthanded hitter, banged out 2,226 base hits in 1,903 games and had a batting average of .312, a sound enough record to earn him Hall of Fame election in 1977.

Amazingly enough, Sewell struck out only 114 times in those 14 years, in over 8,000 total plate appearances (including walks, sacrifices, etc.). He whiffed but three times in both 1930 and 1932, and he struck out only four times in three other seasons—and all these were when he was a regular, playing in well over 100 games per year.

Sewell is the all-time big league champion in being the toughest man to strike out.

When we spoke with Sewell in July 1987 in Cooperstown, we asked him why so many of today's hitters are fanning so frequently, pointing out that some of them roll up 114 strikeouts even before the season winds into August.

"Because they don't keep their eye on the ball!" snapped the 89-year-old Sewell, who is still very much alert, sharp-tongued and sharp-minded. "Too many batters today swing wildly trying for the home run instead of just going with the pitch and meeting the ball. If you're talking about strange baseball, it's strange to me why so many contemporary players lack discipline and refuse to control their swings the way they should."

Sewell added:

"Don't forget that the pitchers I faced in the 1920s and 1930s were just as fast as the ones throwing today. I faced flame throwers like Walter Johnson and Lefty Grove, and they had a hard time striking me out because I had a compact swing and watched the ball the whole way. It's hard for me to imagine that legions of batters in the 1980s are striking out 125 to 150 times and more per season and not getting farmed out."

That may be because they have million-dollar contracts.

Sewell was an authentic "Iron Man" of his day, playing in 1,103 consecutive games from 1922 to 1928. At that time, Sewell's Iron Man performance ranked second only to that of Everett Scott, American League infielder who played in 1,307 games in a row from 1916 to 1925. Even now, Sewell's streak ranks as No. 5 on the all-time list. Lou Gehrig stands as No. 1, of course, with his staggering total of 2,130 straight games.

When asked why his streak finally came to a halt, Sewell replied: "One morning I got up and found out I had the flu real bad, and so I had to crawl right back into bed. Still, no one made a big fuss about playing streaks 50-60 years ago. At that time, my 1,103 straight games plus a dime would be good for a cup of coffee."

(Cal Ripken, Jr., Baltimore Orioles shortstop, established a big league record by playing 8,243 consecutive innings over the course of 908 games, but was pulled out in the eighth inning on a September 14, 1987 game by his father, manager Cal Ripken, Sr., who said: "I wanted to get everybody to stop writing about the consecutive inning streak. The media pressure on us was getting intense, and so we just had to put an end to the streak.")

Sewell also recalled: "Lifetime records didn't attract all that much attention in the old days. I remember when Tris Speaker, our manager and center fielder at Cleveland, got base hit Number 3,000 in 1925 ... there was hardly a ripple about it. The newspapers made passing mention of this milestone, but 'Spoke' received nothing in the way of special tributes."

Accordingly, Clifford Kachline, former Hall of Fame Historian and longtime baseball writer, commented that Ty Cobb received relatively little publicity when he lined out base hit No. 4,000 while playing for the Philadelphia A's in 1927.

"Just check Cobb's file in the Hall of Fame Library and you won't see any banner headlines about that milestone," Kachline said.

Also, there's no record of the President in 1927 calling from the Oval Office in the White House to congratulate Cobb. When Pete Rose broke Stan Musial's National League base hit record of 3,630, Ronald Reagan got right on the White House phone to call Rose before Rose had a chance to take his post-game shower. And when Rose got hit Number 4,192 in 1985 to pass Ty Cobb on the all-time list, Mr. Reagan got on the White House phone again to congratulate Rose again.

"Everybody is statistics-happy today, even the President of the United States," muttered Sewell.

JIMMIE FOXX AND MICKEY MANTLE: WHO HIT THE BALL HARDER?

If Jimmie Foxx had stuck more closely to training rules, he could have piled up even more impressive statistics. Through the 1940 season, when Foxx was only 33, he had already smashed out an even 500 homers. From that point on, he was only able to hit 34 more in the big leagues.

Foxx stood an even 6 feet in height, weighed about 210 pounds, and was proportioned like Charles Atlas, with a massive chest and powerful forearms. Called "The Beast" because of his enormous strength (he developed his physique as a Maryland farm boy), he could hit homers righthanded as far as Babe Ruth could hit them lefthanded.

As a member of the Boston Red Sox in 1938, he lined a shot to the deepest corner of the leftfield bleachers at Cleveland's Municipal

Stadium 435 feet away. Lots of hitters can blast baseballs 435 feet, but Foxx's line drive had so much velocity behind it that it broke the back of a wooden seat at that great distance!

On one occasion in batting practice, Foxx hit a drive back to the box with such force that the pitcher could not get his glove up in time to shield himself (as Mark Eichhorn was able to do), and suffered a fractured skull. The pitcher, a promising youngster, saw his career end on that fateful day.

Billy Martin once said Mickey Mantle could hit a baseball harder than anyone he ever saw ... that may be true, but Martin never saw Ruth and Foxx in action. In deference to Mantle, however, his greatest moment of glory in the power department came on May 30, 1955, at Griffith Stadium when he faced Washington's Pedro Ramos.

Mantle, a switch-hitter batting lefthanded, caught hold of one of Ramos' fastballs and propelled an immensely high drive that appeared to have enough power behind it to clear the rightfield roof, a feat that no player had accomplished in the stadium's half-century history. None of the great sluggers of baseball had even come close to powering a fair ball over the giant-sized filigree, the ornamental work hanging from the lip of the stands, which, in both rightfield and leftfield, hooks into fair territory toward the bleachers. Mantle hit the filigree, and as Joe Reichler, *Associated Press* baseball writer, who witnessed the drive, said: "He came so close to making history that he still made it. The ball struck high on the facade, barely a foot or two below the edge of the roof ... For years after that spring 1955 game, fans who came to Griffith Stadium lifted their eyes and stared at the spot where the ball hit. Likely many of them remembered the 565-foot homer Mantle hit in Washington two years before. Unobstructed, the drive against Ramos would have traveled even further."

WHAT RIGHTHANDED BATTER LAST HIT .380 OR BETTER? JOE D. IN 1939

When Joe DiMaggio, New York Yankees center fielder, won the American League batting championship with a .381 average in 1939, he became the last righthanded hitter in the major leagues to hit .380 or better. Joe played in only 120 games in 1939 because he held out for more than a month at the beginning of the season. He finally settled for a contract calling for $30,000, a small fraction of what he could earn if he were playing today.

DON MATTINGLY: HITS WITH EXTRA OOMPH, SETS TWO HOMER RECORDS IN 1987

Don Mattingly has been noted primarily for his fielding and his high batting average. He smashes hard line drives to every part of the field, with home runs merely a secondary affair until 1987. In his first four seasons with the New York Yankees (1983–86) Mattingly, a 5-foot-11-inch 185 pound lefthanded swinger, belted a good, not great, 93 homers, while batting at a sizzling clip of .332.

In 1987, Mattingly continued his usual high batting average and modest home run-hitting pace. But, while hitting 30 homers, Mattingly, extraordinarily enough, was able to both tie and break two all-time major league home run records.

In July, he hit for the circuit in eight consecutive games, tying the major league mark established by Pittsburgh's Dale Long in 1956. Then on September 29 at Yankee Stadium against Boston, he whacked his sixth grand slam of the season, breaking the record of five that had been shared by Ernie Banks of the Chicago Cubs (1955) and Jim Gentile of the Baltimore Orioles (1961). Oddly, Mattingly had never hit a grand slammer before the 1987 season.

Mattingly's record-breaking sixth grand slam came in the third inning off Boston lefthander Bruce Hurst. The ball carried 11 rows into the third tier of the rightfield stands and powered the Yankees to a 6-0 victory over the Red Sox.

Mattingly had never hit Hurst well in the past, averaging a mere .217 with no homers.

When questioned by reporters after the game about his grand slam slugging splurge, Mattingly modestly replied, "I can't explain it. I basically haven't done anything different, other than to try to hit the ball hard. Before, I would hit a sacrifice fly with the bases loaded. Now, I think of hitting the ball hard. Consequently, if I get the ball in the air, it carries."

BOB BUHL GOES 0 FOR 70

In respect to all-time weak-hitting pitchers, Bob Buhl rates a top spot in that category. While with the Chicago Cubs and Milwaukee Braves in 1962, Buhl "distinguished" himself by going 0 for 70, winding up with a batting average of .000. No other player in major league history, pitcher or otherwise has gone to bat that many times in a season without a single bingle.

Buhl struck out about half the time; 36 K's were registered against him during that ignominious 0 for 70 streak at bat, though he did manage to walk six times, and score two runs.

Over the course of 15 years in the big leagues (1953–67), Buhl went 76 for 857, good for a .089 average, and somehow he managed two doubles, which brought his "slugging" average up to .091. He scored a grand total of 31 runs, drove in 26 and struck out 389 times.

As a pitcher, however, Buhl posted a very competent 166-132 for a .557 percentage, reaching his peak in 1957 for Milwaukee when he went 18-7 as he played a key role in helping the Braves capture the National League pennant. Buhl's record as a batsman literally cried out for the DH (Designated Hitter) rule.

DEL ENNIS LEAVES 500 STRANDED
CLEAN-UP HITTER CAN'T CLEAN UP

Del Ennis, a hard-hitting outfielder, came up with the Philadelphia Phillies in 1946, and reached his peak in 1950 when he helped the Phillies' so-called "Whiz Kids" to the National League pennant. Ennis compiled excellent stats that year—he hit 31 homers, drove in a league high 126 runs, and averaged .311 at bat.

However, a team of sportswriters for the *Philadelphia Inquirer* still felt that Ennis, hitting in the fourth position, wasn't driving in enough runs, particularly since the three batters who ordinarily preceded him in the order (Eddie Waitkus, Richie Ashburn and Willie "Puddin' Head" Jones), always seemed to be on base. The reporters went back and checked the results of every game, and discovered that Ennis left over 500 men on base during the course of the 1950 season.

"If that isn't a record for leaving men on, it sure comes close to it!" one of the writers declared. "If Ennis was a better clutch hitter—and with all those men he had on base—he could have easily broken Hack Wilson's major league record of 190 runs batted in for one season."

The Phillies experienced total disaster in the World Series that year as they were wiped out by the Yankees in four straight games. Ennis didn't help the cause much as he went 2 for 14 and failed to drive in a single run.

SENATORS, WITH WALTER JOHNSON' BIG LOSERS BUT NOT THE WORST

The Washington Senators experienced their worst season in 1909 as they finished dead last under manager Joe Cantillon with a 42-110 record, for a lowly .276 percentage. The Senators wound up exactly 56 games behind the pennant-winning Detroit Tigers.

The Senators started the season poorly, but sagged even more in midseason. Of the 34 games played in July, they managed to lose 29. That still remains as the all-time record for the most games lost by one team in a month.

For the season, the great Walter Johnson, then in his third year in the majors, rolled up a dismal 13-25 won-lost record, while his fellow righthander, rookie Bob Groom, "fashioned" a 7-26 mark. No big league pitcher in the 20th century has lost more games in a season than Bob Groom.

Though they were big losers, Johnson and Groom could justifiably complain about weak hitting support since they posted glittering earned run averages of 2.21 and 2.87, respectively. In team batting, Washington finished last with a puny .223 mark.

Was this baseball's "worst" team? No. Other teams have actually experienced worse months. In August 1890, the National League Pittsburgh Pirates went 1-27, and the Cleveland Spiders tied that record in their final National League year in 1899, when they staggered to a 1-27 record for the month of September.

Pittsburgh for the entire 1890 season, wound up with a miserable 23-113 (.169 percentage), while the 1899 Cleveland Spiders finished with a horrendous 20-134 record (.149 percentage). No other major league team has surpassed this.

SHORTEST GAME IN PRO BALL— 9 INNINGS IN 32 MINUTES!

The average nine-inning major league game today requires about two hours and 45 minutes to complete. However, a game can be played much faster—as was proved by the Southern Association during an experiment conducted on September 19, 1910, which proved that 32 minutes is all you really need.

In this 32-minute game, Mobile edged the home team Atlanta Crackers 2-1. With the score tied 1-1 in the first half of the ninth, Mobile pushed across the decisive run. Both teams hustled every minute of the way. Batters did not wait out the pitchers, but rather swung at every good pitch. There was only one walk; not a single player struck out; and, Mobile even reeled off a triple play. Mobile made 6 hits against 4 for Atlanta. On the same afternoon, Chattanooga at Nashville in another Southern Association game, needed only 42 minutes to complete.

BASEBALL HALL OF FAME
HOUSES STRANGE SPECIMENS OF THE GAME

"Be careful how you hold this," Peter P. Clark, Baseball Hall of Fame Museum Registrar warned us as he handed over an artifact he pulled out of a cabinet in his lower-level museum office. We followed Clark's advice because this particular specimen of diamond game memorabilia turned out to be a Gillette razor blade taped onto a sheet of letter paper. The inscription was a note testifying to the fact that this blue blade was used by Cy Young on September 9, 1953, during a visit to a friend's house in East Cuyahoga Falls, Ohio.

The Cy Young razor blade is among numerous items in the Hall of Fame Museum collection not ordinarily placed on display. A razor blade in a baseball museum? Strange.

But that's not all. After Clark gingerly placed the Cy Young Gillette blade back into the cabinet, he hauled out a chunk of wood, measuring about 16 inches in length and some 6 inches thick. This solid-looking specimen of wood—more specifically red oak—was inscribed in pen as being the last block of wood cut with an axe by Cy Young, and dated November 8, 1954. Moreover, Cy Young, the 511-game winner, who spent his long retirement from baseball as a farmer in Newcomerstown, Ohio, autographed the chunk of oak soon after he chopped it. He was 87 at the time. (Young died on November 4, 1955, at the age of 88.)

"The Cy Young oak is a part of our permanent holdings, but one wonders what a collector would pay for it at public auction," mused

Clark. "Almost any sort of artifact dealing with a Hall of Famer seems to have special appeal," he added.

Cy Young, the hard-throwing righthander is, of course, baseball's all-time winningest pitcher with those 511 victories being rolled up over 22 seasons from 1890 to 1911.

Another highly unusual gift came to the Hall of Fame shortly after Johnny Mize was elected to baseball's shrine in 1981. The gift consisted of a large bucketful of red clay soil from the school playground in Demorest, Georgia, where Mize first began playing on the diamond. The contributor was Demorest's school superintendent.

In a 15-year major league career (1936–53, with three years out for military service in World War II), Johnny Mize slammed out 359 homers and averaged .312, while playing successively for the St. Louis Cards, New York Giants and New York Yankees.

Nelson Fox isn't a Hall of Famer yet, but many baseball experts feel he should eventually gain election to baseball's shrine. During a 19-year big league career (1947–65), mostly with the Chicago White Sox, Fox batted a potent .288, lined out 2,663 base hits, and scintillated as a smooth fielding second baseman. After his premature death in 1975, members of Fox's family contributed a batch of the infielder's mementos to the Hall of Fame Museum. These included an unopened pouch of "Nelson Fox's Favorite Chewing Tobacco." Fox was such an inveterate chewer that one of the major tobacco companies produced and marketed his own special brand of chaw.

DRYSDALE ALMOST FAILED TO MAKE IT TO HIS HALL OF FAME INDUCTION

In the Hall of Fame's first half-century of existence just over 200 players, managers, umpires and executives have been voted into baseball's shrine. A player must wait at least five years after his retirement from the game before he is eligible to be voted upon, and sometimes, unfortunately, a diamond star is elected to the Hall of Fame long after he's gone to the Great Beyond.

In the case of Don Drysdale, the righthanded power pitcher of the old Dodgers from Brooklyn had to endure a waiting period of 15 years before he was elected to the Hall of Fame in 1984. Happily enough, he was very much alive and well when he finally received the call, but he almost missed out.

"Big D," as he was popularly known, posted a 209-166 won-lost record with the Brooklyn-Los Angeles Dodgers over a 14-year period (1956–69), and achieved one of baseball's truly noteworthy records in 1968 when he racked up six straight shutouts while hurling 58 consecutive scoreless innings.

"Election into Baseball's Hall of Fame is the highest tribute an athlete can ever receive." That is not just the opinion of Edward W. Stack, Hall of Fame President, but of thousands of fans as well.

Hall of Fame Induction Ceremonies are always elaborately staged gigantic media events with the newly minted enshrined being called upon to make speeches after receiving the bronze plaques recording

"Let me go. PLEASE let me go."

their deeds on the diamond. Thousands of fans from across the country. always jam their way into tiny Cooperstown, N.Y., when those Induction Ceremonies are held on midsummer Sunday afternoons.

Naturally enough, Don Drysdale, now a radio and television broadcaster with the Chicago White Sox, put together a carefully written speech to make at his induction. When his Chicago White Sox employers heard that "Big D" was planning to take the Sunday off, however, they were irked and told him straight out that his job status would be seriously jeopardized if he didn't show up for work in the broadcast booth that day as scheduled.

"It was touch and go for a while," said Drysdale. But after Drysdale made an emotional plea to his bosses pointing out that this was a one-in-a-lifetime thing (which, of course, they knew), and after a good bit more wrangling back and forth, he was finally given reluctant permission to travel to Cooperstown for his big day! Strange?

BABE RUTH'S "CALLED SHOT" IN THE 1932 WORLD SERIES

The third game of the 1932 World Series still stands as one of the most dramatic clashes in the long history of the Fall Classic. The October 1 game pitted the Chicago Cubs at Chicago's Wrigley Field against the New York Yankees. New York had already won the first two games of the Series played at Yankee Stadium. Babe Ruth smashed a three-run homer off Cubs starter Charlie Root in the first inning, and in the early going, teammate Lou Gehrig also homered.

In the top of the fifth inning, with the scored tied at 4-4, Ruth faced Root again. With a count of two balls and two strikes, Ruth then seemed to gesture toward the center field bleachers, as if to indicate that's where he planned to deposit Root's next pitch. Or was he merely pointing at Root? Or was he addressing the Cubs bench with an exaggerated gesture, since the Cubs bench jockeys were teasing Ruth unmercifully?

Whatever the message, Ruth delivered on Root's next pitch. He swung viciously and the ball sailed like a rocket toward center field—

then went over the bleacher wall. This titanic blast put the Yankees ahead, 5-4.

Lou Gehrig matched Ruth's two homers by following with a drive into the right field bleachers. The back-to-back fifth inning blasts stood up as the margin of victory as the Yankees, after trading runs with the Cubs in the ninth, prevailed 7-5.

Gehrig, the on-deck hitter at the time, obviously thought that the Babe had indeed called his shot. He said, "What do you think of the nerve of that big lug calling his shot and getting away with it?"

Charlie Root, on the other hand, strongly felt that Ruth never pointed to deep center field before the home run pitch. He said soon after the action was over, "If he had pointed to the home run landing spot, I would have knocked him down with the next pitch."

Babe Ruth himself was content to go along with the called shot scenario, although he never really expounded upon the matter in any great detail.

In 1990, we had the opportunity to interview Billy Herman, who was the Cubs second baseman in the historic game. When we asked about Ruth's "called shot," Herman exclaimed without a moment's hesitation, "I never believed that the Babe called his shot. I was standing at second base, maybe 120 feet away from the batter's box, and though Ruth was gesticulating all over the place, I really don't think that any of his actions indicated that he would blast the ball over the center field bleachers. Still, the legend that the Babe did call the shot grew and grew. We'll never really know what was in Ruth's mind."

There's no question, however, that Game 3 broke the Cubs' spirit as the Yankees went on to win Game 4 by a 13-6 count, giving the Bronx Bombers a Series sweep. Now, more than two generations after that October 1, 1932, clash between the Yankees and Cubs, the legend continues to live on. Ruth's homer off Charlie Root remains unquestionably the greatest moment of his illustrious career and the most storied circuit blast in the entire history of the World Series. Babe Ruth played his final game in the major leagues over six decades ago, but the glory of his achievement continues to live on forever.

MARK McGWIRE, HOME RUN HITTER EXTRAORDINARE

During the 1998 season, Mark McGwire reached his peak as one of the premier home run hitters of all time, surpassing records established by such great sluggers of the past as Babe Ruth, Lou Gehrig, and Roger Maris.

Maris' record of 61 homers in '61 stood for 37 years, until it was first broken by McGwire in 1998, and then by Sammy Sosa, outfielder with the Chicago Cubs, who also breached the Maris standard in the same season. Sosa finished with 66 homers, but McGwire went on to virtually demolish the old mark when he concluded the season with an even 70 circuit clouts.

Even more incredibly, McGwire averaged 60 homers per season from 1996 to 1998—slamming a total of 180 balls out of the park. That is far and away a record. With Oakland in '96, McGwire led the National League with 52 homers, and then in '97 he hit 34 homers before being traded to the St. Louis Cards on July 31. For St. Louis, "Big Mac" homered 24 more times, giving him a total of 58. And his 70 in '98 gave him 180, or an average of 60 over three incredible seasons.

McGwire also became the first player in history to hit 50 or more homers in three consecutive seasons. Babe Ruth did hit 50 or more homers four times, but never in three seasons in succession.

Ruth's best 3-year total came during the 1926–1928 seasons when he slammed out 47, 60, and 54 homers, respectively for a total of 161. Many baseball historians felt that record would never be broken, but McGwire's three-season total bettered the Ruth mark by 19.

The big difference between the Ruth era and the McGwire era revolves around the fact that homers were not in vogue at the time. The Babe was at his peak, from 1919 until the early 1930s. (During the first six years of his career with the Boston Red Sox, from 1914 to 1919, Ruth was almost primarily a pitcher—in 1919, he began to pitch sparingly, played the outfield almost every day, and hit 29 homers in 130 games.)

Ruth, in fact, on two separate occasions, in 1920 and 1927, personally hit more homers than each of the seven other teams in the American League. In 1920, the "Sultan of Swat" smacked out a record 54 homers and no team in the league matched that total.

In 1927, the Bambino, at the peak of his long ball power, whacked his then record 60 homers, and in that season no single American League team managed to top that total. Philadelphia "threatened" Ruth with 56 four-baggers.

In 1998, McGwire faced competition for the National League home run crown from Chicago's Sammy Sosa. McGwire and Sosa were tied at 66 going into the final weekend of the season. While Sosa was homerless, McGwire hit four in his last two games, giving him 70.

Because there were so few authentic home run hitters in the Ruth era, The Babe really stood out in the long ball department, but McGwire does his belting in a home run crazy period in baseball history.

Baseball's Funny Moments

Baseball is a zany sport where practical jokes, goofy gags, and loony lines muttered by ballplayers are as much a part of the game as heroic home runs, dazzling no-hitters, and inspiring pep talks. Baseball jokesters range from fabled Hall of Famers and modern superstars to well-traveled reserves and lesser-known bench warmers. Baseball history is crammed full of crazy coaches, oddball owners, and wacky players who have all contributed to the unforgettable mystique of America's favorite and sometimes outrageously funny sport.

HOUSE SITTER

In 1978, the Boston Red Sox, managed by Don Zimmer, met the New York Yankees in a one-game playoff to determine the American League's East Division champion. The game was won by the Yankees on a home run hit by New York shortstop Bucky Dent. In 1983, Don Zimmer was hired as a coach by the New York Yankees, and Bucky Dent was traded from the Yankees to the Texas Rangers. Since Zimmer needed a place to live near New York, he rented Bucky Dent's vacant house in New Jersey. When the Zimmers moved into the Dent's home, they found photographs of Bucky's game-winning home run hit against the Red Sox in 1978 hanging on walls all around the house. The first thing Zimmer did was turn around the photographs of Dent's famous hit—so they all faced the wall!

CATCH PHRASE

Dean Chance was on the mound for the California Angels in a close game against the Minnesota Twins. Chance's battery mate was catcher Hank Foiles. The Angels held a slim lead, but the Twins had the bases loaded. Chance fired a sinking fastball low and outside. Catcher Foiles reached out to catch it, and then jumped up and raced back to the screen to chase down what he figured was a wild pitch.

As Foiles frantically searched for the ball, all three Twins runners scored. The ball seemed to vanish off the face of the earth. It wasn't until the crazy catcher looked into his glove that he realized the ball had never gotten by him. It was wedged in the pocket of his glove the entire time. Foiles only thought he'd missed it!

WORK OF ART

In the 1990s, the St. Louis Cardinals outfield consisted of Del Ennis, Chuck Harmon, and Wally Moon. Ennis, Harmon, and Moon were good players, but they all lacked one vital ability. "The Cardinals have a Venus de Milo outfield," a sportswriter once said. "It's beautiful—but no arms."

GRASS ROOTS

When the Philadelphia Phillies traveled to Houston, Texas, in July of 1966 to play in the Astrodome, some Phillies players were asked their opinions of the revolutionary new artificial turf. Philadelphia third baseman Dick Allen was later quoted as saying, "If cows don't eat it, I ain't playing on it"

SHOE THING

Fresco Thompson, who became vice president of the old Brooklyn Dodgers, was one of baseball's great funny men. His wit was even quicker than his bat. Fresco, who for a while played alongside hilarious Babe Herman in the outfield for the Dodgers, once described Herman's lack of fielding ability this way: "Babe wore a glove for only one reason. It was a league custom." In his later years as a member of the New York Giants, Thompson played for manager Bill Terry and was seldom used. Fresco spent most of his days with the Giants relaxing on the bench in the dugout. One afternoon, he was shocked to hear Bill Terry call for him to go into a game as a pinch runner. Thompson yawned, stretched, and refused to play by saying, "I'd love to Bill, but I just had my shoes shined."

BIRD BRAIN

Joe "Ducky" Medwick was a great player for the St. Louis Cardinals. He also had a wacky sense of humor. During his prime, Medwick visited Vatican City in Rome with a group of famous entertainers. The group was granted an audience with the Pope. Members of the group were introduced to the Pope one by one and announced their occupations. "I'm a singer," said the first member of the group.

"I'm a comic," said the next person to be introduced.

When it was Medwick's turn to meet the Pope, Ducky said, "Your Holiness, I'm a Cardinal."

BULL PENNED

Pitcher Moe Drabowsky, who played for the St. Louis Cardinals during the early 1970s, had a wacky way of passing time, while out in the bullpen. While games were in progress, he often used the bullpen telephone to order a pizza. Once he even called the opposing team's bullpen, disguised his voice, and ordered an opposing pitcher to warm up.

GRIMM HUMOR

Manager Charlie Grimm led the Chicago Cubs to National League pennants in 1932 and 1935, but both of his squads fizzled in World Series play. In 1932, he lost to manager Joe McCarthy's New York Yankees team 4-0. And in 1935, he was defeated by manager Mickey Cochrane's Detroit Tigers team 4-2. Nevertheless, Grimm had a world championship sense of humor. Once a scout called him up to brag about a young pitcher he'd discovered. "The kid is great," insisted the scout. "He struck out 27 batters in one game. No one even hit a foul ball off of him until the ninth inning."

Grimm paused to reflect on the report and then replied, "Sign the kid who hit the foul ball. We need hitters more than pitchers."

SIZE WISE

Huge Ted Kluszewski played for the California Angels in 1961. Kluszewski, who stood six-feet-two inches tall and had massive, bulging biceps, was given a new roommate that season by manager Bill Rigney. Big Klu's roomie was Albie Pearson, a great player who stood only five-feet-five inches tall. When Kluszewski first laid eyes on his new roomie, he told Pearson, "I get the bed in our room. You get the dresser drawer." Pearson laughed at Kluszewski's joke. One night later that season, Kluszewski came into his room to

find Pearson sound asleep in bed. Big Ted lifted Albie out of the bed without waking him and positioned Pearson's dozing form in an open dresser drawer. And that's where Pearson remained until he woke up.

METAL PLATES

The first baseball game in Berlin, Germany, was played in June of 1912, and the wackiest guy on the field that day was the home-plate umpire. No one knows his name, but they know what he wore to call balls and strikes that day. It was a suit of armor.

LET'S SEE

There is more than one way to get an umpire's goat. Skipper Charlie Grimm didn't always argue with the 20 men in blue to make his point. Once umpire Charlie Moran (who had been a college football coach before his umpiring days) made a bad call against Grimm's Chicago Cubs team. As angry players rushed out to fight with umpire Moran, Grimm got between his players and the ump. Charlie raised his hands to calm down his angry squad and stated, "The first person to lay a finger on this blind old man will be fined fifty bucks!"

SICK HUMOR

Seattle Mariners superslugger Jay Buhner is a fun-loving player with a hot temper and a sick sense of humor. Buhner, who clouted 20 or more home runs per season from 1990 to 1995, can't stomach failure. Once while playing golf with some Seattle teammates, he missed a shot and threw his club in disgust. When that display didn't cool his temper, he tried to toss his entire golf bag but found it tightly fastened to his motorized cart. Since Jay couldn't undo the bag from the cart and throw it, he did the next best thing. He flipped over the entire golf cart.

On the field, Buhner's sick sense of humor can be upsetting to those who witness his most famous prank. Buhner can force himself to vomit at will. Jay calls his sick stunt "blurping" and explains it as a combination of burping and vomiting. Buhner usually "blurps" to nauseate rookie players. However, Buhner once pulled his "blurping" gag in the outfield, which caused fellow Mariners outfielders Ken Griffey and Kevin Mitchell to become sick to their stomachs. In a yucky display of team unity, all three players threw up in the outfield during the game.

TALKING BASEBALL

Pitcher Mark Fidrych of the Detroit Tigers was a colorful character during his playing days. While standing on the mound, Fidrych would talk directly to the baseball he held in his hand. On other occasions, if one of his infielders made a good fielding play, Mark would storm off the mound and offer the appropriate player a vigorous congratulatory handshake before continuing to pitch in the game.

CLOWN PRINCES OF BASEBALL
LARRY "YOGI" BERRA

Hall of Famer Larry "Yogi" Berra, who played for the New York Yankees and managed the Yankees and the New York Mets, was not only one of the game's greatest hitting catchers, but also one of baseball's funniest guys. His wacky remarks, side-splitting stories, and nutty exploits are definitely of funny Hall of Fame caliber:

It's a Repeat

When it comes to understated daffiness, Yogi is in a class by himself. He once remarked, "It's déjà vu all over again."

A Swinging Guy

Yogi Berra was famous for swinging at and usually hitting pitches out of the strike zone. However, on one occasion he swung at a terrible pitch way out of the zone and struck out. "Humph," Berra grumbled on his way back to the dugout. "How can a pitcher that wild stay in the league?"

Fan Support

When Yogi Berra visited his hometown of St. Louis in 1947 as a member of the New York Yankees, the fans there staged a celebration in his honor. After he was presented with numerous gifts and mementoes,

Yogi walked up to a microphone to make a speech. Berra took a deep breath and said, "I want to thank all of you fans for making this night necessary."

Crazy Qualifications

When Yogi Berra was named manager of the New York Yankees in 1964, he was asked what qualified him for the position. Said Yogi, "You observe a lot by watching."

Music Man

In 1964, the New York Yankees managed by Yogi Berra suffered though a difficult losing season. After one really disheartening loss, Berra boarded

the team bus and was shocked to hear utility infielder Phil Linz playing happy tunes on his harmonica. Upset by the team's defeat, Berra got into a loud argument with Linz and ended up fining him two hundred dollars for playing the harmonica. The next year when Linz signed his Yankee contract, he got a raise in salary which included a two-hundred-dollar bonus. With the bonus was a letter from Yogi telling Linz to spend the two-hundred dollars on harmonica lessons!

Light Humor

Yogi Berra was playing in a World Series game on an October afternoon when the sinking sun cast a dark shadow across the playing field. Looking out across the diamond, Yogi commented, "Gee, it gets late early out there."

Don't Make Waves

One afternoon in the New York locker room, Yogi Berra was telling some rookie players about his first days with the Yankees. Listening as he worked was Pete Sheeby, the clubhouse man. "I was in the Navy the first time I came in here," Yogi said as he pointed at the clubhouse floor. "In fact, I had on my sailor uniform," Berra added. Then he turned to speak to Sheeby. "I bet you thought I didn't look like much of a ballplayer the first time you saw me, huh Pete?"

Pete Sheeby laughed and answered. "You didn't even look like much of a sailor."

Class Act

Yogi tells a story about his days in school. He said he once took a test and answered every question wrong. The teacher called him up to her desk and said, "Lawrence, I don't believe you know anything."

Lawrence "Yogi" Berra looked at his teacher and replied, "Ma'am, I don't even suspect anything."

JAY HANNA DEAN

Jay Hanna Dean (who sometimes called himself Jerome Herman Dean) more than lived up to the nutty nickname "Dizzy" given to him by an Army sergeant while Dean was serving in the Armed Forces. Dizzy Dean was an All-Star pitcher for the famous St. Louis Cardinals team known as the "Gas House Gang." The Gang included other zany baseball stars like John "Pepper" Martin, Leo "The Lip" Durocher, and Frankie Frisch. When it comes to ranking baseball's all-time wackiest and funniest person, Dizzy Dean's name just might get top billing.

Name Game

In 1934, pitcher Dizzy Dean won 30 games for the St. Louis Cardinals and lost only 7. Dean figured he was due a hefty raise, so he went to see General Manager Branch Rickey. "I want a twenty-thousand-dollar raise," Dizzy said.

Branch Rickey almost fainted. "Judas Priest! You're not worth that kind of money," Rickey shouted.

Dizzy looked Branch in the eye and replied, "I don't know who Judas Priest is. My name's Dean and I'm worth every penny of it."

Punny Position

Dizzy Dean was a great pitcher, but he often had trouble retiring New York Giants slugger Bill Terry. In one game where Dean was matched against Terry, Bill smashed a liner off Dizzy's leg his first time up. The next time he was up, Terry cracked a liner that sizzled past Dizzy's head. On his third trip to the plate, Terry rocked one off Dizzy's glove for a hit. Finally Pepper Martin called time out and walked to the mound from his position at third base. "Hey, Diz," said Pepper, "I don't think you're playing him deep enough."

News Flash

On one occasion, Dizzy Dean was batting when he was hit in the head by a pitched ball. Dean was rushed to a hospital. Baseball fans anxious for medical news about the status of the St. Louis star cheered and laughed when a press report stated that Dean's head was X-rayed and the test revealed nothing!

CHARLES FINLEY

"I don't want to be remembered as a kook," Charlie Finley said, "but as an owner who did his best to make the game better." In a way, Finley got his wish. He is the man mainly responsible for the designated hitter rule which is in use in Major League baseball's American League. However, Finley will also be remembered as one of baseball's wackiest club owners.

Stump the Umps

Boring baseball tasks like re-supplying the home-plate umpire with base-balls were given a hilarious twist in the Athletics' home stadium. Team owner Finley had baseballs delivered to the plate umpire by a mechanical rabbit that popped out of the ground!

The umpires were also given a treat during the fifth inning of every home game thanks to Mr. Finley. Finley had water and cookies delivered to the umps. In fact, the cookies were made by an A's employee named Debbie Fields who later established her own cookie business. Mrs. Fields' baked goods are now very famous.

The Merry Mascots

In the 1960s, Finley was the owner of the Kansas City Athletics. One day, he decided the team might play better if it had a mascot. The mascot Mr. Finley decided on for his Kansas City squad was a mule, whom Finley called "Charlie O.," naming it after himself. He also let the mule

WHAT POSITIONS DO THEY PLAY?

graze in the stadium's outfield.

Charlie came up with another wild animal idea shortly thereafter. Behind the outfield in the Athletics' home stadium was a hill covered with pasture land.

Charlie put a sheep out in that pasture and dyed its wool green and gold—the team colors of the Kansas City Athletics.

What a Pitchman

Charles O. Finley had a soft spot in his heart (others said he had a soft spot in his head) for pitchers. In 1965, he signed one of the game's greatest hurlers to pitch for the Athletics. That pitcher was the immortal Satchell Paige. However, Paige was nearly 60 years old at the time, and Finley signed him to pitch just one game.

When Charlie signed pitcher Jim Hunter to a contract, he decided Hunter needed a nickname. Finley loved baseball nicknames. Charlie asked Jim what he liked to do when he wasn't playing baseball. "I like to go fishing for catfish," answered Jim.

"From now on, you'll be Catfish Hunter," Finley announced. To this day, the nickname "Catfish" has stuck with Jim Hunter.

Finley tried to tag a new name on another of his famous hurlers,

Vida Blue, an All-Star pitcher and a Cy Young Award winner. Finley tried talking his young superstar into changing his first name from Vida to "True" so he would be known as "True Blue." Blue absolutely refused, and he kept his first name despite the protests from the wacky Finley.

Clubhouse Rap

The Kansas City Athletics moved west and became the Oakland Athletics in 1968. Charles Finley was never one to stand in the way of progress. He was also an owner who believed in keeping his players entertained. In fact, a batboy for the A's named Stanley Burrell was encouraged to dance in the clubhouse to entertain Charlie's players. That dancing bat-boy later became rap music mega-star M.C. Hammer.

AH, SKIP IT

Babe Herman's wacky ways are legendary. Babe didn't like to report to spring training, so he seldom signed his yearly contract until the season was about to begin. Everyone thought Babe "held out" each year just to squeeze more money out of the Dodgers team, which might not have been the whole truth. A teammate once asked Babe, "Is it worth skipping spring training every year just to get a few more dollars?"

Wacky Herman, the worst fielder in baseball, replied, "I don't do it for the money. The longer I stay out of training camp, the less chance I have of getting hit by a fly ball."

Bogus Babe

During his heyday, Babe Herman was a well-known celebrity. However, for a short period of time, an imposter made the rounds of New York restaurants and nightclubs claiming to be Babe. "Look," Babe Herman said to the press when asked about the imposter. "Showing up that fake is easy. Just take the guy out and hit him a fly ball. If the bum catches it, you know it ain't the real Babe Herman!"

Smoke Screen

On another occasion, Babe Herman cornered several reporters in the Dodgers' locker room after a game and tried to convince them there was nothing nutty about his behavior. After a long talk, he finished by stating, "I'm just a normal guy." He then pulled a cigar out of his jacket pocket and began to puff on it. Babe didn't have to light the cigar. The stogie was lit the entire time it was in his pocket!

Triple Trouble

Could Babe Herman hit! However, he didn't always think straight. One day the daffy outfielder came to the plate with the bases loaded and no outs. He quickly walloped a triple. Unfortunately for Babe and the Dodgers, the triple turned into a double play when Herman raced past two of his Brooklyn teammates on the base paths in his rush to reach third base. The runners he passed were declared out.

JOE GARAGIOLA

Joe Garagiola may not have been one of the game's greatest catchers, but he is one of baseball's best storytellers.

Dough Boy

After his Major League career ended, Joe Garagiola worked as a broadcaster of major league games. He remembers the early days when the hapless New York Mets had difficulty winning games. During that period, he attended a banquet in New York City. When a waiter laid a basket of breadsticks on his table, Garagiola quipped, "I see the Mets' bats have arrived."

Can't Resist

Sports broadcaster Joe Garagiola tells the story of Smead Jolley, a great fastball hitter. Jolley is up at the plate with runners on first and third. The guy on first breaks from the base to steal second. The catcher throws to second. The guy on third sees the throw and starts to run home. The shortstop cuts off the throw to second and fires a perfect strike to the plate. It's going to be a close play at home. At the plate, Jolley watches intently. When the hard throw from the shortstop comes across the plate, Jolley swings and cracks the ball into the outfield. "Hey," the home-plate ump yells to Jolley, "What are you doing?"

"Sorry, ump," answers Smead. "I couldn't resist. That's the first fastball I've seen in weeks."

PROTEST MARCH

Earl Weaver recorded 1,480 victories in his 17 seasons as skipper of the Baltimore Orioles. As a manager, Weaver was not afraid to exchange heated words with any home-plate umpire in the league. On one occasion, Weaver got into an argument with umpire Ron Luciano. "I'm playing this game under protest," Weaver screamed.

"Protest? On what grounds?" the ump asked.

"On the grounds of your integrity," the Baltimore skipper shouted.

"You know I have to announce the protest," Umpire Luciano replied. "Are you sure that's how you want me to do it?"

"Damn right'" Weaver grumbled. And so the Baltimore Orioles played a Major League baseball game under protest because their manager doubted the home plate umpire's integrity.

MILLER TIME

Having a star player like Babe Ruth on your team can be a mixed blessing, as New York Yankees manager Miller Huggins quickly learned. Ruth, who never paid much attention to training rules or team regulations, made no attempt to hide his off-the-field behavior. Late one night while the Yankees were on the road, Huggins and road secretary Mark Roth were sitting in a hotel lobby when Ruth walked in way after curfew. "I'll have to talk to Ruth tomorrow about the late hours he keeps," Huggins said to Roth.

The next afternoon, the Yankees played a game. In the contest, Ruth clubbed two home runs. That evening Huggins and Roth were again in the hotel lobby when Ruth came strolling in long after curfew.

"He's done it again," Roth said to Huggins. "Are you going to talk to him?"

"I sure am," answered Huggins. As Babe walked by, Huggins yelled out, "Hi, Babe. How are you?"

YOU BURN ME UP

Jamie Quirk, of the Kansas City Royals, pulled the ultimate bathroom joke on pitcher Dan Quisenberry while they were in the bullpen in Boston. When Quisenberry went into a portable toilet in the bullpen, Quirk thought it would be funny to light a fire under Dan. He lit some newspapers and smoked Quisenberry out of the portable bathroom. The crowd roared when Quisenberry rushed out and was caught with his pants down!

FAINT HEART

When Nick Altrock was coaching third for the old Washington Senators, he never missed a chance to take a verbal potshot at an umpire. Once during a game, a Senators batter hit a line shot foul into the stands behind Altrock. An umpire ran over and saw some people in the stands helping a female spectator who was unconscious. "What happened?" the ump asked Nick. "Did that ball hit her?"

"Nah," answered Nick Altrock. "When you yelled foul, she was so shocked that you finally made a correct call, she passed out!"

FUNNY MONEY

In 1970, Bernie Carbo played for the Cincinnati Reds, who were managed by Sparky Anderson. As a skipper, Sparky strictly enforced team rules and regulations. Whenever a player did something wrong,

Anderson was quick to levy a fine. It was also Sparky's habit to donate to charity the money he collected from players in fines. One day, a smiling Carbo came to the Reds' skipper with a question. "My wife keeps asking me why we get so many thank-you notes from the Heart Fund. She can't figure out why I'm making so many contributions. What should I tell her?" Anderson just laughed and walked away.

KINER QUIPS

New York Mets broadcaster Ralph Kiner, who was a great slugger during his playing days, says some of the funniest things. On one occasion, he remarked, "The Mets' Todd Hundley walked intensely his last time up." On another occasion, the ever glib Kiner cracked, "That's the great thing about baseball. You never know exactly what's going on."

KINGS OF DIAMOND DAFFINESS
CHARLES "CASEY" STENGEL

Charles "Casey" Stengel was a daffy outfielder in his playing days, which were spent with the Brooklyn Dodgers, the Philadelphia Phillies, the New York Giants, and other clubs. He also managed the Boston Braves, the Brooklyn Dodgers, the New York Yankees, and the New York Mets. It was Casey's skill as a manager that got him into the Baseball Hall of Fame. He won the World Championship several times at the helm of the

New York Yankees. However, Casey is best remembered for his baffling choice of wacky words and his weird way of explaining things that became known as "Stengelese."

The Gag That Bombed

In 1916, young Casey Stengel was a member of the wacky Brooklyn Dodgers squad managed by future Hall of Famer Wilbert Robinson. Robinson, an outstanding catcher with the old Baltimore Orioles, had carved his niche in the baseball record book on June 10, 1892, when he collected seven hits (six singles and a double) in seven times at bat.

Wilbert constantly reminded his collection of diamond clowns of his many personal achievements as a player, especially his exceptional ability to catch towering pop-ups while behind the plate. Robinson wasn't really a braggart; he just wanted to impress upon his young players that he knew what he was talking about when he gave them advice as a manager.

However, jokester Stengel used Robinson's own words as bait for one of baseball's great practical jokes. Stengel, with the aid of his teammates, goaded their manager into making a really wacky wager. He bet Wilbert he couldn't catch a baseball dropped from an airplane circling above the field. With his reputation as a "guy who could catch anything" on the line, Robinson agreed to the bet. He was determined to prove to Casey and his cohorts what a great catcher he was.

The day of the aerial baseball bombing finally came. Ruth Law, one of America's famous female aviators, was hired to pilot a plane with an open cockpit. In the aircraft with her was Casey Stengel. Standing far below on the Dodgers' training field in Florida was Robinson, wearing his catcher's mitt. Looking on were members of the Dodgers team. When Wilbert was ready to attempt his crazy catch, he signaled the plane above.

Then that sneaky Stengel pulled a shifty switcheroo. Instead of a baseball, he dropped a grapefruit out of the plane. From far below, the grapefruit looked just like a ball.

As the grapefruit plummeted toward the baseball field, Robinson positioned himself directly in its path. The grapefruit slipped through Robinson's outstretched arms, hit him squarely in the chest, and exploded! The force of the impact knocked the Dodgers manager to the ground, where he lay dazed for several seconds. When Robinson regained his senses, his chest was soaked with juice and splattered with squishy sections of grapefruit. Thinking the worst, the future Hall of Famer panicked.

"Help me!" he screamed to the surrounding Dodger players, who were already laughing hysterically. "Help me! I'm dying! The ball split my chest open and I'm bleeding to death!"

When the players continued to howl, Wilbert Robinson smelled a rat, a rat by the name of Stengel. He sat up and, upon quick examination, learned that the only injuries he'd suffered were a bruised ego and a fractured grapefruit. Thanks to kooky Casey Stengel's wacky prank, everyone on the Dodgers squad had a good laugh at their manager's expense. However, Robinson was so infuriated, young Casey had to stay in hiding for several days until the manager forgave Stengel for pulling off one of baseball's funniest gags.

Who's Tired?

Manager Casey Stengel was armed with a quick wit and was always ready to fire off a fast one-liner. On one occasion, the Yankee manager waddled out to the mound to yank a weary pitcher out of the game. "But, Skip," protested the pitcher, who was reluctant to leave, "I'm not tired."

Casey eyed the young hurler and took the baseball from him. "Well, I'm tired of you," Stengel replied as he signaled the bullpen for a relief pitcher.

Bird Brainer

Casey Stengel played some of his best baseball during his years with the old Brooklyn Dodgers. When Stengel was traded to Brooklyn's National League rival, the Pittsburgh Pirates, he knew he'd get booed the first time the Pirates visited the Dodgers. Of course, Casey wasn't the type to take getting booed lying down. When Pittsburgh arrived at Brooklyn's Ebbets Field, Casey cooked up a classic gag guaranteed to please even the rowdy Dodger rooters. When the stadium announcer introduced Casey as a starting outfielder for the Pirates, Stengel hopped out of the dugout. As the Dodger fans began to boo loudly, Casey bowed and tipped his hat. As he raised the cap from his head, a sparrow flew off of his brow and winged its way skyward. The wacky birdbrained stunt quickly won over the hostile crowd. The fans clapped and cheered the return of one of the game's zaniest players … nutty Casey Stengel.

What a Kick!

One day Walter Boom-Boom Beck was having his usual run of bad luck on the mound. Opposing batters blasted pitch after pitch. When the side was finally retired, Beck stormed into the Brooklyn Dodgers' dugout. In a fit of anger, Boom Boom kicked the water cooler. "Hey, calm down! Don't do that," called manager Casey Stengel. Beck smiled, expecting to hear some words of encouragement from Casey. "If you break your leg," Stengel continued, "I won't be able to trade you."

BILL VEECK

Bill Veeck was the P.T. Barnum of Major League baseball. As the owner of the old St. Louis Browns and the president of the Chicago White Sox, Veeck pulled off some of the wildest and funniest stunts in baseball history.

Cool Idea

Bill Veeck had a shower installed in Chicago's center field bleachers in 1977 so fans could cool off on hot days.

Ka-Boom!

The first exploding scoreboard was the brainchild of Bill Veeck. The scoreboard was installed in Chicago, and fireworks exploded every time a White Sox player belted a home run.

Short Game Stopper

The 1951 St. Louis Browns team owned by Bill Veeck and managed by Zack Taylor had some problems. The Browns were in last place in the league and had trouble drawing fans to their games. Showman Veeck decided to spice up the Browns' contests by staging some publicity stunts. One of his all-time best stunts was signing Eddie Gacdel to play for the Browns as a pinch hitter.

Gacdel became famous in the second game of a double-header played between the Browns and the Detroit Tigers at St. Louis in 1951. Eddie Gacdel didn't become a baseball hero for swinging a big bat. He became famous as the smallest man to ever bat in the Major Leagues. Gacdel stood only three-feet-seven inches tall and wore the fraction "1/8" on his back as his number. Since Veeck had listed Gacdel on the official St. Louis roster, the umpire had to let Eddie bat even though the Tigers protested.

Little Eddie Gacdel walked on four straight balls. As the crowd laughed hysterically and cheered loudly, Gacdel trotted down to first base. He was quickly replaced in the game by pinch runner Jim Delsing. The crowd gave Gacdel a loud ovation as he left the field, never to return. Gacdel never batted in another Major League game, but Bill Veeck's little trick on the Tigers was a big success.

VERNON "LEFTY, GOOFY" GOMEZ

Hall of Fame hurler Lefty Goofy Gomez played for the New York Yankees in the 1930s and 1940s. In his 13 seasons as a Yankee, he had only one losing season. As a funny man on the mound, he was never at a loss for producing laughs.

The Naked Truth

One day when the New York Yankees traveled to Boston to play the Red Sox, Lefty Gomez was scheduled to be the starting pitcher in the small, confined Fenway Park. However, when Yankee manager Joe McCarthy went looking for his starter, he couldn't find Gomez in the locker room. After a hasty search of the surrounding area, Joe finally found Lefty. Gomez was crouched in a phone booth, and he was totally naked. "I'm staying in here until game time," explained Lefty. "That way, when I get out on the field, Fenway will look real big to me."

Bright Guy

One dark and dismal afternoon, the New York Yankees took on the Cleveland Indians in a game that pitted Yankee pitcher Lefty Gomez against the Indians' ace fastballer Bob Feller. Feller was one of the hardest throwers to ever hurl a baseball in the Major Leagues. On occasion, some of Feller's pitches went just a bit wild. No batter in his right mind wanted to get "beaned" by one of Bob's blazing bullets. As the skies darkened that gloomy afternoon and the visibility became worse and worse, some of the Yankee hitters started to worry about such a beaning.

Late in the game, Lefty Gomez stepped up to the plate. The field was now covered in shadows. As Feller started to wind up, Lefty lowered his bat, took out a match, and lit it. Gomez held up the burning match to the astonishment of the home-plate umpire. "What are you doing Gomez?" barked the ump. "Can't you see Feller is getting ready to pitch?"

"I can see Feller fine," Lefty replied. "I just want to make sure he can see me!"

Pay Day

Lefty Gomez had lots of funny stories about the days he spent pitching in the Minor Leagues. One of his zany tales was about money problems. Lefty was staying in a boarding house and, due to lack of funds, got way behind in his rent. When the landlady demanded payment, Goofy Gomez tried to talk his way out of the jam. "Just think," Lefty said to the landlady. "Someday you'll be able to say Lefty Gomez the great pitcher once lived here."

The landlady wasn't impressed. According to Lefty's account, she answered, "I know ... and if you don't pay me, I'll be able to say it tomorrow."

Full, Thanks

After Lefty Gomez pitched himself into trouble by loading the bases, New York manager Joe McCarthy called time and walked out to the mound. "I just want you to know the bases are full," said Joe.

"Did you think I thought those guys were extra infielders?" Gomez replied.

IT'S ALL IN HOW YOU INTERPRET THINGS

In the spring of 1994, there was a great deal of talk about a rather unusual situation facing the Los Angeles Dodgers. They had a rookie pitcher named Chan Ho Park, who was from Korea. Since he spoke no English, the big question was whether the pitching coach would be able to communicate with him while making a mound visit during a game. Since baseball officials had ruled Park's interpreter couldn't go along for the conference on the hill, this was a very real concern.

Upon hearing all of the fuss, infielder Graig Nettles, always noted for his humor, came up with a great quip. "I don't know what all this concern about the interpreter is all about," he opined. "George Scott (former Red Sox player) played 15 years and he never had an interpreter." Scott, hardly known for his oratory skills or his dazzling articulation, probably was the only one who didn't enjoy Nettles' wit.

MR. REPLACEMENT

Alan Cockrell was a 32-year-old player who had kicked around in many teams' minor league systems as the 1995 season began. In fact, he had logged 1,199 pro games, of which none took place at the Major League level.

The Colorado Rockies were in need of replacement players to start the season. When Cockrell learned he was being considered by Colorado, he was asked if he felt he could handle the situation. He summed up his situation by saying, "When you look at the replacement guys, I not only fit the mold, I am mold."

THE WRY "RAJAH"

Roger Hornsby was one of the greatest hitters ever to don big-league flannels. His career batting average of .358 ranks behind only the .367 lifetime mark of Ty Cobb. Hornsby attributed much of his success to his single-minded devotion to baseball—they say he wouldn't even attend a motion picture for fear it would somehow hurt his batting eye.

He offered an opinion on why baseball is a better sport than golf by saying, "When I hit a ball, I want someone else to go chase it."

TALES OF LEATHER

Two classic stories stand out when it comes to tales of defensive play.

First, a look at Dick Stuart, a notoriously poor-fielding first base-man. The man nicknamed "Dr. Strangeglove" was a Pirate fan favorite despite his shortcomings with the leather. One day, a bat slipped out of the hands of an opposing batter. The bat whirled through the air towards first base, hit the turf, and then bounced all the way to Stuart. The first sacker came up with the bat cleanly, thus drawing good-natured cheers from a somewhat sarcastic crowd.

When asked if that was the most applause he'd ever heard, he responded, "No, one night 30,000 fans gave me a standing ovation when I caught a hot-dog wrapper on the fly."

Likewise, Johnny Mize could hit a ton, but was a leather liability at first base. When Mize was playing with the Giants for manager Leo Durocher, he also became the target of sarcasm. A fan mailed a letter to Leo The Lip which read: "Before each game an announcement is made that anyone interfering with or touching a batted ball will be ejected from the park. Please advise Mr. Mize that this doesn't apply to him."

A'S INSULTS

Two players from the Oakland Athletics came up with scathing insults. First, relief specialist Darold Knowles summed up Reggie Jackson's personality quite succinctly by saying, "There isn't enough mustard in the world to cover him." The flamboyant Jackson was the personification of being a baseball "hot dog" according to detractors and teammates as well.

During the glory days of the Athletics in the 1970s, the team owner was Charlie Finley, a controversial figure. Even though the A's won the World Series for an amazing three consecutive years (1972–1974), Finley was not exactly loved by many of his players. One such player was pitcher Steve McCatty. When McCatty learned Finley had undergone heart surgery, McCatty took this stab at his boss, "I heard it took eight hours for the operation ... seven and a half to find the heart."

Nettles on Steinbrenner

Like Finley, New York Yankees owner George Steinbrenner is constantly making headlines and enemies. Over the years, more than a few of his players have said they detest Steinbrenner because of his volatility and insensitivity. Some of those players went on to change their minds. Others simply changed their teams, at times being traded due to their public comments concerning their boss.

It should be noted, though, that Steinbrenner, a very wealthy man, is also capable of being quite generous. He must have felt generosity (or a forgiving sense of humor) towards Graig Nettles because he put up with a lot from the veteran Yankee infielder. For example, Nettles once said of his owner, "It's a good thing Babe Ruth still isn't here. If he was, George would have him hit seventh and say he's overweight."

The outspoken Nettles is most remembered for his view of the chaotic atmosphere playing for Steinbrenner's Yankees. "When I was a little boy," he said, "I wanted to be a baseball player and join the circus. With the Yankees, I've accomplished both."

MORE SADISM

During a 1995 baseball game, Philadelphia Phillies relief pitcher Norm Charlton was on the mound. He wasn't in the contest long before he let loose with a pitch to San Diego Padres' Steve Finley that was hit back to him a whole lot faster than it had been pitched.

The liner off Finley's bat smacked Charlton directly on his forehead, shocking everyone in attendance. Observers noted they couldn't ever recall so much blood gushing from an injury. Such a blow had ended players' careers in past cases. Remarkably, Charlton was relatively unscathed.

In fact, he was back at the ballpark the next day joking with the media. "I've had worse headaches than this," said the lefty, who broke into the majors with Cincinnati, where he became part of a wild crew of bullpen inhabitants nicknamed "The Nasty Boys." When reporters pointed out that his bruised appearance was quite a sight, he responded, "I guess I'll have to cancel that GQ cover.

Charlton even insisted he came to the park because he felt he was capable of pitching even with injuries less than 24 hours old. With that thought in mind, reporters approached the Phillies manager Jim Fregosi. "Would you actually use him tonight?" they queried. Fregosi showed his ability to employ gallows humor by saying, "Why not? He didn't throw that many pitches last night."

KEN GRIFFEY, JR. SIGNS FOOTBALL UNDER THE MOST UNUSUAL CIRCUMSTANCES

Baseball fans often go to unusual lengths to obtain a free autograph from a diamond star, with one of the strangest attempts coming during a Sunday, August 30, 1998 game between the New York Yankees and the Seattle Mariners before a packed house of more than 50,000 screaming fans at Yankee Stadium.

In the bottom of the fifth inning, a fan wearing a No. 24 Ken Griffey, Jr. jersey bolted from the grandstand along the left field line foul directly at the Mariners center fielder. Almost immediately, security guards descended upon the interloper from all sides. Griffey stood in place, hands on hips, stunned, unsure of what to expect. "You never know," he said later.

The fan proceeded to hand Griffey a regulation-size football and a pen and asked for an autograph, just before being tackled and heaved to the ground. As the security detail gained control of the fan, Griffey inscribed his signature on the football.

As the fan was hauled away to custody, he stretched out one free hand and Griffey handed him the ball. Alas, the souvenir was later taken away by the tightly disciplined Yankees security contingent.

Griffey Jr. has always been regarded as "fan friendly." John Sterling and Michael Kay, who were doing the radio broadcast for the Yankees, guffawed throughout the curious incident.

Incidentally, the Mariners thrashed the Yankees 13-3 in that game. And the hitting star for Seattle? Why, none other than Ken Griffey, who smacked two homers and drove in five runs!

ZANY UMPIRING IN THE JAPANESE LEAGUES

Umpiring practices in Japan are somewhat different compared to the umpiring ways in the U.S. professional leagues. For example, in a 1973 game played at Tokyo's sprawling Korakuen Stadium, a player began punching an umpire as the result of a disputed call. Several teammates joined in on the pummeling. Then the team's manager came storming out of the dugout. What did he do? Stop the fight? Heck, no. He also began punching the beleaguered ump!

Unlike American umpires, their Japanese league counterparts change their decisions—sometimes two or three times, depending upon the arguments put forward by the players, coaches, and managers. At a June 1974 game between the Tokyo Giants and the Hanshin Tigers at Korakuen, we witnessed a 45-minute game delay because of umpire indecision. All the while, the Japanese fans remained in their seats, quite complacent.

In 1974, Joe Lutz, a former major league player and a Cleveland Indians coach, became the first American to manage a team in Japan when he was appointed pilot of the Hiroshima Toya Carp of the

Central League. Lutz resigned before the season was over. Why? Because of a controversial call at home plate that went against his team. On that one call, the umpire changed his mind three times.

MARK McGWIRE'S SYNTHETICALLY MARKED HOME RUN BALLS

During the 1998 home run race between St. Louis Cardinals' Mark McGwire and Chicago Cubs' Sammy Sosa, fans became obsessed with catching the home-run baseballs hit into the grandstands by that duo (especially by McGwire, who outpaced Sosa in the homer derby for most of the time).

From a historical perspective, Sal Durante, a New York fan, became a minor celebrity after he retrieved Roger Maris' 61st home run ball in the right field bleachers at Yankee Stadium on October 2, 1961. Durante reportedly sold the historic baseball for $5,000.

National League officials were cognizant of the fact that any record-breaking McGwire homer baseball would undoubtedly be worth a lot of money on the open market. As the St. Louis slugger passed the 50-homer mark, every ball pitched to him was marked with synthetic DNA to make it identifiable. Thus, there would be no chance for any-one to pass off a "fake" McGwire home run ball.

On the last day of the 1998 season, on Sunday, September 27, at Busch Stadium in St. Louis, McGwire, in his final time at bat, lined his 70th home run into a deep left field luxury-box suite. After a ferocious scramble, Philip Ozersky, a 26-year-old technician at the St. Louis University School of Medicine, came up with the ball.

Within two weeks, after gaining possession of the ball, he received some 400 inquires from dealers and collectors. Three St. Louis collectors got together and offered Ozersky a cool $1 million. Ozersky hired a lawyer to help him sort through all the offers.

The baseball is considered to be worth far more than $1 million, and now ranks as the single most valuable bit of baseball memorabilia.

One of the wackiest offers for the ball came from a man who identified himself as a distributor for a major American doll maker. Ozersky's lawyer commented, "This guy thinks he can get a million threads out of the ball, and insert one tiny thread into a million dolls. And sell them as Mark McGwire dolls with a piece of the ball in each one. That's not all. Then he wants to put the ball back together with other thread and sell it!"

THE NEW YORK YANKEES— TIGHT WITH A BUCK

The New York Yankees, baseball's most successful franchise, had the reputation of being extremely "tight with a buck"—at least until George Steinbrenner bought the team in 1973.

Take the tale of Babe Ruth, whose relations with the Yankees were strained after he retired from active play in 1935. At the beginning of the 1939 season, he wrote to the Yankees offices and requested a pair of complimentary tickets for opening day at Yankee Stadium. Ruth was curtly told via return mail that he must include his check with his request. Naturally, Ruth, who felt he was grievously insulted, was not present for opening day ceremonies.

Then we have the case of Phil Rizzuto, who often recounted this story when he was doing play-by-play for the Yankees on radio and TV. He recalled the time he hit his first homer for New York at Yankee Stadium early in 1941, his rookie season. As Rizzuto rounded third base, a fan ran onto the field, grabbed Phil's cap off the top of his head, and ran into the stands with it.

The next day Rizzuto received a note form George Weiss, Yankees general manager, saying that $5 would be deducted from his pay for losing the cap. Rizzuto said, "I couldn't help it. That fan came after me like a madman."

Weiss said firmly, "You've got to hold onto your stuff better." The $5 charge stood.

HENRY AARON—AUTOGRAPHS, YES. REGISTRATION SIGNATURES, NO.

When anyone registers at a hotel or motel just about anywhere in the world, he must sign the registration book. But not Henry "Home" Aaron, the great home run slugger.

When Aaron appeared as an autograph guest at a show featuring all living major leaguers who had rapped out at least 3000 base hits, an event staged at Atlantic City's Showboat Hotel and Casino in the fall of 1995, he flat out refused to sign the registry. "No way I'm going to sign that book!" Henry told the hotel clerk.

It seemed that Aaron's fee per autograph at the Showboat ranged from about $50 to more than $100, depending upon the nature of the item to be signed. (Autographed bats are the most expensive.) Aaron simply wasn't going to sign anything for free.

The matter was settled when Aaron's agent signed the registry for him.

IT'S ALEXANDER CARTWRIGHT, NOT ABNER DOUBLEDAY, WHO INVENTED BASEBALL!

John Sterling and Michael Kay have been partners on Yankees radio broadcasts for a decade. Although we appreciate their general knowledge of the game and its wide array of intricacies, they have their zany moments on the radio.

Kay once went into a soliloquy on the beauty and symmetry of the game during a Yankees broadcast early in the 1998 season. Toward the midpoint of the game, a player hit a grounder to deep short, with the shortstop coming up with the ball and throwing in time to the first baseman to get the out. Kay in effect said, "That's beautiful … in the great majority of the cases, if an infielder handles the ball cleanly, his throw to first will get the batter out. The space between the bases, 90 feet apart, is just perfect. Thank you, General Doubleday, for inventing this great game."

The only problem with Kay's analysis is that General Abner Doubleday did not invent the game at Cooperstown, New York, in 1839, where the first ballgame was supposed to have been played. It has been proven that Doubleday (1819–1893) never set foot in Cooperstown and had nothing to do with the development of baseball. Even historians at the Hall of Fame in Cooperstown agree, although Doubleday's mistaken connection with the diamond game is legendary.

Credit for the development of modern baseball, as we know the game, must go to Alexander Joy Cartwright (1820–1892) who organized the first baseball team, the Knickerbocker Ball Club of NewYork City, in 1845. Cartwright's Knickerbockers played the first organized game on June 19, 1846, at the Elysian Fields, Hoboken, New Jersey, against a club called the New Yorks.

It was Cartwright, an engineer and New York city volunteer fireman, who set the basic rules of the game that stand today, including ending the practice of putting a man out by hitting him with a thrown ball. He introduced the nine-man team with an unalterable batting order, a nine-inning game, three outs per side, and a 90-foot baseline. He also dressed his team, made up of local firefighters, in the game's first uniforms. Most New York teams of that era came out of various firehouses. Barry Halper, the indefatigable New Jersey memorabilia collector, has a wide array of Cartwright materials, including his fireman's hat and horn!

For his contributions to baseball, Cartwright was inducted into the Hall of Fame in 1938. Though there is a Doubleday exhibit in the Hall of Fame, Abner Doubleday was never elected into baseball's shrine.

The next time Kay muses about the wonder of the 90-foot baselines, he should say instead, "Thank you, Mr. Cartwright."

You're the Manager

Baseball fans love to second-guess managers while they are watching a game. After all, part of the charm of the game is deciding what you would do if you were the manager.

Some fickle fans offer their opinions only after a negative outcome. For example, it isn't unusual to hear a spectator bellow, "I never would've stuck with that reliever," after the pitcher has just given up a home run. That second-guess scenario is all too familiar.

On the other hand, some knowledgeable fans will go out on a limb and declare their managerial intentions before a situation has run its course. This chapter affords you the opportunity to be a big league manager and make decisions based on real-life situations.

Read all the pertinent details about a given situation, then make your move. Next, read on to learn what really happened—or what most big league managers would've done in a certain situation.

Of course, the real-life job of managing entails more than just making calls. Consider the plight of Phil Cavarretta, manager of the Chicago Cubs for the 1954 season. As the team entered spring training, Cubs owner Phil Wrigley asked Cavarretta what the outlook was for the Cubs that year. Cavarretta made a serious mistake when he answered his boss honestly, reporting that things didn't look too bright.

Wrigley, who wanted optimism from his field generals, gave him the proverbial ax. Cavarretta became the first manager ever to be fired during spring training. Still want to be a big league manager? If so, read on and begin making your decisions.

TOUGH CALL

Let's begin with a very difficult call, one that confronted San Diego Padres manager Preston Gomez back on July 21, 1970. His pitcher, Clay Kirby, was methodically mowing down the New York Mets. Through eight innings, the Mets had not chalked up a hit.

Now comes the dilemma. Despite the no-hitter, Kirby was losing, 1-0. In the bottom of the eighth, the host Padres came to bat, and, with two men out, Kirby was due to hit. What did Gomez do? Did he pinch hit for Kirby in an effort to rev up some offense, or did he let Kirby remain in the game so the 22-year-old second year pitcher could try to secure his no-hitter?

What Happened

Gomez made a gutsy move that was criticized a great deal—he lifted Kirby for a pinch hitter. What really gave second guessers ammunition for their anger was the fact that the move made no difference. The Padres went on to drop the game 3-0, and the bullpen went on to lose the no-hit bid. Through 1998, the Padres were one of just three teams (not counting 1998 expansion clubs) that had never recorded a no-hitter. (The others were the Mets and Rockies.)

Change of Scenario

If you voted emotionally to let Kirby try for the no-hitter and felt the choice was easy, you aren't alone—tons of fans feel this way. Now, however, let's change the scenario a bit. Would you remain as liberal if the game had entered the bottom of the ninth and was scoreless? Are you still sticking with him? Let's further assume Kirby is tiring a bit, and his pitch count is rapidly climbing.

Finally, for stubborn fans clinging to the thought of staying with Kirby, would it change your mind if you had a hot pinch hitter salivating, anxious to come off the bench? This time, there's no right or wrong answer—it's your call.

Similar Scenario

In 1974, the Houston Astros manager faced a situation much like the Clay Kirby near no-hitter. Don Wilson had worked his way through eight innings of no-hit ball and was due up to bat in the fifth inning. The manager lifted Wilson for a pinch hitter. Moments later, the new pitcher, Mike Cosgrove, began the ninth by issuing a leadoff single to Cincinnati's Tony Perez for the only hit they'd get that day. The Reds also wound up winning the game, 2-1. The punch line here is that the Astros manager was none other than Preston Gomez.

Perhaps there's no connection, but Gomez managed Houston again in 1975 for part of the season (127 games), then went nearly five years before being hired again as a big league manager. After 90 games as the Cubs' manager, he never had a job as a major league skipper again.

WAS VIDA FEELING BLUE

Oakland A's manager Alvin Dark had a dilemma similar to Gomez's. On the final day of the 1975 season, Dark sent his ace, Vida Blue (with his 21 wins), to the mound. The A's had already clinched the Western Division, so Dark decided to have Blue pitch just 5 innings, then rest him for the upcoming playoffs.

At the end of those five innings, Blue had a no-hitter going. Dark didn't change his mind, though. He went to the bullpen for Glenn Abbott, who worked a hitless sixth inning. In the seventh, Dark brought in Paul Lindblad before turning the chores over to his closer, Rollie Fingers, to wrap it up. The quartet of pitchers managed to throw a highly unusual no-hitter with Blue getting the win. This game marked the first no-hitter by four men.

INTENTIONAL WALK LUNACY

Intentional walks are a big part of a manager's strategic repertoire. Frequently, with first base unoccupied, a team will deliberately walk a dangerous hitter and take its chances that the next batter will hit the ball on the ground. If he does and the defense turns a double play, a volatile situation is defused, and the team is out of a dangerous inning.

Would a situation ever call for intentionally walking a man with the bases loaded? As is the case with many of the plays that follow, this call is based on opinion. However, 99.99 percent of all the managers who ever filled out a lineup card would feel such a move was positive proof of temporary insanity. Believe it or not, such a move has taken place in a big league game, and on more than one occasion!

Two Intentional Incidents

A recent occasion took place on May 28, 1998, when the San Francisco Giants faced the Arizona Diamondbacks. The score was 8-6 in the bottom of the ninth. With two outs and the bases loaded, Arizona manager Buck Showalter ordered an intentional walk to the always-dangerous Barry Bonds.

After Bonds had moseyed down to first, the Giants were within one run. However, the next batter, Brent Mayne, made Showalter look good by lining out to right fielder Brent Brede on a payoff pitch, ending the contest.

The Second Bold Intentional Walk

Showalter wasn't the only manager who made a brazen strategic move in 1998. On May 24 in the 14th inning of a chaotic game, San Francisco manager Dusty Baker definitely went against accepted baseball wisdom. In the top of the 14th, with the game still tied, Giants pitcher Jim Poole handled St. Louis hitters Ron Gant and Delino DeShields with no problem. Mark McGwire stepped up to the plate, and that's when it happened. Baker ordered an intentional walk to the hot-hitting McGwire.

Baker was deliberately allowing the potential game-winning run to reach base. Traditionalists were apoplectic, but Baker had his reasons for the walk. First of all, anybody who followed the game in 1998 knew McGwire was one bad dude. In fact, he had already homered in the 12th inning. That gave him a major league-leading 24 blasts. With a full week to go in May, he was tied for the record for the most homers ever hit by the end of that month. (Later, he did break that record.)

In addition, Baker was following the baseball adage that you just don't let certain superstars beat you—you take the bat out of their hands. On that day, Baker took McGwire's bat away three times with intentional walks.

When Ray Lankford followed with a single, things appeared to be shaky. However, Poole managed to strike out Willie McGee to end the inning without further damage. Ultimately, the move worked since the Giants went on to win 9-6 in 17 innings. Poole said of the walk, "Your first instinct is like, 'No!' Then you realize it's him [McGwire], and you say, 'Oh, well, I guess so.' He's going pretty good right now." Clearly that was an understatement.

Veteran pitcher Orel Hershiser captured the spirit of the event. He said, "Walk McGwire with nobody on? That's a legend. Jim Poole and Dusty Baker will be trivia, and McGwire will be the legend."

WHEN NOT PITCHING IS GOOD

Along the same lines as the Ott intentional walk issue, sometimes not pitching to a slugger or a particularly hot hitter is as much a case of good strategy as, say, knowing when to yank a tiring pitcher from the hill.

In 1969, when San Francisco first baseman Willie McCovey was wielding a lethal bat, opposing managers avoided him as if he were a coiled, angry python. Not only did "Stretch" go on to win the National League's Most Valuable Player award (45 HR, 126 RBI, and a lofty .656 slugging percentage), he was awarded first base intentionally a record 45 times as well. That works out to about three intentional walks every 10 games.

Foxx Hunt

Consider, too, what American League managers did to Jimmie Foxx. During his 20-year career, spent almost entirely in the "Junior Circuit," Foxx amassed 534 homers, enough even now to rank in the all-time top ten. Knowing how powerful "Double X" was, managers often had their pitchers work around him.

On June 16, 1938, Foxx, by then with the Boston Red Sox, was well on his way to an incredibly productive season that included a .349 average, 50 home runs, and 175 runs batted in. On that day, the feared Foxx was issued six walks during a nine-inning game, still good for a major league record. While the walks were not officially listed as intentional walks, it's pretty obvious that pitchers worked him quite carefully. Again, not pitching can be a wise move.

TO PITCH OR NOT TO PITCH, THAT IS THE QUESTION

After all the talk about pitching or not pitching to blistering hot hitters, here's a real-life case. In the best-of-seven National League Championship Series (NLCS) back in 1985, the Los Angeles Dodgers squared off against the St. Louis Cardinals. The winner would head to the World Series.

The NLCS stood at 3 games to 2 in favor of the Cardinals. The Dodgers had to have a win. They were leading 5-4 as the top of the 9th inning rolled around. Then a critical situation developed. With two men out and runners on second and third, the Redbirds mounted a major threat. Even a single would probably score two, giving St. Louis the lead.

To make matters worse for the jittery Dodgers, the batter was Jack Clark, the Cardinals cleanup hitter, who had already crushed 22 homers and driven in 87 runs that year to go with his .281 batting average in just 126 games.

RUTH'S WORLD SERIES LARCENY

It's the 9th inning of the seventh game of the 1926 World Series. Today's winner will be the new World Champion. The St. Louis Cardinals are leading the New York Yankees by a score of 3-2. You are the Yanks skipper, Miller Huggins, winner of 91 regular-season games.

Despite all that success, you are down to your last out. But all is not lost yet—Babe Ruth is on first base after drawing a walk. The game is still alive. If the "Bambino" could reach second base, he'd be in scoring position. A single could tie it up. Not only that, the batter now in the box is your cleanup hitter, Bob Meusel, and Lou Gehrig is on deck.

Meusel missed part of the season with a broken foot, but he still drove in 81 runs. Gehrig, meanwhile, had 83 extra base hits in 1926, his second full season in the majors. As for Ruth, he had swiped 11 bases during the season and was considered a pretty good base runner in his day.

Final Factors

The St. Louis pitcher was Grover Cleveland Alexander. Although he would come back in 1927 to post a stellar 21-10 record, the 39-year-old Alexander was on the downside of his career. He had recorded a complete-game victory just the day before our classic situation unfolded. Baseball lore states he had celebrated the win by going out on the town that evening… and into the morning. They say he didn't even witness the events prior to being called into the game because he was by then soundly sleeping in the bullpen.

Now, having worked flawlessly for 2 innings prior to the walk to Ruth, the game was on the line. He peered in to get the signal from his catcher, Bob O'Farrell, who had a .976 career fielding percentage.

Armed with all the data, what would you have done if you were in charge? Call for a hit-and-run play? Do nothing and let Meusel swing away? Have Meusel take a strike (not swing at a pitch until Alexander throws a strike)? This last would show whether Alexander was getting wild and/or tired; after all, he had just walked Ruth. Would you have Ruth steal to get into scoring position? Any other ideas?

What Happened

Ruth took his lead. Alexander fired a pitch, and Ruth, who had stolen a base the day before, took off for second. O'Farrell's throw easily beat Babe as St. Louis player-manager Rogers Hornsby applied the tag. The Series was over with the Yankees losing on a daring play that most experts felt was also a very foolish play.

Accounts of the game indicate that Huggins actually had Meusel hitting away and did not have Ruth running. The story goes that Ruth was running on his own, creating a terrible blunder. Few, if any, managers would have had Ruth running —it was way too risky.

The Outcome

The Sox skipper, Ed Barrow, made a good call. Although Ruth grounded out early in the game, he tripled-in two of Boston's three runs. In his final at-bat, he sacrificed. Meanwhile, the man who did hit in the ninth spot was a catcher by the name of Sam Agnew. He went 0-for-2 after hitting .166 on the year.

On the mound, Ruth worked eight innings, got in trouble in the ninth, was relieved, then moved to the outfield as the Sox held on to win, 3-2. Boston also went on win the Series 4 games to 2. By the way, during this game, Ruth's streak of 29⅔ consecutive scoreless innings (a record at the time) came to an end.

Quick Quiz

Do managers normally try to steal home in a situation like this? The runner on third can be anyone you choose. If you'd like, select Ty Cobb, who stole home an all-time record 50 times during his illustrious career. (Who wouldn't like that prospect?)

Now, does it matter if the batter is a lefty or righty as long as you have the fiery Cobb barreling down the line as soon as the pitcher commits to throwing the ball to the plate?

○ **ANSWER:** Yes, it matters. Most managers feel they'd definitely prefer a right-handed batter in the box when they attempt a steal of home. Back in the 1940s, Jackie Robinson was known to have done it with a lefty in the batter's box, but he was special.

Incidentally, stealing home was rather common in the Cobb era, a dead-ball era in which you'd scratch for runs any way you could come by them.

Lately, swiping home is a rarity. Wade Boggs, a sure future Hall of Famer, says that nowadays, you just don't see it done. "It's probably a lost art. Mostly it's done now with first and third. The guy on first takes off, then the guy on third takes off."

Nevertheless, when an attempt to steal home does occur, you still don't want a lefty at bat. A left-hander stands in the batter's box to the right of the catcher. Conversely, a right-handed hitter stands on the left side of the catcher.

What's the logic involved here? Kevin Stocker of the Tampa Bay Devil Rays explained, "If you're on the right side of the plate, and you're straight stealing, the catcher can see the runner coming and has no one to go around." In other words, there's nothing obstructing his tag.

Or, as Atlanta Braves manager Bobby Cox, perennial winner of division titles, put it, "You want the batter in the right hander's box to help block out the catcher." A righty obstructs the catcher's view of the runner dashing down the line. The catcher may not realize a play is on until it is too late to do anything about it.

There was once a runner who stole home standing up. This happened because the pitcher threw a pitch that was so wild, the catcher was only able to grab it after lunging out of the line of action. Thus, he couldn't even come close to tagging the runner.

THE PLAYER-PITCHER SWITCH

Let's say that the starting southpaw of the Phillies is in trouble late in a game against the Braves. Atlanta has runners on first and second, one out, and their clean-up hitter, a right-handed batter, at the plate.

The Phillies manager decides to relieve his star lefty with his best bullpen hurler, a righty. But he does not remove his star pitcher from the game. He puts him at first base and moves his first baseman to play third base. The relief pitcher gets the batter to hit a short fly ball to left field for an out. There is no advance. Then the manager returns the fielder from third to first and restores his star to the mound, to pitch to the next batter, who is a left hand hitter.

Can a manager switch pitchers this way?

○ **ANSWER:** As long as he stays in the game, a pitcher can return to the mound. The pitcher who replaced him, however, has to have hurled to at least one official batter.

Manager Paul Richards of the White Sox used to be noted for that switch. One day he substituted left-hander Billy Pierce for right-hander Harry Dorish when southpaw-swinging Ted Williams was at the plate. Richards kept Dorish in the game, placing him at third base. When Pierce retired Williams, Dorish returned to the mound, retiring Pierce. The displaced third baseman, however, could not come back into the game.

Sometimes Richards used to keep Pierce, a good-hitting pitcher, in the game, too. Richards would put his pitcher at first base. When the situation was right, he would return his good-hitting pitcher to the mound.

THE ELEMENT OF SURPRISE

The Yankees are at bat with a runner on third base.

With a count of two balls and two strikes on the batter, the runner on third tries to steal home. The batter, totally surprised, takes the pitch which the umpire calls a ball. Meanwhile the runner is tagged out.

"Don't s...w...i...n...g."

What's wrong with that play?

○ **ANSWER:** The runner never—repeat never—tries to steal home with two strikes on the batter. A hitter, when he has two strikes on him, has to protect the plate. So if the ball is close, he has to swing. If he does, the runner could be hit by either the ball or the bat. In either event, the consequences could be disastrous.

The Yankees were guilty of that mistake a few years ago. Roy Smalley was the runner; Graig Nettles, the batter. Don Zimmer was the third-base coach. With a count of two balls and one strike, Nettles jumped out of the way of a pitch under his chin. Zimmer and Smalley assumed that the pitch was a ball, but the umpire called it a strike. On the next pitch, Zimmer thought that the count was three-one, instead of two-two, and he sent Smalley in.

Realizing the situation, Smalley, while running home, was pleading, "Graig, Graig, please don't swing."

Nettles didn't. But the strategy definitely took the possibility of a hit away from Nettles.

IT COULD HAVE BEEN

How important is it that a pitcher be able to cover first base well? It's ultra-important. It's so important that it might have cost the Yankees the 1985 pennant.

In this case, the Yankee pitcher breaks to his left on a ball hit to the first baseman. The throw is in time. But the pitcher, who had run directly across to the bag, overruns the bag in his haste to beat the runner. The ball then comes loose from his glove and rolls down the right-field line. Two Blue Jays score as the game turns around.

What mistake did the pitcher make?

○ **ANSWER:** The pitcher should have "bellied" into the catch. That is, he should have run to a spot on the foul line midway between home and first and cut to his left, running parallel to and inside the foul line.

Then, he could have caught the ball while his right foot could be touching the second-base side of the base. In that way, the pitcher avoids contact with the runner and makes the play the safe way.

Ron Guidry had outduelled Dave Stieb in the first game of the big September series with the pennant at stake, and it looked as though the Bronx Bombers were going to finally overtake the Blue Jays. But this basic play turned the game—and perhaps the season—around.

Don Mattingly, one of the best fielding first basemen in recent memory, made the play going to his right, turned and threw. Mattingly made a high throw, very uncommon for him. Phil Niekro, an accomplished fielder, in running straight towards the bag, got his hands up slowly. Normally he would have made that play. When the ball bounced off the pitcher's glove and trickled into the dugout, it allowed two runs to score.

Those runs decided the game, preventing Niekro from recording his 300pth career victory and stopping the Yankees from creeping to one-half game from the American League lead.

The Yankees went on to lose eight consecutive games and were virtually eliminated from the race.

If he had made that play, he would have won his 300th game, and the Yankees might have won the pennant.

That's how important it is for a pitcher to be able to cover first base!

THE BOUNCE SLIDE

In the top of the tenth inning in a tight game, a runner races home on a single and slides without a play being made on him.

The catcher, receiving the late throw, notices that the umpire does not make a call. He rushes after the runner, who is walking to the dugout, and tags him.

Why, in this case, does the umpire not make a call? Is the runner safe or out?

○ **ANSWER:** No call by the umpire indicates that the runner is neither safe nor out. On this play, the runner misses touching home plate, so he isn't safe. But since he wasn't tagged initially, he isn't out, either. When the catcher runs after him and tags him, then the runner is out.

When Gil Hodges was managing the Washington Senators, he was victimized by such a play. One of his players slid "across" the plate without a play being made. When the Oriole

The bounce slide

catcher realized that a call hadn't been made; he tagged the surprised runner out.

Hodges angrily faced the umpire and demanded to know how his runner could be out when a play hadn't been made on him. The umpire informed Hodges that when the Senator runner slid, he bounced over the plate.

EVERYTHING TO GAIN

Imagine that Pete Rose, who is known for his hustle, is on first for the Reds with two out.

The batter hits a long fly ball to right field. Rose breaks on his teammate's contact. Just about everyone in the park thinks that the ball is foul. But a strong wind pulls the ball back into fair territory. The ball lands right inside the foul line as Rose, who never stopped running, scores from first on the play.

What's the moral?

O **ANSWER:** Run hard on every play, especially if you've got nothing to lose. In this case, it turns out that Rose had everything to gain.

Actually, the Yankees' Steve Kemp was the real-life hero of this script. He scored on a wind-blown fly ball hit by Don Baylor.

Asked why he was running all-out on the play, he said, "There were two outs. I had nothing to lose."

My kind of ballplayer.

EIGHT MEN ON THE FIELD

Marty Barrett of the Red Sox hits very few home runs. Understandably, he was very upset when the Yankees' Ken Griffey Jr. dived into the left-field stands at Yankee Stadium to rob the Boston second-baseman of a long ball blast.

Can an outfielder leave the playing field to make a catch?

○ **ANSWER:** Yes, an outfielder, or any other player, can leave the playing field to make a catch. The determining factor is whether the fielder's momentum carries him into the stands while he is making the play. If it does, it is a good catch. If the player establishes a stationary position in the stands before he makes the catch, however, the grab is disallowed.

In the situation described above, Griffey timed his jump perfectly and made a sensational catch while bouncing off a fan who was trying to snatch the ball from him. It was a legitimate catch.

If Griffey had mistimed his jump, landed in the stands early, and then caught Barrett's drive, the hit would have been ruled a home run.

But Griffey played the ball perfectly. Only his landing, back on the playing field, was a little less than smooth. Dave Winfield, playing the part of an Olympic judge, gave Griffey a ten on his dive, but only a five on his landing.

UNAWARE

In a real game, in August 1979, the Reds were leading the host Pirates in the bottom of the fourth inning. But the Pirates had runners on first and third with two out. Pitcher Fred Norman had a three-two count on hitter Omar Moreno. On the pay-off pitch, Lee Lacy at first was off-and-running. Catcher Johnny Bench instinctively threw the ball to shortstop Dave Concepcion, who applied the tag to the sliding Lacy. The umpire called Lacy out.

Lacy, thinking his side was out, then got up and walked towards the first-base line, waiting to be delivered his glove for the field. Lacy was unaware that the pitch to Moreno had been wide and high for ball four. He had been forced to advance on the walk.

When his teammates yelled that fact to him, and that he should return to second, Concepcion was waiting for him at the bag with the ball. The umpire called Lacy out for the second time.

Pirate manager Chuck Tanner argued the call for a long time.

Did his argument prevail?

○ **ANSWER:** No. When it didn't, he protested the game. But National League President Chub Feeney overruled it on two grounds: one, there had been no misinterpretation of rules, and two, Lacy should have known what was going on.

THEY WON BUT THEY LOST

In a late-season game in 1979, Yankee first baseman Chris Chambliss was warming up his infielders in between innings when the webbing of his glove broke. While he ran to the dugout to get a new glove, Lou Piniella came out to first to continue the warm-ups. When Chambliss resumed his first-base position, Tiger manager Sparky Anderson came out to the plate umpire and said that once a substitute took the place of a player on the field, he was in the game. When the umpire didn't remove Chambliss from the game, Anderson filed a protest. The Yankees went on to win the game, 3-1.

Did Anderson win the protest?

○ **ANSWER:** Yes, he did, but the league office considered it a technicality and elected not to play the game over. Sparky won but he lost.

QUICK EXIT?

On this day Tigers manager Sparky Anderson selects a light-hitting batter as this designated hitter, and he putting him in the no.8 spot in the batting order. But when his time at-bat comes in the second inning, the bases are loaded, and Sparky decides to go for the big inning. He sends up a long-ball hitter, Mickey Tettleton, for his DH.

Can he do this?

○ **ANSWER:** No, he can't. The designated hitter named in the starting lineup must come to bat at least one time, unless the opposing club changes pitchers. Rule 6.10 (b).

THE UNKINDEST TOUCH

The Mets have a runner on second base, one out, and Eddie Murray at the plate in a game against the host Phillies. Murray lofts a soft fly ball to left-center field. The runner, thinking that the ball might drop for a base hit, goes halfway to third, but the center fielder makes a good running catch.

His subsequent throw to third base, however, strikes a stone and bounces wildly past the third baseman into the Mets' dugout. The runner from second advances two bases on the play, scoring a run. But he doesn't retouch second before he makes his advance.

The Phillies realize this, so the pitcher, when he puts the ball in play, throws it first to second base and files an appeal with the umpire.

Is the run taken off the scoreboard?

○ **ANSWER:** Yes, the runner had to retouch second after the catch. Then, while the ball was dead, he could advance. The award of two bases would have been made from his original base. Rule 7.05 (i).

FORCE OUT?

With one out, the Cardinals have Felix Jose on third base, Todd Zeile on second base, and Ozzie Smith on first base. Pedro Guerrero then hits a ground ball to Met shortstop Dick Schofield, who throws to second baseman Willie Randolph for the start of a double play, but Smith beats the throw. Randolph, however, relays the ball to first baseman Eddie Murray for the out on Guerrero.

Murray notices that Smith has overslid second base, throws to Schofield, who applies the tag to the runner before he can scramble back to the base.

In the meantime, Jose and Zeile have scored on the play. However, the Mets argue that the runs shouldn't count, since the inning ended on a force-out double play.

Are they right?

O **ANSWER:** No, they are not right. The runs score. It is not a force play. It is a tag play. Rule 7.08 (e) play

TWO TRIPS PER INNING

Scott Erickson, the pitcher for the Twins, is in trouble in the bottom half of the sixth inning. The Brewers have Jim Gantner on third, Paul Molitor on second, and Robin Yount on first with one out. Before Erickson pitches to clean-up hitter Rob Deer, Minnesota manager Tom Kelly comes out to the mound, explaining to his right hander how he wants him to throw to Deer.

Erickson, perhaps thinking too hard, proceeds to walk Deer on four straight pitches. Kelly then comes out to the mound for the second time in the inning, and everyone in the ballpark knows what's going to happen.

What?

○ **ANSWER:** A second trip by the manager to the same pitcher in the same inning causes the hurler's automatic removal. Rule 8.06 (a).

ONE TRIP PER BATTER

Suppose in the preceding example, manager Tom Kelly had come out to the mound for the second time just after Erickson had thrown ball three to Deer.

○ **ANSWER:** The penalty would be greater. The manager or coach can't make a second trip to the mound while the same hitter is at the plate. Rule 8.06 (a). If the manager does, he is automatically ejected from the game, but the pitcher can remain for the duration of the hitter's at-bat. After the batter either reaches base or makes an out, the pitcher is ejected, too.

THE MANAGER'S CLONE

Let's take the preceding situation one step further. Suppose Kelly has already made his one trip to the mound, but after Deer runs the count to 3-0, Kelly yells some instructions to shortstop Greg Gagne, who runs to the mound to converse with Erickson.

Is there any penalty?

○ **ANSWER:** Yes. Gagne's trip to the mound would be considered Minnesota's second conference during the same at-bat, and the same penalties that were imposed when Kelly visited the mound twice during the same hitter's at-bat would apply here. Rule 8.06 (a).

The rule wasn't always applied so rigidly. Casey Stengel frequently used to manage through his infielders, who didn't always relish the role of playing manager.

Once during the 1949 World Series, when Tommy "Wild Man" Byrne had walked the bases loaded against the Brooklyn Dodgers, Casey whistled to second baseman Jerry Coleman. That was his signal that he wanted Coleman to visit the mound. Byrne wasn't too happy to see his teammate, though. "What do you want?" he snapped. "I just wanted to know how you're doing," Coleman said. "Fine. You?" "Fine." "Well, since we're both fine," Byrne said, "I guess we've got business to do." "Yes."

Coleman ran back to his position, Byrne released the pitch, and Gil Hodges hit into an inning-ending double play.

Three years later, in the 1952 World Series, when Yankee starter Vic Raschi was struggling, Stengel whistled to second baseman Billy Martin, who dreaded to visit Raschi, who was a martinet on the mound.

"What do you want?" Raschi greeted him, irritated.

I just wanted to know how you're doing," Martin said. "Well, you're having enough trouble playing your own position. Don't come in here and tell me how to play mine."

Martin, with his tail between his legs, scurried back to his position at second. Later he whined to Stengel, "Don't ever send me to the mound again when Raschi's pitching. He'll punch me in the head."

So Stengel didn't get himself in trouble with the rules— but Martin did.

THE PLAYING MANAGER

Don Kessinger, the last playing manager in the major leagues, removes himself from the White Sox lineup in the top half of the eighth inning, then assumes the third-base coaching reins in the bottom half of the inning.

Can he do this?

○ **ANSWER:** Yes. Here is Rule 3.03: A manager under those circumstances may continue to lead his team and may go to the coaching lines via his own directions.

THE FAIR FOUL

Suppose the host Padres, in the bottom of the ninth inning, are tied with the Cubs.

The Padres' shortstop leads off the inning with a single to right. The Cubs look for the bunt, but the hitter slaps a single past the drawn-in infield. The next batter moves the runners up a base with a sacrifice bunt.

The Cubs elect to pitch to the Padres' power hitter. He slaps a soft fly ball down the left-field line. The Cub left fielder thinks that he can catch the ball and hold the runner at third. But the ball bounces off the fingers of the glove, in fair territory, into foul territory for the game-winning hit.

The Cubs argue, however, that since the ball landed in foul territory, the umpire must call it foul.

Is it?

○ **ANSWER:** No, the Cubs are wrong. The determining factor is where the ball was touched. In this case, the ball was touched within the chalk lines, so it's a fair ball. Sometimes a fielder will be in fair territory, but touch and drop the ball while reaching across the chalk line into foul territory. In that instance, the ball is foul. At other times the fielder may be in foul territory, but touch and drop the ball while leaning over the foul line into fair territory. In that instance, the ball is fair.

In 1984 the Yankees encountered that problem in Milwaukee. In a tie game, in the bottom of the ninth, first baseman Mike Felder led off the inning with a single. The Yankee infield, expecting Paul Molitor to bunt, was surprised when the third baseman singled Felder to second. Randy Ready then sacrificed the runners to second and third, respectively.

The Yankees, with lefty Dave Righetti on the mound, elected to pitch to dangerous Cecil Cooper, a left-handed hitter. Cooper hit a

Righetti fast ball down the left-field line. The left fielder attempted to make the play, but he deflected the ball, in fair territory, into foul ground, where it bounced. In the meantime, Felder scored the winning run.

Yankee manager Billy Martin argued wildly that the ball was touched in foul territory, so it should be a foul ball. But the umpire disagreed and stuck by his decision.

It's a good thing that he did. The video replay showed that the ball was touched in fair territory.

Fair ball. Fair call.

YOU CAN'T DO THAT

The batter singles sharply to right field with a runner on second base. The team's manager, who happens to be coaching at third, waves the runner home.

But when he sees the right fielder charge the ball and fire on the run, the coach changes his mind. He cannot hold up his hands, however, because the runner is not looking at him at the time. So he reaches out and grabs the runner by the right hand and yanks the runner back to third as the outfielder throws a strike to the catcher.

Can the coach legally do this?

○ **ANSWER:** No, a coach cannot physically aid a runner in any way while the ball is a live ball. If he does, as he did here, the runner is called out. You will see the third-base coach pat a player on the rump after a home run. But that is a dead-ball situation. If the coach had done the same thing during a live-ball situation, the runner would be declared out.

Harold "Peanuts" Lowrey, a third-base coach for the Cubs in the 1970's, did that one day to Bobby Murcer, who was trying to score.

THE HASTY RETREAT

Oakland's center fielder is on second base ready to steal third. He gets a good jump on the Yankee pitcher as the batter flies out to the outfield. Running with his head down, the A's player doesn't see the fly being caught, and is decoyed into sliding by the Yanks' third baseman.

In doing so, he overslides third. The third-base coach, seeing what had happened, helps the runner to his feet; since the fly was caught, and the A's outfielder has to return to second, he goes directly back.

What two things are wrong with this play?

O **ANSWER:** The two things wrong are 1) the third-base coach cannot physically aid the runner, and 2) the runner must retouch the base he has overslid before returning to second.

That very play occurred in a game between Oakland and New York. The A's Mike Davis overslid third, the Yankees' Graig Nettles applied the decoy, and Clete Boyer, a former Yankee third baseman, was the Oakland third-base coach.

The umpire didn't notice Boyer help Davis to his feet, but he did see that the runner fail to retouch third.

Nettles appealed the play. The umpires upheld the appeal. Davis was called out.

MORE DELAYS

Albert Belle, Baltimore's volatile slugger is at the plate. Let's say he gets irate over a strike call you, the umpire, just made. He starts to jaw with you. After a few moments, you get fed up with the delay and tell Belle to get in the box and quit squawking.

What do you do if Belle refuses to obey your orders ?

○ **ANSWER:** In this case, you would order the man on the mound to pitch the ball. As a punishment, you would call that pitch a strike even if it isn't in the strike zone. In addition, if the batter still refuses to step in and face the pitcher, every subsequent pitch is ruled a strike until the recalcitrant batter whiffs.

You're the Umpire

Even fans who constantly boo the men in blue must realize how difficult their job is. To paraphrase a famous quote, umpiring is the only game where you must be perfect on your very first day on the job, then improve during the rest of your career.

This chapter provides you with the vicarious opportunity to become an umpire. You'll be presented with some facts, then you make the call. Good luck—you're probably about to learn that it isn't as easy as it looks.

PICKOFF CHICANERY

Say Ken Griffey, Jr. of the Seattle Mariners pounded a ball into the right field corner. The ball kicked around a bit, and Griffey kept digging around the base paths, sliding into third in a cloud of dust. Let's further imagine he called time-out to brush the dirt from his uniform.

Now the third baseman tosses the ball back to the pitcher, a righty. The pitcher straddles the rubber for a moment, then, seeing Griffey stroll off the bag, throws over. Griffey is doomed—or is he? You're the umpire.

What's the call?

O **ANSWER:** It is not an out; Griffey can stay at third base. In order for play to resume after a time-out, the pitcher must come in contact with the rubber, not merely straddle it. Thus, time is still out, and the play never happened.

AARON AND HIS 756 HOMERS

Every good fan knows Hank Aaron is the all-time home run king with 755 career blasts. But, here's a situation involving Aaron and home runs that many fans don't recall.

Back on August 18, 1965, in St. Louis, Aaron faced Cards pitcher Curt Simmons. Simmons lobbed a blooper pitch to "Hammerin Hank." The superstar right fielder slashed the ball on top of the pavilion roof at Sportsman's Park for a tape-measure blow. As Aaron stepped into the pitch, he actually wound up making contact with the ball while one foot was entirely out of the batter's box.

Does this matter? Was Aaron permitted to trot around the bags with a home run, was it a "no pitch" call, or was he ruled out?

○ **ANSWER:** When a batter makes contact with a pitch while outside the box, he is declared out. Aaron would own 756 homers if it weren't for the sharp eyes of home plate ump Chris Pelekoudas.

GREAT CATCH NULLIFIED

Back in 1982, Terry Harper of the Atlanta Braves made a great catch that, due to an umpire's call, wasn't a catch. On September 26, in the middle of a pennant race, the Braves were playing the San Diego Padres. In the third inning, San Diego's Gene Richards lofted a ball to left field. Harper speared the ball after making a long run. He caught the ball in fair territory, then crossed into foul territory.

Running as quickly as he was, he needed a good four long strides to slow down. Those strides, though, put him in contact with a low bullpen railing. He grabbed at the railing to brace himself before tumbling into the bullpen area.

At about that time, he dropped the ball. Now the rule states that a ball that is dropped by a player immediately following contact with a wall is a live ball—no catch has been made. That's why umpire Ed Vargo ruled Harper's play a "no catch," and that's why the speedy Richards was able to cruise around the bases with an inside-the-park home run. To this day, Braves fans feel cheated by Vargo's interpretation that Harper hadn't held on to the ball long enough to validate the catch. They believe that the time that passed from the "catch" in fair territory until Harper hit the fence, including his many long steps holding on to the ball, were sufficient to prove it was a catch. Even an NBA official would've called Harper for traveling on this play, but the ump's call stands, as always.

ANOTHER TRICKY OLDIE

The year is 1930, and the pitcher is Burleigh Grimes, a man who later retired with 270 career wins. Grimes goes to his mouth and loads up the baseball with a nasty concoction of chewing tobacco and saliva.

If you were working that game, what would your call be?

○ **ANSWER:** Absolutely nothing. Although the spitball was outlawed in 1920, there was a grandfather clause that permitted a handful of pitchers to continue to throw their specialty pitch. The last man to legally throw a spitter was none other than Hall of Famer Burleigh "Ol' Stubblebeard" Grimes in 1934.

MONDAY, MONDAY

On May 10, 1977, the Montreal Expos were at home facing the Los Angles Dodgers. Warren Cromartie tattooed a long drive to center field. Rick Monday gave chase. Although he got close to the ball, it struck the wall over his head. Then it ricocheted off the wall, cracked Monday on his forehead, and rebounded over the wall. Is this play basically the same as Canseco's, or does the fact that it first bounced off the wall change things?

What do you award Cromartie?

○ **ANSWER:** Once it hit the wall, it was considered to be a "bounding ball." Such plays result in a ground-rule double, not a home run.

ANOTHER HIT-BY-PITCH SCENARIO

Must a batter make a legitimate effort to avoid getting hit by the ball, or is the fact that he was hit sufficient to earn a free trip to first base?

○ **ANSWER:** The batter must try to dodge the pitch. Perhaps the most famous case involving this rule occurred in 1968. Don Drysdale, Los Angeles's standout right-hander, was in the midst of a fantastic streak of shutout innings.

In a game versus the Giants, he faced a bases-loaded, no-outs situation. Dick Dietz, the San Francisco catcher, was at the plate with a 2-and-2 count. Drysdale came in tight with a pitch that hit him. Dietz got ready to stroll to first base, forcing in a run.

But wait a minute—home-plate umpire Harry Wendelstedt ruled that Dietz had made no move to avoid the pitch. Despite an argument that raged on and on, the ruling stood, and the pitch was ball three.

When Dietz proceeded to fly out, Drysdale's shutout streak continued, eventually stretching to 58⅔ innings. Incidentally, that record was later broken by another Dodger, Orel Hershiser.

THE FAKE OUT

Let's suppose that in the top of the 15th inning, in a game between Minnesota and Chicago, the Twins take a one-run lead.

But in the bottom half of the inning, Chicago's right fielder singles with one out. Then on a long fly ball, he tags up and runs to second. It is obvious to almost everyone in the ball park, including the runner, that he had left first too soon.

The Indian manager comes out to the mound to show the relief pitcher how to properly appeal the play. The pitcher takes his stretch, steps off the rubber, and, instead of throwing to first for the appeal, looks at second. When the runner sees the hurler look at second, he fakes a run to third. The pitcher reacts by faking the runner back to second.

What effect does the fake have on the appeal at first?

○ **ANSWER:** The Indian pitcher cannot now make an appeal at first. When he bluffs a throw to second, he forfeits his legal right to make an appeal play at first.

In a real 15-inning contest in the American League, the Brewers tried to come from behind against the Indians.

Charlie Moore, the runner, left too soon on a fly ball. After the ball was returned to the infield, Cleveland manager Jeff Torborg went out to the mound to show pitcher Victor Cruz how to conduct an appeal. When Cruz looked at second, however, he forgot everything he was told. He bluffed a throw to catch Moore at second and thereby lost the right to appeal at first.

No appeal play, no out.

THE RUN STEALER

Sometimes, though a runner misses a base, he can change a negative into a positive.

Let's say one man is at first base, with a runner in front of him at second. That was the scene in a game at Detroit. There are two out. A Tiger batter lines a single to left center. One run scores and the hitter ends up on third. But he missed touching second. Both the Brewers and the Tigers know it.

The Brewers appeal the play. But, as the Brewers pitcher steps off the rubber, the runner dashes for home. The pitcher throws to the catcher just in time to nip the speedy runner.

What mistake did the pitcher make?

○ **ANSWER:** The pitcher should have thrown the ball to second. If he had continued his appeal play, the runner would have been out at second, and no run would have scored. As it is, the runner is called out at the plate, the inning is over, but one run counts. Give the runner credit for a heads-up play. He is the reason why one run scores. If he had been safe at home, he would have scored another run.

In an actual game, Ron LeFlore of the Tigers got credit for that identical heads-up play against the Brewers. After he had missed second and was on third, the Brewers, appealing, put the ball in play. As their pitcher turned to throw to second, LeFlore broke for home. The startled pitcher broke his stride toward second, whirled, and fired to his catcher just in time to nip the runner.

LeFlore had nothing to lose. He was already out at second. If he had beaten the throw to home plate, he would have scored a second run for the Tigers.

THE INFIELD FLY

The Tigers, with men on second and first, have no out in the top of the eighth inning. The batter lofts a soft fly ball behind second base. The center fielder of the Brewers comes in; the second baseman goes out. Either one of them can catch the ball easily.

When the umpire sees the second baseman settle under the ball, he calls the batter automatically out on the infield fly rule. But the fielder drops the ball, and other players on the field lose their train of thought. The runner on second, believing the batter is safe on the error, runs to third, thinking that he is forced. The second baseman's throw beats him to the base, but the third baseman commits an error, too. He doesn't tag the runner. Instead, he steps on third for the "force."

Three questions: 1) *Can an umpire call the infield fly rule when the defensive man is in the outfield?* 2) *Who gets charged with errors on the play?* 3) *Is the runner called back from third base?*

○ First, the umpire can call the infield fly rule on an outfield play. The rule permits the umpire to make the call any time the infielder can make the play with ordinary effort.

○ Second, there were two errors on the play: one of commission (the second baseman's) and one of omission (the third baseman's).

However, since the second baseman's error confused the runner into running, he is charged with a miscue by the official scorer.

○ Third, the runner on third base is not called back to second. In an infield fly play, the runner can advance at his own risk.

That play occurred in a 1956 game between the Braves and the Pirates. The Braves, with Frank Torre at bat, had Bobby Thomson on second and Bill Bruton on first. Pirate Dick Groat, an MVP winner four years later, dropped the ball and threw it to third baseman Gene Freese in time for the out. But Freese didn't tag Thomson; so the runner at third was safe, and Bruton moved up to second on the play.

There were three errors on the play: Groat's, Thomson's, and Freese's. But only Groat got officially charged with one.

The Pirates won the game, though, 3-1.

Not often is the league president in the stands when something peculiar happens.

THE UMPIRE ALWAYS WINS

The batter takes a pitch that is called a strike. The hitter disagrees with the call. The hurler pitches again and the batter takes again. The umpire calls another strike. By this time, the batter who is furious with the umpire's calls against him, steps out of the batter's box and argues vigorously. The umpire orders him to resume his hitter's position. He refuses.

What does the umpire do?

○ **ANSWER:** The umpire orders the pitcher to throw the ball. The arbiter calls an automatic strike for every pitch that is made while the hitter is out of the batter's box. At any time, the hitter can step into the box and resume the count from that point.

Frank Robinson, when with the Reds, got called out on such a play in 1956, his rookie year. He argued about a called second strike in a game against the Giants. Umpire Larry Goetz told him to get back in the box. Robinson refused.

Goetz ordered the Giants' Steve Ridzik to pitch, and called "Strike three" while Robinson was still disputing the previous call!

"Get up off second base...you don't own it"

WHAT'S THE PITCH?

In a hypothetical case, the star hitter of the Red Sox is on third base, with the next batter at the plate.

When the Texas pitcher goes into his windup, the third-base umpire calls, "Balk!" But the hurler pitches the ball anyway and the batter bloops a double to left. The runner on third, who had heard the umpire call a balk, remains on third. The batter who hit the double clutches second. In fact, he refuses to leave the base.

How does the umpire resolve

this predicament?

○ **ANSWER:** Once again, the balk takes precedence; so the umpire lets the runner from third score and returns the batter to the plate. When the batter refuses to leave second base, the umpire ejects him from the game, and places his substitute at the plate.

In a real-game situation, Lou Piniella of the Yankees, who relished every hit he ever got, refused to leave second under similar circumstances. He had to be kicked out of the game before he would give up his double.

THE CUNNING CATCHER

The Mets' catcher is noted for thinking all the time. The following hypothetical example points it out:

The Braves' clean-up hitter is at bat with a man on first, one out, and a three-two count on him. As the Mets' hurler pitches, the runner breaks for second. The batter checks his swing and the plate umpire calls, "Ball four!" The Braves' first-base coach yells to the runner to stand up. But the catcher throws to second anyway; and the Mets' second baseman makes an easy tag on the runner, who has slowed down.

Then the Mets appeal the swing. The first-base umpire says the batter broke his wrists, which constitutes a swing. Strike three.

Is it a double play?

○ **ANSWER:** No, it is not a double play. The runner cannot be penalized for the umpire's mistake. The runner, misled by the false signal, slows down. But there is no guarantee that the runner would have stolen the base had he run hard all the way. The umpire calls the batter out, but puts the runner back on first.

Thurman Munson of the Yankees was such a catcher. In the mid-1970's, he pulled off the identical play. He thought he should have had a double play.

On defense, as an offense, Munson was always thinking one out ahead of the game.

TEAMWORK

The Red Sox have a runner at third base, and one out. The batter hits a long fly ball to right center against the Yankee pitcher. The ball deflects off the right fielder's glove and floats into the center fielder's mitt.

Two questions: 1) *Is the batter out?* and 2) *can the runner tag up after the ball touches the right-fielder's glove?*

○ A fly ball that is deflected off one outfielder's glove into another one's is a legal out. The batter is out.

○ A runner can legally tag up and advance as soon as a fielder touches the ball. He does not have to wait until a fielder "possesses" the ball.

On a play just like this, at Yankee Stadium in the late 1950's, Hank Bauer got the assist and Mickey Mantle, the putout. There was no runner on third. The batter got "put out."

INSIDE THE LINES

Suppose the Red Sox are at bat with runners on second and first with no out in a game against the White Sox.

The batter drops a bunt down the first-base line. The White Sox catcher picks the ball up and throws it to the first baseman. But the batter, who is running inside the first-base line, is hit by the throw. The ball bounds down the right-field line, allowing the runner on second to score. That run turns out to be the deciding one.

Does it count?

O **ANSWER:** The run shouldn't count, if the umpire sees the play the same way we do. In running the last 45 feet to first base, the batter-runner has to run within the three-foot line that parallels the base line for that distance. If he is hit by the throw when inside or outside that area, he should be called out and the ball declared dead.

This controversial play occurred in the 1969 World

"That's my elbow"

Series between the Mets and the Orioles. With runners on first and second, no out, and a tied game in the bottom of the tenth inning, J. C. Martin, the Mets' batter, dropped a bunt down the first-base line.

Pete Richert, the pitcher for the Orioles, fielded the ball and threw it to first. Martin was running inside the first-base line. The throw hit Martin on the arm and bounced into foul territory while Jerry Grote of the Mets sprinted home with the winning run.

Most observers thought that Martin was clearly out of the base lines and should have been declared out. The umpire saw the play differently, however. His was the vote that counted.

The Mets' run counted, too.

A CATCHY SITUATION

The Reds and Red Sox are tied 1-1 in the bottom half of the ninth inning. In Game 3 of the 1975 World Series, they are also tied at one game apiece.

Cesar Geronimo leads off the Reds' inning with a bloop single. Then the next batter drops down a bunt right in front of the plate. But he is slow to move out of the batter's box. Red Sox catcher Carlton Fisk has to shove the batter out of the way with his glove hand and pick the ball up with his bare hand. Fisk's throw beats Geronimo by plenty of time at second; but because of the bodily contact at the plate, his off-balance throw goes into center field. Geronimo continues to third. The Red Sox want the batter to be called out for interference. In fact, they want two outs, for that's what they would have gotten, if Fisk's throw were on the mark.

What did they get?

○ **ANSWER:** They got nowhere. The plate umpire disallowed the appeal, claiming that the contact was accidental, not purposeful. Joe Morgan, the next batter, singled, Geronimo scored, and the game was over.

That play might have cost the Red Sox the 1975 World Series. The Reds went on to win the World Series in seven games. Had the call gone the other way, the Red Sox might have won Game 3. If they had, they would have won the World Series in six games.

THE TRAP-BALL TRAP

Let's suppose there is a runner at first base with one out; the batter is hitting against the opponents' star pitcher.

The hitter loops a ball to right field, and the outfielder either catches it or traps it. One umpire calls the play a catch; another, a trap. The runner at first, who is confused, finally decides to run to second. One umpire calls him safe; the other umpire, out.

How do the umpires resolve this contradictory situation?

○ **ANSWER:** The umpires are in a tight spot on this one. The only way out is compromise. They allow the runner to stay at second, but call the batter out.

The Mets and the Reds had a similar situation. The Cincinnati out-fielder made such a good try that he confused the umpires. He also confused the Met base runner.

The only way out, the umpires concluded, was to give a little and to take a little. Neither the Mets nor the Reds argued too long, since each got something: the Mets, a base; the Reds, an out.

INSTANT REPLAY

Can the instant replay camera cause a pitcher's ejection?

O No, but it certainly created a furor during the 1992 season. Tim Leary, a pitcher for the New York Yankees, got off to a bad start early in the season. Suddenly he righted himself with three consecutive victories toward the middle of June. Then, in defeating the host Orioles one night, he threw an errant pitch that broke Chris Hoiles's wrist. Johnny Oates, Baltimore's manager, was suspicious of the pitch that sidelined Hoiles. While the game continued, he began to collect the discarded balls and place them in a bucket. According to him, they were all defaced. When he had enough evidence, he presented the balls to the homeplate umpire.

The umpire, who didn't have to go out to the mound, did so anyway a few pitches later to search Leary. He found nothing! The diamond-vision camera on the center field scoreboard, however, detected Leary removing a substance—it was thought to be sandpaper—from his glove and putting it in his mouth. The umpire didn't see Leary do it. Oates, who saw it on the screen, asked the umpire to look in Leary's mouth. The umpire, who said it was beyond his authority, refused.

The next day the diamond-vision film excerpt was shown on television stations all over America. There was a demand for action on the part of the league office. President Bobby Brown called Leary in for a meeting, but he let him off with a warning.

Nothing in the rule book says an umpire's or league office's decision can be influenced by the view on an instant replay camera.

After the incident, Leary was no longer effective with the Yankees, though, and in late August he and his huge ERA were shipped to the Mariners.

SHARING AN AT-BAT

Casey Stengel is playing with his batting order and alternating Phil Rizzuto and Billy Martin in the number-one and number-eight spots. On Friday, he had Martin batting first and Rizzuto eighth. On Saturday

"Casey says it's my turn to bat."

Martin steps into the batter's box to begin the game at Briggs Stadium in Detroit. Tiger pitcher Hal Newhouser runs a count of no balls and two strikes on Martin before Rizzuto realizes he is the named lead-off batter for the Yankees for this game. The "Scooter" rushes up and takes Martin's place in the batter's box. On Newhouser's next pitch Rizzuto swings and misses.

Is anyone called out for batting out of order here? Who is charged with the strikeout?

○ **ANSWER:** Rizzuto, as the proper batter, gets charged with the strikeout. No one is called out for batting out of order. The proper batter may take his place in the batter's box at any time before the improper batter becomes a runner or is put out, and any balls and strikes shall be counted in the proper batter's time at bat. *Rule 6.07 (a)(1).*

THE QUICK PITCH

Reggie Jackson used to take a lot of time to get ready in the batter's box. In this hypothetical situation, he is still a Yankee, and he is batting with a three-two count with no one on base against a crafty Red Sox hurler.

The Red Sox pitcher fires a strike right down the middle of the plate before Jackson is set, but the umpire calls it a quick pitch.

What's the penalty?

○ **ANSWER:** The umpire calls the pitch a ball. That makes four on Jackson, so he goes to first base. *Rule 8.05 (e).*

Would there have been a ball call if there had been runners on base? No, it would have been a balk. A runner at third would score, a runner at first would go to second, etc. Reggie would remain at the plate with a three-two count. *Rule 8.05 (e).*

It happened in the fourth and final game of the 1928 World Series, Bill Sherdel of the Cardinals "slipped" a third strike by Babe Ruth, but plate umpire Charles Pfirman disallowed the offering, calling it a quick pitch. A ball was added to the Babe's count, and then Ruth hit his third home run of the game (for the second time in World Series play). All of his homers that day were solo shots.

HOW HIGH CAN A PITCH GO?

Is there any height limit to the trajectory of a hurler's pitch?

○ **ANSWER:** No, the rule book doesn't cover the subject. Truett "Rip" Sewell of the 1943 Pirates was delighted to find that out. One day during the season, he became the first major league pitcher to throw a lob to the plate. Some viewers said that the pitch rose almost thirty feet above the ground.

Sewell had a number of other pitches that were effective: fastball,

"Why can't he pitch it straight"

curveball, slider, forkball, and change-up. In fact, he posted a league-leading 21 wins that season. But he wanted the hitter to be thinking of his "eephus pitch." It helped to set up some of his other pitches.

Sewell frustrated National League hitters for four years with the lob pitch. None of them ever hit it for a home run. One day Eddie Miller of the Reds was so frustrated that he caught the pitch and fired it back to Sewell. The home-plate umpire called that pitch a strike.

There's a climax. It occurred in the 1946 All-Star Game, which the American League won, 12-0. In that game, Ted Williams hit two home runs and drove in five runs in his home stadium, Fenway Park. One of his home runs came against Sewell's "eephus pitch." Williams had thought about the possibility of seeing the pitch before the game. He concluded that the only way anyone could hit the ball out of the park was by running up on it. When he faced Sewell, he guessed right on the pitch, ran up on it, and with his feet in the batter's box timed it perfectly. The ball sailed deep into the right-center field bleachers for a home run—the first and only one that was ever hit off Sewell's "eephus pitch."

How high can a pitch go? Williams proved that it could go very high.

HOW CLOSE CAN "THE BARBER" THROW?

Sal Maglie, pitcher with the New York Giants in the early 1950s, was called "The Barber," for two reasons. One was because he didn't shave on the day of a game, and he had a heavy dark beard. The second was because his pitches "shaved" the heads of opposing hitters, especially those of the Brooklyn Dodgers.

Quite often the Dodger players suspected that Maglie's "purpose pitches" were signaled by Giant (skipper) Leo Durocher, who managed the Dodgers from 1939 to 1948. Dodger fans and players had a love-hate relationship with Durocher.

Let us hypothesize that in 1954 Maglie knocked down slugger Gil Hodges three straight times. Then, with the winning run on second base and two out in the bottom of the ninth inning at Ebbets Field, he threw so close to Hodges' head that he had to fall to the ground.

Would Maglie have been ejected from the game? Would Durocher have been thrown out, also?

○ **ANSWER:** Probably not. The plate umpire undoubtedly would have warned the pitcher and turned in a report to the league office, which would have resulted in a fine being levied against him. Durocher may or may not have been fined, also. *Rules 9.01 (d) and 9.05 (a).*

But umpires and head-hunting pitchers got away with much more in those days than they do today. Dizzy Dean of the Cardinals, for example, once knocked down eight consecutive Giant batters in the mid-1930s.

Back in the 1950s, hitters were supposed to retaliate with their own methods. One summer afternoon in 1956, when Maglie was pitching for the Dodgers against the Giants, "The Barber" knocked Willie Mays down on two consecutive pitches. The umpire warned Maglie, who defended himself by saying that "my fingers were sweating and the balls just slipped out."

"Tell Willie I'm sorry," Maglie said to the plate umpire.

Willie hit the next pitch for a long home run. As Mays circled the bases, he delivered his own "knockdown" to Maglie, when he told the third base umpire, "Tell Sal I'm sorry."

BATTER'S INTERFERENCE?

The Cincinnati batter, trying to protect Barry Larkin, who is running from first on the pitch, swings at Phillie's pitcher Terry Mulholland's offering. His big swing misses, but his bat comes all the way around and hits Darren Daulton in the head just after he has released the ball on his throw to second base. Nevertheless, Daulton manages to throw Larkin out.

In another incident Mackay Sasser of the 1992 Mets got a bloody nose when a Pirate batter, Barry Bonds, hit Sasser's nose on his back swing.

Was the batter called out in these cases?

○ **ANSWER:** No. If the batter had interfered with the catcher's fielding or throwing by stepping out of the batter's box or making any other movement which hinders or impedes the catcher's play, he is out. Also, he is out if the umpire thinks his act is intentional. However, the batter is not out if any runner who is attempting to advance is thrown out. *Rule 6.06 (c)*

Exception: If Larkin had reached second safely, the batter would have been called out.

In May of 1986, there was an enactment of this play. The Yankees, who were playing the Rangers, had Henry Cotto at the plate and Gary Roenicke at first. Roenicke was running on the pitch, Cotto swung through the pitch and hit catcher Don Slaught, who was attempting to throw the runner out, in the head. Slaught's throw sailed into center field, and Roenicke raced to third on the play.

In this case, Cotto was called out on batter's interference, and Roenicke was returned to first base. The ball became dead as soon as the interference took place. *Rule 6.06 (c).*

BAT COLOR

Ball players are superstitious about many things, some about their bat. Babe Ruth used a black bat that he called "Black Betsy." It was his special home run stick. George Foster used black bats, too. They helped him to hit 52 home runs in 1977. Bats like the ones he used are known to have a "Foster Finish."

Tan bats that have a light stain are said to have the "Hornsby Finish." They were named after Rogers Hornsby, who used them en route to compiling a .358 lifetime batting average.

Two-tone bats are modeled after the ones that Harry "The Hat" Walker used. Walker won a batting title in 1947.

These natural shades are allowed.

Are there any shades that are disallowed?

○ **ANSWER:** No colored bat may be used in a professional game unless it has been previously approved by the Rules Committee. *Rule 1.10 (d).*

There are exceptions to every rule, though. In 1947, Jerome "Dizzy" Dean was broadcasting baseball games for the St. Louis Browns, who were having their typically dismal season—both in the league standings and at the gate. For the Browns' final game of the season at Sportsman's Park, management asked Dean to suit up and pitch three innings. Always happy to provide a lark, Dizzy willingly went along with the gimmick to lure 20,000 or more paying customers to the park.

Six years after Dean had officially retired, he pitched three scoreless and hitless innings. He also went one-for-one at the plate. (During his career, he batted .225 and hit eight home runs.) The color of the bat he used that day was red, white, and blue. Up until the end, the Diz was "colorful."

One additional story of bat shades comes to the author's mind. When he was a teenager, he and his family were listening to a Phillie vs. Pirate's game on the radio. Going into the bottom of the tenth inning, the score was tied 1-1. Suddenly the Philadelphia broadcaster got excited. He gushed, "Uh-oh, Ralph Kiner's coming to the plate, and he's carrying his black bat with him. That's his special bat, his home run bat. That's the one he uses when he wants to end the game."

It was hard to believe that the announcer actually thought the shade of Kiner's bat could dictate the outcome of the game, as though it were some sort of talisman. But two pitches later, Kiner hit a ball over the roof in left field to end the game. It could make one a "true believer" overnight.

DOUBLE PENALTY

An Oakland A's batter is at the plate in the top half of the seventh inning with two out, a three-two count, and the bases loaded. Just as the Mariner pitcher is about to go into his wind-up, the batter steps out of the box and requests the umpire for time-out. The arbiter doesn't give it to him! The pitcher pitches. Scott Bradley, the Seattle catcher, has to jump to prevent the pitch from sailing for a wild pitch.

What happens next?

○ **ANSWER:** The pitch, though wild, is called an automatic strike. The batter is out and the inning is over. The umpire doesn't have to give the batter time-out if he feels that it was requested too late or for the wrong reason. It is the batter's responsibility to know whether the time-out has been granted. *Rule 6.02 (b) and (c).*

Jose Canseco of the A's got called out on such a play during the 1992 season.

THE CHECKED SWING

The visiting Braves are playing the Mets at Shea Stadium. Atlanta's John Smoltz is pitching to Vince Coleman, the New York center fielder. With two strikes on him, Coleman checks his swing on a borderline pitch. Plate umpire Gary Darling calls the pitch a ball, but catcher Greg Olson appeals the call.

The plate umpire asks third-base umpire Dana DeMuth for his angle on the swing. DeMuth signals that the batter swung at the pitch. Strikeout. Coleman then engages in a heated argument with DeMuth. Darling, who is a spectator to the argument, eventually throws Coleman out of the game.

Can he do this?

○ **ANSWER:** Yes, he can. The home-plate umpire is the umpire-in-chief.

Afterwards, Terry Pendleton, the Braves third baseman and a friend of Coleman's, said, "I don't know why Darling even threw him out. He [Coleman] was arguing with the third-base ump. Darling should have no authority to throw him out."

Only the authority of being the umpire-in-chief.

THE WAY THE BALL BOUNCES

On August 22,1992, Charlie Hayes of the Yankees, with no runners on base in a scoreless tie, hit a pitch by Chuck Finley of the Angels high and far down the left-field line at Yankee Stadium. The ball hit the "wire netting extending along the side of the pole on fair territory above the fence to enable the umpires more accurately to judge fair and foul balls," and rebounded to left fielder Luis Polonia in fair territory.

Did the third-base umpire rule the hit a foul ball, a home run, a double, or a ball that was still in play?

○ **ANSWER:** A home run. Today, the foul poles in all major-league parks are placed in fair territory, behind the fence or wall. Thus, any batted ball that hits either the foul pole or the wire netting extending from it is a home run. *Rule 2.00 A FAIR BALL*

SWINGING THIRD STRIKE

One of the most famous plays in baseball history took place in the bottom of the ninth inning of Game Three of the 1941 World Series. The Brooklyn Dodgers, down to the Yankees 2-1, were leading, 4-3, with two out and no one on base. Tommy Henrich was the batter for New York;

Hugh Casey was the pitcher for Brooklyn. The count ran to three-and-two on Henrich. Then Casey broke off a hard curve—some said it was a spitter—and Henrich swung and missed. The game would have been over—but the ball got away from catcher Mickey Owen and rolled back to the screen, as Henrich ran safely to first base.

Then the roof fell in on Brooklyn. Joe DiMaggio singled and Charlie Keller doubled two runs home. After Bill Dickey walked, Joe Gordon doubled two more runs across the plate. The Yankees ended up winning the game, 7-4. When Henrich swung and missed, it appeared that Brooklyn had tied the Series at two games apiece. Instead, the Yankees held a commanding three-game-to-one lead. The next day, the Yankees won 3-1 and wrapped up a Series they very well could have lost.

In retrospect, though, wasn't Henrich's swinging strike the third out of the inning, and the final out of the game?

○ **ANSWER:** No. To conclude a strikeout, the catcher must hold the third strike or pick up the loose ball and throw it to first base before the runner for the out to count. Henrich was safe at first base because he reached it before the throw. *Rule 6.09 (b).*

A NO-WYNN SITUATION

Hal Morris of the Reds is at the plate with one out and a teammate on third base. Before the Pirate pitcher releases his next pitch, he balks, but Morris lines a drive off center fielder Andy Van Slyke's glove for a double. The runner at third starts for home on the play, but when he sees that Van Slyke has a possible play on the ball, he returns to third. When Van Slyke doesn't catch the ball, Morris tags and starts for home again. However, the Pittsburgh outfielder makes a quick recovery and throws to the plate while the runner retreats to third.

Red manager Lou Piniella comes out of the dugout after the play and tells the plate umpire he is waiving the balk call. He wants to take the play instead. But the umpire says he can't.

Why?

○ **ANSWER:** In order for the play to supersede the balk, all runners who were on base had to advance at least one base. *Rule 8.05 (m)* PENAL-TY. The runner at third would score on the balk, but Morris would have to come back to the plate and try all over again.

In April 1977, Jimmy Wynn of the Yankees was the runner at third base, and Lou Piniella was the hitter. Jerry Garvin of the Blue Jays was the pitcher with two out in the bottom of the fourth inning. Piniella "doubled" off the center fielder's glove, but Wynn didn't score on the play. He did score on Garvin's balk, though, while Piniella had to be tossed out of the game before he would give up second base and the double he had hit. Piniella's replacement struck out, and the Yankees went on to lose both the game and their protest.

YOU'VE GOT TO RUN 'EM OUT

In a 1992 game between the White Sox and the host Yankees, New

York's Randy Velarde singles to right field, a run scoring on the play. Dan Pasquats relay throw misses the cut-off man, however, and Velarde continues on to second base on the play.

When catcher Carlton Fisk realizes that there is no White Sox teammate backing up the play, he races to retrieve the ball as it rolls toward the visitors' third-base dugout. At the last possible second, he slides feet-first into the dugout in order to stop and recover the ball. Ultimately, he takes firm possession of the ball, which had come to rest on the top step of the dugout.

Velarde, who thinks that the ball has gone into dead territory, and that he is entitled to a free base, trots to third base, but Fisk now steps out of the dugout and throws the ball to third baseman Robin Ventura for an easy tag-out.

The Yankees don't protest the call. Should they have?

O **ANSWER:** No. A fielder or catcher may reach or step into, or go into, the dugout with one or both feet to make a catch (play), and if he holds the ball, the catch (play) shall be allowed. The ball is in play. *Rule 7.04 (c).*

BALL HITS HELMET

Ivan Calderon, Spike Owen, and Tim Wallach are on third, second, and first bases, respectively, when Gary Carter hits a tailor-made double-play ball to the second baseman. But Wallach, in running from first to sec-

ond, accidentally loses his batting helmet; the ball hits it and then bounces past the fielder into the outfield while two runs score and Tim advances to third base on the play.

Legal play?

○ **ANSWER:** Yes. In cases where a batting helmet is accidentally hit by a batted or thrown ball, the ball remains in play. It is the same as if the helmet were not hit by the ball. *Rule 6.05 (h).*

"The ball is still in play when it hits a helmet by accdent."

Willie Mays, of course, was known for losing his hat while running the bases. Later, it became mandatory for players, beginning with the 1972 season, to wear a protective batting helmet. While with the Mets, in 1973, in Mays's last major-league season, he lost his helmet in the above situation while running between first and second base. Instead of a double play ensuing, the batter got credited with two runs batted in.

LINES ARE LINES

David Cone is the pitcher for the Mets. Mackey Sasser is the catcher. Cone blows the batter away with a swinging strike on a hard slider that goes down and away, but Sasser has trouble holding onto the pitch and it bounces about five feet to his right.

Since there is no one on base and no out, the batter runs out the play, but in running the last half of the distance from home to first, he runs "outside" of the three-foot line, and Sasser's throw to first baseman Eddie Murray hits him and bounces down the right-field line. The batter goes to second base on the play.

Does he have to give up his base?

O **ANSWER:** Yes, he is called out because he has interfered with Sasser's throw. The only time a batter can run inside or outside the three-foot line is when he is trying to avoid a fielder trying to play a batted ball. *Rule 6.05 (k).*

A few years back, that same play occurred in a Mariner vs. Yankees game at Yankee Stadium. Don Slaught was the Yank catcher and Don Mattingly was the first baseman. The Seattle batter-runner was called out for interference.

TWO FOR THE PRICE OF ONE

John Kruk of the Phillies hits what appears to be a certain double-play ball to Jose Lind, the Pirates' second baseman. Lind fields the ball cleanly and gives a perfect toss to shortstop Jay Bell, who has enough time to take two full steps to touch second on the right-field side of the base. But before Bell can relay the ball to first for the inning-ending double play, the base runner from first veers deliberately out of his path to take out Bell, preventing him from making the throw.

What's the umpire's call, if any?

○ **ANSWER:** The umpire calls the batter out because of the runner's interference. *Rule 6.05 (m).*

This play has happened thousands of times in the major leagues. Today, the umpires are more likely to penalize the flagrant runner. At one time, it was merely considered part of the game.

In 1949, for example, the Yankees thought that the Red Sox were roughing up their shortstop, Phil Rizzuto. One day, in retaliation, Joe DiMaggio slid directly at Red Sox shortstop Vern Stephens, who was well out of the base path, to break up a double play. Stephens made no throw to first, and the umpire assessed no penalty against DiMaggio and the batter-runner.

DiMaggio's slide had a twofold result: The runner was safe at first and the Red Sox left Rizzuto alone from that day forward.

But today it's different.

A MATTER OF JUDGMENT

In a game at the Oakland Coliseum, Kelly Gruber of the Blue Jays hits a soft pop foul towards the third-box seats. The A's third baseman, Carney Lansford, makes a running catch about 10 feet from the boxes, but his momentum carries him into the wire protecting fence, the ball drop-

"Sorry, folks, but I've got to catch this."

ping out of his glove upon contact.

Is it a legal catch?

○ **ANSWER:** It's a matter of judgment on the umpire's part. The rule book says that if the fielder has contact with another fielder or wall immediately following his contact with the ball—and drops it—it is not a legal catch. Ten feet would seem to be a considerable distance, but it wasn't in the following application. *Rule 2.00 CATCH.*

Late in the 1982 season, the host Braves were leading the Padres when San Diego's Gene Richards, with no one on and two out, sent a twisting fly ball down the left-field line. Terry Harper made a running catch inside the foul line, but his momentum carried him across the line into the bullpen railing. Trying to cushion his landing, he grabbed the railing but dropped the ball. Umpire Ed Vargo called the play a no-catch, and by the time Harper retrieved the ball and returned it to the infield, Richards had circled the bases. The official scorer ruled the play a four base error, but the league office overruled the scoring, and called the play an inside-the-park home run.

THE BOOTED PLAY

The San Francisco Giants have Willie McGee on second base, Will Clark on first base, and Matt Williams at the plate. While the host Cubs have Dave Smith on in relief, Smith's first pitch to Williams bounces in front of the plate, and off the Bruin backstop's shinguard towards the first-base dugout. McGee and Clark move up a base on the wild pitch. But the Cub catcher, in running down the ball, accidentally kicks it into the Cubs' dugout.

What's the ruling? Is it true that runners can advance only one base on a wild pitch?

○ **ANSWER:** Yes, runners may advance only one base on a wild pitch that goes into dead territory. However, if the wild-pitch ball remains on the playing field, and is subsequently kicked or deflected into dead territory, the runners shall be awarded two bases from the position the runners are in at the time of the pitch. *Rule 7.05 (h).* *APPROVED RULING.* McGee scores and Clark advances to third.

Early in the 1992 season, a Yankee catcher inadvertently made the above faux pas.

A VACANT RULE

In this hypothetical case, with two out in the bottom of the ninth inning, the home team Phillies are trailing the Pirates, 7-6. John Kruk is the Philadelphia batter, and Lenny Dykstra the runner at first base.

On the first pitch, from Pittsburgh hurler Doug Drabek, Kruk lifts a high pop foul towards the Phillie dugout. As Pirate first baseman Orlando Merced and catcher Don Slaught converge on the ball, the on-deck batter, Darren Daulton, gets caught in the crossfire. Merced runs into Daulton and drops the ball. The Pirates demand of the home-plate umpire that Kruk be called out because of offensive interference.

Does the umpire comply with the Pittsburgh request?

○ **ANSWER:** According to the language of Rule 7.11, he should, but he probably doesn't. The rule says: "The players, coaches or any member of an offensive team shall vacate any space (including both dugouts) needed by a fielder who is attempting to field a batted or thrown ball.

Penalty: Interference shall be called and the batter or runner on whom the play is being made shall be declared out."

But quite often, the umpires don't interpret Rule 7.11 literally. If they feel that the on-deck batter made a legitimate attempt to get out of the ball's way, they probably won't call offensive interference. In the above example, Kruk would probably get at least one more swing at a pitch.

Baseball Trivia

WHO SAID IT?

Baseball has always produced colorful, funny, and interesting quotes. Some of these lines have worked their way into everyday lingo, and some have even become a part of Americana. Who can forget such bits of wisdom as Satchel Paige's "Don't look back. Something might be gaining on you"?

Now it's your turn to read a quote and to match it up with the person who uttered it. So, get started. (Match-up answers are given at the end of the chapter.)

MATCH-UP: MANAGERS' WORDS

1 Who said, in discussing his team's home park: "When you come to the plate in this ballpark, you're in scoring position"?

2 Who made the egotistical comment "Stay close in the early innings, and I'll think of something"?

3 What diminutive skipper said these fiery words: "I think there should be bad blood between all teams"?

4 What manager, saddled with an inept team, moaned, "Can't anyone here play this game?"

5 Who said, "You don't save a pitcher for tomorrow. Tomorrow it may rain"? Big clue: He's also famous for saying, "Nice guys finish last"—although that wasn't exactly what he said.

6 After suffering through a tough road trip, what Reds manager of 1997 said, "When it rains it pours, and we're in the midst of a monsoon"?

A Charlie Dressen
B Don Baylor
C Earl Weaver
D Casey Stengel
E Ray Knight
F Leo Durocher

MATCH-UP: HUMOR

1 When told his salary was more than the earnings of President Hoover, this man stated, "Oh, yeah? Well, I had a better year than he had."

2 On his disdain for artificial grass, this slugger commented, "If a cow can't eat it, I don't want to play on it."

3 When asked for the highlight of his career, this player responded, "I walked with the bases loaded to drive in the winning run in an intrasquad game in spring training."

4 Although he probably wasn't trying to be humorous, this good ol' country boy once said, "They X-rayed my head and didn't find anything."

5 Speaking of his dislike for hitting in Comiskey Park, this player said, "At Wrigley Field, I feel like King Kong. Here, I feel like Donkey Kong."

A Gary Gaetti
B Bob Uecker
C Babe Ruth
D Dick Allen
E Dizzy Dean

MATCH UP: MORE MANAGERS

1 Even though he'd won a World Series in the 1990s, this manager once muttered, "I'm not sure whether I'd rather be managing or testing bulletproof vests."

2 This man's team was injury plagued in 1989, prompting him to observe, "If World War III broke out, I'd guarantee you we'd win the pennant by 20 games. All our guys would be 4-F. They couldn't pass the physical."

3 In 1997, this White Sox skipper philosophized, "I learned a long time ago, in this game you might as well take the blame because you're going to get it anyway."

4 His pitcher entered the game with the bases loaded. Two wild pitches later, the bases were empty because all three men had scored, leading to this managerial quip: "Well, that's one way to pitch out of a bases-loaded jam." Clue: He was managing the Brewers when this occurred.

A Terry Bevington
B Tom Trebelhorn
C Whitey Herzog
D Joe Torre

MATCH UP:
LAST CALL FOR MANAGERS' QUOTES

1 Lucky enough to be the manager of George Brett, this man was asked what he told Brett regarding hitting. The Royals manager replied, "I tell him, 'Attaway to hit, George.'"

2 Never known for his use of grammar, this great manager once said of a player's injury, "There's nothing wrong with his shoulder except some pain, and pain don't hurt you."

3 On what it takes to be a successful manager, an all-time big-name manager opined, "A sense of humor and a good bullpen."

4 Two quotes from the same man. A) "I'm not the manager because I'm always right, but I'm always right because I'm the manager."

B) "The worst thing about managing is the day you realize you want to win more than your players do."

5 This manager-for-one-day naively believed, "Managing isn't all that difficult. Just score more runs than the other guy."

A Ted Turner   **D** Jim Frey
B Whitey Herzog   **E** Sparky Anderson
C Gene Mauch

MATCH UP: THIS AND THAT

1 Who said: "Baseball statistics are a lot like a girl in a bikini. They show a lot, but not everything"?

2 Two quotes from an ex-catcher: A) "When Steve [Carlton] and I die, we are going to be buried 60 feet, 6 inches apart." B) On Bob Gibson: "He is the luckiest pitcher I ever saw. He always pitched when the other team didn't score any runs."

3 During 1998 spring training, this man came to camp overweight. He joked, "I must have had five coaches come up to me and say, 'I expected to see you floating over the stadium tied to a string…'"

4 Who was so arrogant that he once proclaimed, "The only reason I don't like playing in the World Series is I can't watch myself play"?

5 Soon after being traded, a disgruntled player, asked about the condition of his shoulder, replied, "My shoulder's O.K., but I've still got a scar where the Mets stuck the knife in my back."

A Dante Bichette   **D** Tim McCarver
B Toby Harrah   **E** Reggie Jackson
C Tug McGraw

MATCH UP: MORE THIS AND THAT

1 This manager summarized the futures of two 20-year-old prospects, saying, "In ten years, Ed Kranepool has a chance to be a star. In ten years, Greg Goosen has a chance to be thirty."

2 This Hall-of-Famer said, "So what if I'm ugly? I never saw anyone hit with his face."

3 Tired of being reduced to sitting on the bench, and ignoring his lack of productivity, this man said his team was guilty of the "worst betrayal by a team in all sports history. It's not fair to Deion Sanders. It's not fair to teammates or to the fans, either. It's one of the worst things ever done to a player." P.S.: His team went on to win the World Series without him.

4 After fanning in a two-out, potential game-winning situation in the bottom of the 9th inning, this Pittsburgh Pirate of the past lamented, "It's what you dream of right there, either you're Billy the Kid or Billy the Goat."

A Glenn Wilson
B Casey Stengel
C Deion Sanders
D Yogi Berra

MATCH UP: MORE HUMOR

1 Who said: "I've never played with a pitcher who tried to hit a batter in the head. Most pitchers are like me. If I'm going to hit somebody, I'm going to aim for the bigger parts"?

2 This West Virginia native wasn't too worldly when he broke into the majors. During his ride to Wrigley Field for his first visit there, he spotted Lake Michigan and asked, "What ocean is that?"

3 Who was the player Dante Bichette was referring to when he said: "He's the kid who, when he played Little League, all the parents called the president of the league and said, 'Get him out of there, I don't want him to hurt my son.' I had my mom call the National League office to see if she could do it for me"?

4 What player was former pitcher Darold Knowles talking about when he uttered these words: "There isn't enough mustard in the world to cover him"?

5 Who said: "We live by the Golden Rule—those who have the gold make the rules"?

A Bert Blyleven
B Buzzi Bavasi
C John Kruk
D Mark McGwire
E Reggie Jackson

MATCH UP: COLORFUL QUOTES

1 What American League pitcher said of his first trip to Yankee Stadium, "The first time I ever came into a game there, I got in the bullpen car, and they told me to lock the doors"?

2 This pitcher apparently got tired of being asked trite questions from reporters. Once, after surrendering a home run that cost him a 1-0 defeat, he was asked what it was he had thrown to game hero Tony Conigliaro. The succinct reply was, "It was a baseball."

3 This manager did so well, he was rewarded by the Cardinals. Owner August Busch, who was eighty-five at the time, told the manager he could have a lifetime contract. The St. Louis skipper countered with, "Whose lifetime? Yours or mine?"

4 This colorful character was a fine pitcher. His World Series ledger was golden: 6-0 with a 2.86 ERA. When asked to explain his success, he attributed it to "clean living and a fast outfield."

A Joe Horlen
B Mike Flannagan
C Lefty Gomez
D Whitey Herzog

MATCH UP: FINAL INNING

1 This peppery manager would upstage umpires at the drop of a hat. He even loved to peck umps with the beak of his hat. He offered one of his most famous lines after he showed up the umpires by taking a rule book out on the field. He stated, "There ain't no rule in the rule book about bringing a rule book on the field."

2 This umpire had a rivalry with the manager from the above quote. He once said, "That midget can barely see over the top of the dugout steps, and he claims he can see the pitches."

3 An ex-pitcher, this announcer butchered the English language. In one case, he said a player had "slud into third" instead of "slid." Another remark was, "Don't fail to miss tomorrow's game."

4 After hitting four homers in a game to tie the single-game record, this power hitter said quite correctly, "I had a good week today."

A Earl Weaver
B Marty Springstead
C Dizzy Dean
D Bob Horner

HAS IT EVER HAPPENED?

There are things that have happened in baseball that are incredibly hard to believe. Just imagine: Chicago Cubs outfielder Hack Wilson once actually drove home 191 runs during a single season, and he did it in a mere 155 games. This section tests your knowledge of similarly improbable events.

To keep you honest, every once in a while we'll throw you a wicked curveball, such as a trick question. Then, we'll try to fool you with a change-up in which one of the "facts" in the question will be off by a gnat's eyelash. Your job is to determine the truth and figure out if our events ever really happened.

Potent Lineup

Has a team ever had as many as six players in the lineup drive in 100 or more runs during a season?

ANSWER: No, but the 1936 Yankees featured an incredibly productive lineup with a record five men who had more than 100 ribbies.

The men included three future Hall of Famers: first baseman Lou Gehrig, who amassed 152 RBI; center fielder Joe DiMaggio, who added 125; and catcher Bill Dickey with his 107 RBI. In addition, Tony Lazzeri had 109, and George Selkirk contributed 107.

No-Hit Glory

Has a pitcher ever come up with a no-hitter during his very first start?

○ **ANSWER:** Amazingly, the answer is yes. More amazingly, the pitcher wasn't very good at all. Alva "Bobo" Holloman had pitched exclusively out of the bullpen. Then, after begging owner Bill Veeck to give him a start, he came up with his gem back in 1953. Although Holloman succeeded that day, his luck didn't last; he was gone from the majors for good just a short time later that same year.

His career statistics are paltry: 3 wins versus 7 losses, an ERA of 5.23, and twice as many walks (50) as batters struck out. His no-hitter was his only complete game ever.

Fanning Infrequently

Has a major-leaguer gone an entire season while striking out fewer than, say, 25 times?

○ **ANSWER:** Not in a long time, but yes, it has been done. In fact, Cleveland's Joe Sewell did this with ease. Sewell was known for his bat control, and, in 1925 and 1929, he truly showcased that talent. During those seasons, he struck out a mere eight times, four each year. Men have been known to strike out four times in a day; it took an entire year for Sewell to do that. Furthermore, he had 608 at bats in 1925 and 578 in 1929.

Impotent Bats

Has there ever been a season in which nobody in the entire American League hit .300 or better? Could such a season of pitchers' domination occur?

○ **ANSWER:** Although there was never a season without at least one .300 hitter, there was a year in which only one man topped that level. The year 1968 was known as the "Year of the Pitcher." That season, the American League batting title went to Boston's Carl Yastrzemski, who hit .301. The next best average was a paltry .290. The A.L. pitchers prevailed that year; five of them had ERAs under 2.00.

That was also the season that one of every 5 games resulted in a shutout. It seemed as if every time St. Louis Cardinal Bob Gibson pitched, he tossed a shutout (he had 13). His ERA (1.12) was the fourth lowest in baseball history. Finally, that season also featured the game's last 30-game winner, Detroit's Denny McLain (31-6).

WHO AM I?

1 People stand next to me and realize just how small they are. I'm six-foot-five, weigh about 245 pounds, and have arms as big as some guys' legs. For the most part, I've had my way with pitchers, especially lately. I hit 52 home runs in 1996 and came back in 1997 with 58 long balls. In 1998, I matched that figure by September 2, and then, under the glare of the national spotlight, thrilled the baseball world by adding a dozen more the last three and a half weeks of the season. I cooled off in 1999 and only hit 65 homers. *Who am I?*

2 I have a brother who is an identical twin, but our careers are hardly identical. He played in just 24 games With the A's and Cardinals in the early 1990s. On the other hand, I, who am bulkier than my brother, won the American League MVP in 1988 when I belted 42 home runs, drove in 124 runs, and added 40 stolen bases for good measure. I pounded a league-leading 44 home runs in 1991, but didn't win the MVP. I've been on the disabled list a lot in recent years (seven times since 1993), but still have racked up my share of homers—I hit a career-high 46 in 1998 and slugged 34 in 1999, even though I missed almost one-third of the season. *Who am I?*

3 Stan Musial, Robin Yount, and I are the only players who rank first all-time for a franchise in singles, doubles, triples, and home runs. In my long and distinguished career, I amassed 2035 singles, 665 doubles, 137 triples, and 317 home runs, for a total of 3154 hits, which earned me induction into the Hall of Fame in 1999, the first year that I was eligible. Home run number 200 came off Mitch Williams in his rookie campaign of 1986, after he had been misquoted in my team's local newspaper. The Rangers were coming to town and one of the writers who covered my team asked Mitch how he felt about facing me for the first time, and he answered, "The rumor is that I'm wild and I throw hard, so he might not be too comfortable in there his first at bat." The paper twisted Mitch's words and printed a headline the next day which said that I was scared of Mitch. When I faced Mitch during the series, he threw me a fastball, and I hit it 440 feet over the center field fence for a home run. After the game, the writer commended me on the home run, and I joked, "Yeah, but I was scared doing it." ***Who am I?***

4 I had a laundry list of accomplishments. To name a few, I hit a grand slam in my first big league game in 1968, scored 110 or more runs five straight years (1969–73), and hit 25 or more home runs in a season for five different teams, including the Yankees, Angels, and Indians. Believe it or not, I lost my stroke so badly late in my career that I was sent back to the minors. My son has shown no signs of losing his stroke, though—in 1996, he hit his 333rd career home run to pass me, and in 1999, he moved up to 22nd on the all-time home run list, finishing the year with 445. ***Who am I?***

5 To win a Rookie of the Year Award, a Cy Young Award, an ERA title, two strikeout titles, fan 16 in a game three times, and pitch on a World Series winner in a career is pretty good—I did all that before I turned 22. Too much success so quickly was kind of hard to handle, and caused me some off-the-field problems and cost me some wins for a few years. Things hit rock bottom in the mid-1990s when I missed most of two seasons, but I got back on track in 1996 when I won 11 games and no-hit Lou Piniella's Mariners. ***Who am I?***

6 I have a unique distinction: I'm the only pitcher who has won a Cy Young Award and guest-starred on The Brady Bunch. I won the Cy Young in 1962 when I led major league pitchers with 25 wins and 232 strikeouts. In 1965, I won 23, two less than my teammate Sandy Koufax. In 196S, I set a record—since broken by Orel Hershiser—when I pitched 58⅔ consecutive scoreless innings. And then in 1970, a year after I retired, I gave 15-year-old Greg Brady some tips on pitching. A lot of good it did him— he got a big head and his next game went out and was rocked for 12 runs in the first inning before the manager came out and gave him the hook. *Who am I?*

7 A lot of fans think I'm cocky and a showboat for my antics on the field, but in fact I'm so unpretentious that one year while some of my teammates drove to games in their fancy cars, I rode my bicycle. Here are a few tidbits about my career: I was originally drafted by the Royals, but first played for the Yankees. I led the National League in triples with 14 in 1992. I stole 56 bases for the Reds in 1997 to finish second to Tony Womack. Finally— and I don't mean to sound cocky—I'm the only man who has played in both a World Series and a Super Bowl. *Who am I?*

8 Every time I turned around in 1973, some pro sports team was drafting me. The Padres selected me in the first round of the baseball draft (I was first-team All-American my senior year as a pitcher tout fielder for the University of Minnesota), the NBA's Atlanta Hawks and ABA's Utah Jazz chose me in the fifth and sixth rounds, respectively, and even though I didn't play football in college, the Minnesota Vikings picked me in the 17th round of the NFL draft. In between signing with the Padres in 1973 and stroking my 3000th hit for the Twins in 1993, I hit 25 or more home runs nine times, drove in 100 runs eight times, and feuded with George Steinbrenner almost as much as Reggie and Billy. *Who am I?*

9 1982 was a pretty good year for me: I was voted one of the 10 best casually dressed men in America, and my Cardinals team won the World Series. Other notables on the best dressed list included Alexander Haig and Johnny Carson. As a matter of fact, Johnny hosted The Tonight Show in Burbank, not far from where I grew up and went to Locke High School in Los Angeles. By coincidence, Lonnie Smith, one of the guys I played ball with as a teenager in L.A., was a teammate on my 1982 team. Lonnie had a long career in the majors—17 years— but I played 19 years. I only hit 28 home runs in those 19 seasons, and my lifetime average was less than .270, but my friends tell me I'll probably be voted into the Hall of Fame; I'll be up for induction in 2002. *Who am I?*

10 Major league scouts weren't exactly beating a path to my door when I was playing high school ball for Phoenixville High, outside Philadelphia—I was picked in the 62nd round (the 1389th player) of the 1988 draft. I hung in there, though, made it to the majors, and after the 1998 season I signed a longterm contract for mega-millions. What did I do to justify that mammoth contract? I averaged .335, 33 home runs, and 106 RBIs a year over the previous six seasons, playing a position where guys usually hit .260 with half that many homers and runs batted in. I owe a lot to my godfather, who turned out to be my manager for the first four years of my major league career. *Who am I?*

11 We couldn't have written a baseball quiz book without including one question on "The Bambino" himself, George Herman "Babe" Ruth. Here are 10 statements about the Babe. We want to know if they're true or false.

    A He stole more than 100 bases in his career.

    B He finished his career with the Boston Braves.

C He was born in New York and died in Baltimore.

D He was a 20-game winner for the Red Sox.

E His career average was higher than teammate Lou Gehrig's.

F He is the all-time career leader in RBIs.

G He holds the American League record for most strikeouts in a season by a batter.

H He was six feet, two inches tall.

I He hit .400 in a season once.

J He didn't drink, smoke, or carouse.

12 From the late 1940s until the early 1980s, there were three sure things in life: death, taxes, and this colorful character going to the World Series. Over a 35-year period (1947–81), he suited up for 21 Fall Classics: 14 as a player, five as a coach, and two as a manager, and his team came out on the long end of the stick 13 times. One final hint, which should clinch it for you. The story has it that one time he went to pick up a pizza for one and was asked whether he wanted it cut in four or eight slices. "You better make it four," he said, "I could never eat eight."

13 All right, quick now, name the only two players who started their careers in 1975 or later who collected at least 3250 hits. We'll add that they combined for 738 home runs and 614 stolen bases.

14 The Yankees closed out the century in a grand fashion. In 1998, they set an American League record with 114 regular-season wins and then swept the Rangers in the Division Series, beat the Indians four games to two in the League Championship Series, and swept the Padres in the World Series. Their two losses in the post-season was the fewest since the three-tier post-season system was first used in 1995. In 1999, the Yankees were less of a juggernaut during the season as they won 98 games, but they were even more dominating in the post-season. They again swept the Rangers in the Division Series, beat the Red Sox four games to one in the League Championship Series, and whitewashed the Braves in the World Series; thus, the 1999 Yankees lost only one game in the postseason. From 1969 to 1993, when baseball utilized two post-season rounds (there were three rounds in the strike-shortened 1981 season), only one team went undefeated by sweeping both the League Championship Series and the World Series. *Who was it?*

15 Every dog has his day, and every star doesn't always shine. Hank Aaron is the all-time home run leader, Cal Ripken Jr. holds the iron-man streak, and Brooks Robinson set some records with his amazing defense at third base. But Aaron, Ripken, and Robinson, along with Mickey Mantle and Reggie Jackson, each hold at least one record that they would just as soon not. Match the player with the record.

Hank Aaron	**A** Holds record for most strikeouts in World Series play
Cal Ripken Jr.	**B** The mark for most double plays grounded into in a career belongs to him
Brooks Robinson	**C** Set record for most at bats in a season without a triple
Reggie Jackson	**D** Hit into a record four triple plays
Mickey Mantle	**E** All-time leader in lifetime K's 70

16 What's more exciting, watching Juan Gonzalez or Manny

Ramirez go deep, or seeing Kenny Lofton or Tony Womack steal second on a bang-bang play? Because we already have a lot of questions on home run hitters, we're going to ask you about some great base stealers. These would be hanging curveballs if we asked you who the top three all-time base thieves are (Rickey Henderson, Lou Brock, and Ty Cobb; you knew that, right?), so try to answer these questions about four other players in the top 15.

A This shortstop stole 104 bases for the Dodgers in 1962 to set the single-season record, which Brock broke in 1974.

B Starting in 1985, he won six straight stolen base titles for the Cardinals, averaging 92 per year with three 100-steal seasons. He's fifth on the career list with 762.

C He's first among players who never won a stolen base title, with 689 steals.

D This outfielder pilfered 668 bases, most of them for the Royals in the late 1970s and 1980s.

17 The first 80 years of the 20th century, perfect games were a rare commodity—only eight pitchers twirled perfectos. But the hurlers picked up the pace over the last two decades by throwing seven—or one approximately every three years. All good pitchers in the group, but it's unlikely that any will go to the Hall. We've given you the year and the team for whom each of the seven pitched the gem.

YEAR	TEAM	YEAR	TEAM
		1981	Cleveland Indians
		1984	California Angels
		1988	Cincinnati Reds
		1991	Montreal Expos

1994	Texas Rangers
1998	New York Yankees
1999	New York Yankees

18 In 1999, Sammy Sosa led his Cubs team in home runs for the seventh consecutive season. Impressive stretch by Slammin' Sammy, but a long way from the record. In the first half of the century, a player led his team—the same team—in home runs 18 consecutive seasons. Seven of those seasons, he had at least twice as many homers as the number-two man on the team. He averaged about 28 per year over the 18-year period. He managed the team the last four years. Any idea who it is?

19 Isn't it about time some player won the Triple Crown? After all it's been more than 30 years—since 1967—when a player led his league with a .326 average, 44 home runs, and 121 RBIs. These were the only home run and RBI titles this player won in his long and accomplished career, but he also won batting titles in 1963 and 1968. He's second to Pete Rose on the all-time games played list with 3308, seventh in career hits with 3419, and 11th in lifetime RBIs with 1844. Can you name him?

20 Name the team: They have only been to one World Series since 1919 and they lost. Luke Appling is their all-time hit leader. Ted Lyons is their all-time wins leader. Nellie Fox won the MVP for them in 1959. Tommie Agee won the Rookie of the Year for them in 1966. Jeff Torborg and Jim Fregosi have managed the team. If we told you much more, we'd give it away.

ANSWERS

Managers' Words:

1 **B**
2 **A**
3 **C**
4 **D**
5 **F**
6 **E**

Humor: 1 C   2 D   3 B   4 E   5 A

More Managers: 1 D   2 C   3 A   4 B

Last Call for Managers' Quotes: 1 D   2 E   3 B   4 C   5 A

This and That: 1 B   2 D   3 A   4 E   5 C

More This and That: 1 B   2 D   3 C   4 A

More Humor: 1 A   2 C   3 D   4 E   5 B

Colorful Quotes: 1 B   2 A   3 D   4 C

Final Inning: 1 A   2 B   3 C

Who Am I?

1 Mark McGwire
2 Jose Canseco
3 George Brett
4 Bobby Bonds
5 Dwight Gooden
6 Don Drysdale

7 Deion Sanders

8 Dave Winfield

9 Ozzie Smith

10 Mike Piazza

11 **A** True **B** False **C** False **D** True **E** True **F** False
G False **H** True **I** False **J** False

12 Yogi Berra (14 as a player for the Yankees, four as a coach of
the Yankees, one as a coach of the Mets, one as a manager of
the Mets and one as a manager of the Yankees.)

13 Paul Molitor (3319 hits, 234 home runs, and 504 stolen bases)
and Eddie Murray (3255 hits, 504 home runs, and 110 stolen
bases.)

14 The 1976 Reds; they swept the Phillies in the League
Championship Series and the Yankees in the World Series

15 Aaron–**B** (328 Ripken–**C** (646 in 1989) Robinson–**D**;
Jackson **E** (2597) Mantle: **A** (54)

16 **A** Muary Wills **B** Vince Coleman **C** Joe Morgan **D** Willie
Wilson

17 Len barker (Indians), Mike Witt (Angles), Tom Browning
(Reds), Dennis Martinez (Expos), Kenny rogers(Rangers),
David Wells (1998 Yankees), and David Cone (1999 Yankees).

18 Mel Ott (New York Giants)

19 Carl Yastrzemski

20 Chicago White Sox

Baseball
Bafflers 2
THE SECOND INNING

*Quizzes, Trivia, Other Ballpark
Challenges, and the Strangest Moments
in Baseball History*

EDITED BY "SLAMMIN" SAM WEISER

Baseball Bloopers

OFFBEAT HUMOR

At times, the brand of humor exhibited in baseball is rather offbeat. The wit can be clever, cruel, self-deprecating, wry, almost philosophical, and even a bit baffling. No other game is as rich in humor as baseball. To paraphrase an interesting theory of writer George Plimpton, in sports, the smaller the size of the ball, the better that sport is in terms of possessing interesting and humorous quotes and stories.

To support his theory, Plimpton pointed out that there are many golf and baseball anecdotes; some football and basketball anecdotes; and, he added whimsically, absolutely none about beach balls.

Aside from the fact that there are no great Ping-Pong stories, his theory seems sound.

A HEADS-UP PLAY

A batter hits a long fly ball that bounces off the center-field fence, strikes the outfielder on the head, and bounces into the stands. The umpire awards the batter a ground-rule double.

Is the ruling a good one?

The umpire is right when he rules that a "bounding" fair ball that is deflected by a player into the stands in fair territory is a double. Once a fly ball hits the fence, it is considered to be a "bounding" ball, not a ball "in flight," and cannot be ruled a home run. A ball "in flight" — that is, a fair fly ball that is deflected by a player into the stands in fair territory — is a home run.

The Expos' Andre Dawson, in a 1977 game at Montreal's Olympic Stadium, rocketed

Is it "bounding" or "in flight"?

a long fly ball to center field that bounded off the wall, struck Dodger outfielder Rick Monday on the head, and bounced into the stands.

Dawson got a double, Monday a headache.

OFF-THE-FENCE INSIDE-THE-PARK HOMER

A batter hits a line drive that bounces out of the glove of the left fielder and flies over the fence. The umpire rules the hit a double.

Is he right?

The umpire, in this case, is wrong and should be overruled. When an umpire miscalls a book rule, another arbiter may reverse his call. This hit should be declared a home run. In the next example, one umpire actually did overrule another one.

In a 1953 game between the Cardinals and the host Braves, Milwaukee's Bill Bruton hit a fly ball that deflected off left fielder Enos Slaughter's glove and bounced over the fence. One umpire called the hit a double; another arbiter reversed the call and awarded the batter a home run.

The second umpire's decision, based upon the rule that a fair fly ball "in flight" that is deflected by a fielder into the stands in fair territory is a home run, was the correct one. Bruton was awarded a game-winning home run.

WHO IS THAT MASKED MAN?

The teams are tied, 3-3, in the bottom half of the 12th inning.

The Giant pitcher, who is in a groove, is mowing down batter after batter. He continues until he gets to the potential second out. The batter lifts a foul fly behind the plate. The Giant catcher quickly discards his mask and circles under the ball. But he steps into his upturned mask and tumbles to the ground as the ball falls to earth untouched.

The catcher has made a physical mistake on the play. But he has committed a mental error, too.

What was the mental mistake?

On a foul pop the catcher should never relieve himself of his mask until he knows the direction of the ball. Then he should flip the mask in the opposite direction.

Such a mistake cost the Giants the 1924 World Series. With the seventh game, against the host

"Look where you're going!"

Senators, tied 3-3 in the 12th inning, Giant pitcher Jack Bentley was in a groove. But with one out in the inning, the Giants let the game get away. The Senators' Muddy Ruel, who had had only one hit in seven games, lifted a harmless foul behind the plate. Hank Gowdy, the Giant catcher, stepped into his discarded mask and fell to the ground. Ruel took advantage of his second chance by doubling to left field. Earl McNeely, the next hitter, bounced a ball to third, but it struck a pebble and ricocheted over Freddie Lindtrom's head for the game-winning and Series-winning hit.

Bentley should have been out of the inning in one-two-three style. Instead, he was the loser in the decisive game of the World Series.

WHAT'S THE SCORE?

A fast-racing outfielder appears to catch a looper hit into center field by the home-team's slugger, but the umpire rules that the speedster trapped the ball after it touched the grass.

The hometown fans, who are furious with the call, hurl objects, such as fruit and bottles, onto the field. Some of the missiles hit two of the umpires. When appeals to the fans, by way of the public address system, fail to quiet the angry spectators, it is evident that something drastic has to be done.

What drastic action do the umpires take?

The umpires, when unable to quiet rioting fans who pose a danger to participants and spectators alike, must rule a forfeit — in this

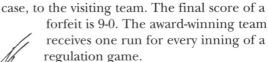

case, to the visiting team. The final score of a forfeit is 9-0. The award-winning team receives one run for every inning of a regulation game.

The Giants of 1949 picked up this type of forfeit when the fans at Connie Mack Stadium in Philadelphia could not be calmed down after an umpire ruled that Phillie center fielder Richie Ashburn had trapped a ball.

Ashburn was one of the greatest defensive center fielders of all time. The Phillie fans, we can suppose, thought that Ashburn could catch any ball that came near him.

THE WAYWARD BALL

A famous player drags a bunt down the first-base line. The pitcher fields the ball and lunges to tag him. But the pitcher loses control of the ball, and it rolls inside the shirt of the runner.

Now, seeing he is in control of the ball, the runner circles the bases while the infielders, in a state of confusion, don't know whether they should chase him or tackle him.

Does the run count?

No, the run doesn't count. When the ball becomes the possession of the runner, he is limited to the base to which he is advancing. In this instance, the runner has to return to first base.

In 1933, Rabbit Maranville, reaching the end of a distinguished Hall-of-Fame career, laid down such a bunt and circled the bases while Dodger pitcher Van Lingle Mungo chased him indecisively from first to home.

The play caused some indecision on the umpires' part, too, and sent them scurrying to the rule book for a verdict on the play.

One base.

WINFIELD GETS THE BIRD

A Yankee outfielder, playing against the host Blue Jays, is warming up between innings. Suddenly a seagull lands on the grass, just a short distance away.

Not knowing the bird is wounded, he impulsively throws at it, believing that he does not have a chance of hitting it. But the bird, which doesn't move, is killed by the thrown ball.

What is the outfielder's punishment, if any?

Canadians have a fondness for seagulls. So, first, the legal authorities arrest the outfielder. Then the player posts a $500 bond and faces a cruelty-to-animals charge.

Dave Winfield, believe it or not, is the one who faced that charge in Toronto. He suffered a lot of bad publicity before he finally was absolved of the offense.

After that, he limited his putouts to runners, not grounded flyers.

THROWING BEHIND THE RUNNER

Trick plays can be "tricky." Take the catcher's pick-off move, for example.

A Mariner catcher was trying to contain the Royals' base runner, who was on first base. What the catcher decided to do was to look at the pitcher, as though he were throwing to the moundsman, and to throw to first base instead. The first time he attempted his trick move, his first baseman was daydreaming. The catcher's throw sailed past the unsuspecting first baseman and rolled into the right-field corner while the runner scored.

How could the catcher have prevented this unfortunate set of circumstances from taking place?

He should have informed his first baseman in advance, and he would have avoided the disastrous consequences.

Choo-Choo Coleman, catcher for the 1962 Mets, tried to hold the Dodgers' speedster Maury Wills close by using that play. Coleman actually executed the play well. The throw was hard and accurate. There was only one problem: the Mets had a first baseman by the name of Marv Throneberry.

The "Marvelous One" was daydreaming, and he caught the throw right on his forehead. The ball glanced off his head and rolled between the right and center fielders. Wills laughed all the way around the bases.

The moral is, the catcher can look the wrong way, but the first baseman can't.

"Playing first base is such fun!"

KICK BALL

The lead-off batter for the Cubs in a late-season game in Philadelphia bunts toward the right side, but as he breaks out of the batter's box, he accidentally kicks the ball up the first-base line. By the time the pitcher fields the ball and throws to the first baseman, the runner has crossed the bag.

Does he get an infield hit or is he out for interference?

The runner is out when his fair ball touches him before touching a fielder.

In an Indian-A's game in Cleveland, Bert Campaneris, the lead-off batter, stepped into the batter's box as the umpire set himself up behind the plate. As the pitcher went into his windup, the umpire in the field, seeing that his partner behind the plate didn't have his mask on, called "Time." The pitch came anyway, and Campaneris proceeded to push a bunt towards first before running into the rolling ball.

Ordinarily the batter would be called out, but in this instance, the time out preceded the play. So the umpire called the offering no pitch and started the game all over again.

LITTLE LEAGUE PLAY

Some plays that work on a lower level of baseball simply don't work at the Major League level — or at least they shouldn't work. Still, with the right ingredients, anything goes. For example, on May 12, 1998, the Pittsburgh Pirates were playing the Colorado Rockies. Kirt Manwaring laced a ball into right field for an apparent single. Pittsburgh right fielder Jose Guillen came up with the ball quickly and rifled it to first base. Embarrassingly, Manwaring was gunned out. Later, he likened the experience to the feeling you get in a dream where you run as hard as you can, but you don't move at all.

The play worked because of four factors. First, Manwaring, a catcher, is slow-footed. Second, the ball got to Guillen in a hurry.

Third, Guillen fielded the ball quickly, charging in to make the play. Finally, Guillen's arm resembles Roberto Clemente's — it's that good.

MORE EMBARRASSMENT

In 1993, Tom Candiotti was on the mound for the Los Angeles Dodgers when a runner took off for second, attempting a steal. Mike Piazza, who was a rookie catcher that year, came up gunning the ball. The throw was on line, but it never reached second because it struck Candiotti in his derriere.

The knuckleball pitcher later said, "I couldn't help but laugh at that one. I've dodged line drives before, but never a throw from a catcher."

HIT YOUR CUTOFF MAN

When Dave Winfield was with the San Diego Padres, he once went through a bad stretch of games in which he had difficulty hitting his cutoff man.

Shortly after a workout focusing on hitting cutoffs, Winfield had a chance to snap out of his defensive woes. On a hard-hit single to the outfield, Winfield quickly and smoothly came up with the ball in shallow center field.

Darrell Thomas lined himself up with Winfield to take the throw. But he saw that Winfield was very close to the infield, and Thomas knew the strong-armed outfielder would not need him for a relay throw. So, Thomas ducked and spun around to watch the play at the plate.

Meanwhile, Winfield's throw came in hard, low and right on target for the relay man. The ball hit Thomas directly on his backside, much like the Candiotti scenario.

After the game Winfield joked, "I finally hit the cutoff man."

A MICKEY MANTLE TALE

Longtime Detroit Tiger announcer Ernie Harwell recalled what had to be one of the longest singles in the history of the game. He said, "I saw Mickey Mantle hit a ball that bounced into the center-field bleachers at Yankee Stadium. He hit it with the bases loaded in an extra-inning game.

"At first, they gave him a ground-rule double, then they looked it up and could only award him a single." According to the rule book, the batter is awarded a single because it only took a single to drive in the run from third. The only exception to this rule is a game-winning home run. In that situation, they do not take away the homer even if a lesser hit would have won the game (as was the case with Mantle).

"HIDDEN" BALL PLAY

On July 1, 1998, the Chicago White Sox were playing the Houston Astros when, in a weird variation on the old "hidden" ball play, an umpire, not a player, "hid" the ball. Doug Henry was on the mound for Houston, and the Sox had Ray Durham on third.

Atlanta Braves coach Pat Corrales picks up the play-by-play from there: "It looked like the pitch was a sinker, and it hit the ground and bounced up. The ball got by the catcher and went in the umpire's [front] pocket and got buried there.

"The hitter didn't know where it was, the catcher didn't know, and the umpire [Gerry Davis] didn't know. The runner crossed the plate, then everybody realized where the ball was."

Durham scored easily and the befuddled catcher, Brad Ausmus, was the loser in this zany game of hide-and-seek. In reality, according to baseball rules, once the ball was "lost," it was also, in medical terminology, DOA. And once a ball is declared dead, searching for it was pointless. As Corrales pointed out, "If it gets stuck like that, you get one base, once they figured out where the ball was." He called it one of the strangest things he'd ever seen in the majors.

RUNNING WILD

Most fans love to watch displays of power. Many fans also enjoy the speed game in baseball. Getting a chance to see a Lou Brock blaze around the bases is a thrill. One of the craziest plays involving speedy runners took place in 1985 when the Chicago Cubs were hosting the St. Louis Cardinals.

With Vince Coleman on second and Willie McGee on first, the Cards put on the double steal. Coleman stole third easily, but he ran so rapidly that he slid past the bag. Realizing he couldn't get back to third without being tagged, Coleman jumped up and dashed towards home plate.

Meanwhile, the fleet-footed McGee, who was on second, saw what had occurred and scampered for third. Amazingly, Coleman made it home, and McGee went into third unscathed. The end result, due to a unique scorer's decision, was four stolen bases on one pitch!

Don Slaught calls the next play one of the funniest moments he ever saw on a diamond. It was funny in two ways: It was "odd" funny, and it was also "gallows humor" funny.

Slaught, the catcher that day, relates what happened on July 27, 1988: "I was in New York with the Yankees when Tommy John had . . . three errors on one play. I think the ball was hit back to him; and he bobbled it for an error, then threw it wild to first for another error. The right fielder [Dave Winfield] caught the ball, threw it in. John cut if off, wheeled and threw it to me, but [he] threw it in the dugout for his third error on one play."

That play made John the first pitcher in the modern era to be guilty of three errors in an inning, and he did it all in a matter of seconds on one zany play.

A NOT-SO-GRAND SLAM

Cesar Cedeno of the Houston Astros hit what has to be one of the strangest hits, and perhaps the shortest grand slam ever. It happened on September 2, 1971, when Cedeno hit a fly ball 200 feet with the bases loaded. Two Dodgers, second baseman Jim Lefebvre and right fielder Bill Buckner, converged on the ball.

They collided, and the ball fell in safely. By the time the Dodger defense could come up with the ball, it was too late. Cedeno had already circled the bases with a rather tainted grand slam.

MORE INSIDE-THE-PARK WILDNESS

On July 25, 1998, Turner Ward came to the plate as a pinch hitter for the Pittsburgh Pirates. He faced Dennis Martinez. What followed was about as bizarre as it gets. He hit the ball down off the plate, causing it to resemble a kid on a pogo stick, bouncing up the middle.

Atlanta Braves second baseman Tony Graffanino got to the ball, but he was only able to get a glove on it. That caused the ball to change directions, caroming past center fielder Andruw Jones.

Reportedly, Jones didn't hustle after the ball when it got by him, and Ward waltzed home with a strange inside-the-park homer.

BUCK RODGERS ON THE HIT-AND-RUN WITH THE BASES FULL

Most managers wouldn't dream of calling for a hit-and-run with the bases loaded. But Buck Rodgers, who managed in the National League East when he was with the Montreal Expos, makes an exception when the situation includes certain favorable factors. Rodgers pointed out three vital elements: "A batter at the plate who usually

makes good contact, a pitcher who has good control and is usually around the plate with his pitches, and a pitcher who isn't a big strike-out pitcher."

Furthermore, the count on the batter would have to be one that would require the pitcher to come in with a strike — a count of 3-and-1, for example.

Dwight Gooden remembered a time when Don Zimmer, a much admired managerial peer of Rodgers, pulled off this trick: "One year when Zimmer was with the Cubs, with less than two outs, he sent everybody. It was the hit-and-run with the bases loaded. Lloyd McClendon was the hitter. I'd never seen that. It worked," Gooden marveled with a grin.

Such moves don't always pay off, of course. Rafael Palmeiro remembers playing for Don Zimmer when Zimmer was managing the Chicago Cubs: "I was playing . . . in '88, and we had the bases loaded in New York against the Mets. Manny Trillo was the batter, and the count was 3-and-2, I believe, when Zimmer put the hit-and-run on. Trillo swung through a pitch up in the zone, and Gary Carter caught the ball and tagged the runner for a double play, and we were out of the inning."

TWO MORE MEN'S THOUGHTS

Finally, on the topic of the bases loaded hit-and-run, the thoughts of another manager, Larry Rothschild: "I think Don Baylor did it in Colorado a couple of times [this would make sense since Zimmer served as Baylor's bench coach from 1993 to 1995]. You don't see that — the odds of it backfiring and costing you dearly are too great.

"I don't think that's having guts [to run such a play]. I think it's [a matter of] intelligence." Rothschild did concede that it depends on whether a manager such as Baylor has the right situation. "It's more of a calculated risk. If it works, great. If it doesn't, you really screwed up."

Bobby Cox disagrees. "There's nothing wrong with that strategy. Why not try something. I like that type of stuff. There's no 'book.'" He added, "It's a lot more fun." Of course, being with the successful Braves, Cox could afford to try any kind of play.

SPARKY'S HIT-AND-RUN

Another legendary manager who employed unorthodox plays at times was Sparky Anderson. Travis Fryman, who played for Anderson, said the only two men he could think of who used unique plays such as a hit-and-run with a man on third were Zimmer and Anderson.

Johnny Goryl said of Anderson, "He'd put on a hit-and-run with a runner on third so the runner could score on a ground ball. The disadvantage is if the hitter misses the ball, you're 'out to lunch,' or you could have a line-drive double play.

"The situation has to be with a contact hitter at the plate who'll put the ball in play on the ground," stated the longtime coach and manager. "Of course the count must also be favorable to the hitter — a count where the pitcher is going to throw a strike."

Frank Howard summed up the play: "What they're really doing is, rather than wait for contact to be made before you start the runner at third base, he's getting his runner in motion in case contact is made on the ground." And, if that contact is made, says Howard, "It's a walk home."

Baseball Oddities

PITCHER TURNED SLUGGER

When the 1997 season opened, Chicago Cubs center fielder Brian McRae felt safe concerning a promise he had made three years earlier. He had told teammate Frank Castillo he would buy him a Mercedes Benz if Castillo, a pitcher and notoriously poor hitter, could ever swat a home run (even during batting practice).

Well, on May 30th, Castillo, a .108 hitter, went deep twice during his rounds in the batting cage prior to a game. This hitting display pleased the man who normally couldn't hit a lick, but brought dismay and utter disbelief to McRae. When asked what he made of the whole situation, McRae simply stated, "He's still the worst hitting pitcher I've ever seen!"

DISAPPEARING BASEBALL

Larry Biittner was manning right field for the Cubs in a 1979 game against the New York Mets when another baseball performed a vanishing act. A low line drive off the bat of Bruce Boisclair came Biittner's way, but eluded his diving effort. He knew the ball had to be near him because he had deadened it when it glanced off his glove. So, he pounced off the turf and back to his feet, losing his hat during that motion.

He began looking around for the ball so the batter couldn't advance to second base. No matter how hard he looked, no matter in which direction he gazed, he could not find the ball. It took on comic proportions as the crowd roared with delight, even as Boisclair raced past second and on towards third.

About that time Biittner, like Wagner, finally figured it out. The ball had deflected off his glove and trickled under his cap. He had found it (as a cliche goes) in the last place he looked for it. Interestingly, his timing was perfect in that he was able to throw out the runner at third.

THE BERRA BRAND OF HUMOR

Yogi Berra truly was as famous as anyone was when it came to having his own brand of baseball humor. Many of the tales of Berra are apocryphal, but remain classics, nevertheless. One little-known story deals with the time the Yankee Hall-of-Fame catcher met Robert Briscoe, the mayor of Dublin, Ireland.

Upon learning Briscoe was the city's first Jewish mayor, Berra beamed, "Isn't that great." He paused and then added in all seriousness, "It could only happen in America."

The craggy-faced Berra wasn't afraid to make himself the source of a laugh. Once a photographer told Berra to pose for a picture. "Look straight into the camera," he instructed. Berra thought for a moment, and then said, "Oh, I can't do that. That's my bad side."

PAINFUL HUMOR

An embarrassing injury took place during a 1989 exhibition game to Milwaukee Brewer Bill Spiers. He was in the on-deck circle as a close play at home plate developed. He got close to the action and began signaling to a teammate racing in from third that it was going to be a bang-bang play, and that the runner should slide into the plate. At the moment he was indicating a slide was in order, he got plunked on the head by the umpire's face mask.

The umpire wasn't out to get Spiers. He had simply flung off his mask to get a better view of the play, something umpires normally do. Observers said they had never before seen such a bizarre play.

THOU SHALL NOT WALK

In 1995, Indian catcher Tony Pena helped engineer a replication of a very famous decoy. California's Chili Davis was in the batter's box facing veteran right-hander Dennis Martinez. The count was full, at three balls and two strikes, with a runner on third.

Pena crouched behind the plate for the payoff pitch, and then suddenly stood and signaled for an intentional walk.

Seeing he was about to be given a free pass to first, Davis relaxed. And, at that moment, Martinez quickly slipped strike three by Davis. The irate batter later stated, "I got suckered. I've never seen it before and I'll never see it again."

Well, if he was watching baseball highlights a year later, he certainly did see that play executed again. On July 30, 1996, Pena, who said he performed this play once with Roger Clemens in Boston and several more times in winter ball, did it once more. This time, the victim was John Olerud, then with the Toronto Blue Jays. Martinez and Pena again worked the con game to perfection on a two-out payoff delivery.

Olerud contended he wasn't fooled as two of his coaches had yelled a warning. "Martinez made a great pitch down and away," claimed Olerud. "It might have looked like I was tricked, but I wasn't."

At any rate, the ironic part of it all is the fact that this trick is extremely famous. When Chili Davis, Tony Pena's victim in 1995, was 12 years old, the Oakland A's pulled it off during the 1972 World Series. It's almost as if Davis (and Olerud?) were proving the axiom that those who don't learn from events of the past are doomed to repeat such errors.

The World Series Deception of 1972 took place in the fifth inning of the fifth game. The A's superlative reliever Rollie Fingers was on the mound, trying to help his team cling to 4-3 lead over Cincinnati. Fingers was clearly in a jam as the Reds had Bobby Tolan leading off first base with the highly feared Johnny Bench at the plate. A few moments later, Tolan swiped second as the count reached two balls and two strikes.

It was then that the Oakland skipper, Dick Williams, went to the mound for a conference. As he strolled off the field, he pointed to first base and said, "Okay, let's put him on." Needless to say, Bench fell for it — after all, the situation obviously did call for an intentional walk. The bat lay on his shoulders as Rollie Fingers slipped a third strike past him.

Seconds later, a job well done, Fingers and his catcher Gene Tenace were jogging to the dugout as Bench stared at the plate in sheer disbelief, a strikeout casualty.

WHAT ARE THE ODDS?

Joe Niekro was a pitcher for 22 seasons in the Major Leagues. While he did possess a splendid knuckleball, allowing him to chalk up 221 victories, he was certainly not much of a hitter. Throughout his career, he could muster just one home run (on May 29, 1976). What's so odd here is his only shot came against a fellow knuckleball artist who wound up winning 318 games and who just happened to be Joe's brother, Phil.

ANNIVERSARY EVENTS

Lou Gehrig swatted his first career home run on September 27, 1923. On that same day 15 years later, he hit his final blast. That truly is an incredible coincidence.

Likewise, on September 13, 1965, Willie "The Say Hey Kid" Mays hit his 500th home run. Exactly six years later, fellow longball artist Frank Robinson launched his 500th.

Meanwhile, Eddie Mathews pelted his 500th home run on July 14, 1967. The next year on that day, longtime teammate Hank Aaron reached the 500 home run plateau. By the way, these two men hit more four baggers than any other teammate duo — even more than Babe Ruth and Lou Gehrig.

UNLIKELY EVENTS

Vic Power was a journeyman who lasted for 12 years in the majors. He was never known for his speed, stealing only 45 lifetime bases with a season high of just nine. Despite that, in August of 1958 while with Cleveland, he stole home twice in the same game. Not only that, for the entire season he wound up with just one additional stolen base.

Balks are hardly the most interesting of baseball topics. Yet there is one balk that was so unusual it's still talked about. During the All-Star game of

1961, Stu Miller, a diminutive pitcher, was on the mound for the National League. The game that year was held on San Francisco's home field, Candlestick Park.

Miller, a member of the Giants pitching staff, was well aware of the gusting winds in Candlestick. However, when one especially strong burst of wind struck him, the 165-pounder was blown off the mound. Since that movement was considered illegal, a balk had to be called on him. What was so odd about it was that it was the first balk of Miller's nine years in the majors — and he'll never live it down.

GRIDIRON OR DIAMOND?

Don Mattingly of the New York Yankees was an outstanding hitter and a fine first baseman. Even before he made it to the big leagues, scouts knew he would be a star. Still, there were several players drafted before him and, amazingly, three of them became professional football stars, forsaking the game of baseball. They were, by a strange coincidence, all quarterbacks: John Elway, Jay Schroeder and Dan Marino.

Furthermore, yet another college grid star, Rick Leach, was selected ahead of Mattingly. While the quarterbacks had a great deal of National Football League success, Leach was a bust. The only baseball organization that came out of this most unusual draft looking good was the Yankees.

THE GREAT GREG MADDUX

In 1994, Greg Maddux was almost unbeatable. His final statistics read like a line from Walter Johnson's page in the record book. The Atlanta ace went 16-6 during the strike-shortened season. Not only did he win nearly 73% of his decisions, his ERA glittered at a nearly invisible, league-leading 1.56.

In 1995, his ERA went up — to a still-microscopic 1.63. His record, however, was simply unbelievable as his ledger read 19-2 for a won-lost percentage of .905! Seldom has a pitcher dominated the game as Maddux did in that era.

Frustrated batters showed awe and respect by their actions (often shaking their heads in disbelief as they dragged themselves back to their dugouts after making outs), and their words — consider, for example, what Danny Sheaffer said.

First, though, some background. In 1995, Maddux had just gone through an especially impressive four-game stretch during which he averaged just 97 pitches per game. That worked out to an average of 10.7 pitches each inning. Further, over that stretch he walked only one batter. Two of those four games resulted in 1-0 shutouts of St. Louis. Now, the Cardinals catcher, Sheaffer, normally not much of a batter, somehow hit safely in both games. When he was asked if he had ever seen a pitcher better than Maddux, Sheaffer calmly stated that he had. "In Nintendo," he smiled. "There's a guy on my computer about that good."

A ROOKIE OF THE YEAR WHO ALMOST WASN'T

The 1997 recipient of the Rookie of the Year Award in the National League was Philadelphia's stellar shortstop Scott Rolen. The ironic circumstance in his situation involves the fact that he came within inches of being denied the award.

It all started on September 7, 1996, when Rolen stood in the batter's box against the Chicago Cubs and pitcher Steve Trachsel. The right-hander reared back, fired the ball, and plunked Rolen with a pitch. The ball shattered Rolen's right forearm, ending his season.

At the time Rolen had chalked up 130 at bats, which just happens to be the maximum amount of trips to the plate a man can have before losing his rookie status. Had Rolen cracked a hit, or even made an out, instead of being hit with the pitch, he would have been ineligible for the rookie honors in 1997.

Only joking slightly, Rolen accepted his kudos saying, "This would be a good time to thank Steve Trachsel, who was a big part of this. At the time, I wasn't really happy with him. Now, I might give him a call and thank him."

UNANIMITY

Not only did Rolen win the Rookie of the Year Award unanimously in 1997, so did the American League winner, Boston's Nomar Garciaparra, also a shortstop. Garciaparra, whose first name is actually his father's name spelled backward (Ramon), sizzled all year long for the Red Sox.

The Rolen-Garciaparra duo marks only the third time both rookie winners were unanimous selections. The other times came in 1993 with Piazza and the American League winner, Tim Salmon of the Angels; and in 1987 when Mark McGwire won in the American League as an Oakland Athletic, and Santiago won in the National League while with the San Diego Padres.

MORE UNANIMITY

The most prestigious of all baseball's postseason awards is the Most Valuable Player. In 1997 Ken Griffey, Jr. impressed the voters so much, he won this award by gaining all 28 of the first-place votes. In doing so he became just the 13th unanimous MVP recipient. Clearly, he deserved such honors. He smacked the ball to a .304 tune while banging out 56 home runs, to lead the American League. Those 56 blasts are also among the highest single-season totals ever. In addition, he drove home 147 runs, first in the majors.

Not only that, Griffey led his league in runs with 125, total bases with 393, and slugging percentage at .646. The versatile center fielder also captured his eighth consecutive Gold Glove award.

WORLD SERIES ODDITY

When the Cleveland Indians played the Florida Marlins in the seventh game in the 1997 World Series, they gave the all-important starting assignment to Jaret Wright. What made that so unusual is: a) he hadn't even been on the 40-man roster of the Indians as of the spring of 1997; b) the son of former big-league pitcher Clyde Wright had just climbed from the low minors to the majors, all in one year; and c) his career victory total in the majors was a meager eight (no pitcher in the 93 World Series played had ever started the seventh game with fewer lifetime wins). Despite the Indians loss, Wright pitched well. He had definitely made a name for himself over the course of one highly charged season.

Incidentally, the Indians outscored the Marlins in the Series by a 44-37 margin, outhit them .291 to .272, and outpitched them with a 4.66 ERA versus a 5.48 ERA, yet lost the title to Florida. Of course, in the playoffs against the Orioles, Cleveland was outscored, yet won the pennant anyhow.

More Baseball Trivia

1. Of course you remember the Marlins won the 1997 World Series in just their fifth year in existence, and the Cubbies haven't been to the Fall Classic since 1945, but can you remember how these teams fared in the Series over the last two decades?

Cleveland Indians   A. Lost two Series in the 1990s
Minnesota Twins   B. Won a Series in the 1990s
San Diego Padres   C. Won a Series in the 1980s
New York Mets   D. Lost a Series in the 1980s and the 1990s
Cincinnati Reds   E. Won a Series in the 1980s and the 1990s

ANSWERS

Indians – A (Lost 1995 and 1997 Series)
Twins – E (Won 1987 and 1991 Series)
Padres – D (Lost 1984 and 1998 Series)
Mets – C (Won 1986 Series)
Reds – B (Won 1990 Series)

2. If you don't know which National League team won the most regular-season games in the 1990s, you've been watching too much football. Figuring out which American League team won the most games in the decade will require more thought. Were the Yankees' strong seasons with Joe Torre at the helm enough to make up for the years in the early '90s when they struggled? How about the Indians, who also came on strong in the mid-'90s? Or could it be the steady Red Sox? What about the 1960s? The Dodgers won the World Series in 1963 and 1965, but did they win more games during the decade than the Cardinals? Looking back over the last five decades, tell us which team in each league won the most regular-season games.

DECADE	NATIONAL LEAGUE	AMERICAN LEAGUE
1950s	Dodgers (913)	Yankees (955)
1960s	Cardinals (884)	Orioles (911)
1970s	Reds (953)	Orioles (944)
1980s	Dodgers/Cardinals (825)	Yankees (854)
1990s	Braves (925)	Yankees (851)

ANSWERS

3. Somebody should sue the Yankees for unfairly monopolizing winning the World Series. In 2000, the Yanks won the Series for the 26th time, more than a quarter of all World Series. Two teams rank second with a very distant nine world championships. Some teams have only won it all once or twice since the Series was first played in 1903. Match these five teams with the number of World Series that they have won.

Chicago Cubs	A. 9
St. Louis Cardinals	B. 6
Brooklyn/Los Angeles Dodgers	C. 4
Philadelphia Phillies	D. 2
Detroit Tigers	E. 1

ANSWERS

Cubs – D
Cardinals – A
Dodgers – B
Phillies – E
Tigers – C

4. When Mitch "The Wild Thing" Williams was with the Cubs, he used to get some golfing in with his teammates, especially during spring training in Arizona. One of the Cubs was the best golfer Williams ever walked the fairway with. Another Cub is the son of an outfielder who was one of two players traded for Hank Aaron. Match these Cub teammates of Williams's with the brief bits of information we've provided.

Greg Maddux	A. Father was traded for Hank Aaron
Derrick May	B. Had three stints with the Padres; also played for the White Sox and Tigers before joining the Cubs
Paul Assenmacher	C. In top 15 on all-time games pitched list
Luis Salazar	D. Best golfer Williams ever played with
Calvin Schiraldi	E. Lost Games 6 and 7 of 1986 World Series

ANSWERS

Maddux – D
May – A (The Brewers traded Dave May and pitcher Roger Alexander to the Braves for Aaron in November 1974.)
Assenmacher – C
Salazar – B
Schiraldi – E

5. Hank Aaron never did it. Willie Mays never did it. Neither did Ted Williams nor Reggie Jackson. In fact, in the history of baseball, the feat of banging out 100 extra base hits in a season has been accomplished just eight times. One player, in the 1930s, did it twice, with 107 extra base hits in 1930 and 103 in 1932. An active player turned the trick in 1995 when he hammered 52 doubles, one triple, and 50 home runs. He came within a whisker of hitting the century mark again in 1998, as he finished with 99.

Can you pick out the old-timer who reached the 100 extra-base-hit plateau twice, and the active slugger who has almost done it twice?

A. Al Simmons and Barry Bonds
B. Chuck Klein and Moises Alou
C. Hank Greenberg and Sammy Sosa
D. Lou Gehrig and Ken Griffey Jr.
E. Hack Wilson and Juan Gonzalez

ANSWER – B

6. Here's one for you fans to debate: Who has been a better pitcher, smoke-throwing Roger "The Rocket" Clemens or Mr. Finesse, Greg Maddux?

Through 2001, which pitcher has ...

A. won more Cy Young Awards?
B. led his league in innings pitched more?
C. won more post-season games?
D. walked fewer batters per nine innings in his career?
E. won more strikeout titles?
F. a better career winning percentage?
G. won more Gold Gloves?
H. had more 20-win seasons?
I. won an MVP?
J. a better career ERA?

ANSWERS

A. Clemens (6-4)
B. Maddux (5-2)
C. Maddux (10-6)
D. Maddux (1.93-2.91)
E. Clemens (5-0)

F. Clemens (.658-.638)
G. Maddux (12-0)
H. Clemens (6-2)
I. Clemens (1-0)
J. Maddux (2.84-3.10)

7. Next time you peruse a list of Major League players and their birthplaces, take note what a large percentage of players hail from California, Puerto Rico and the Dominican Republic. You'll also see no shortage of players from Florida, Arizona, New York and Connecticut. What you won't see are many players from Alaska, Hawaii and Australia, but there are some. Match these players with their unusual birthplaces.

Curt Schilling	A. Honolulu, Hawaii
Dave Nilsson	B. Brisbane, Queensland, Australia
Chili Davis	C. Würzburg, West Germany
Ron Darling	D. Anchorage, Alaska
Mike Blowers	E. Kingston, Jamaica

ANSWERS

Schilling – D
Nilsson – B
Davis – E
Darling – A
Blowers – C

8. The following is not a typographical error: I put together a 58-game hitting streak. Don't worry, Joe DiMaggio fans, because I compiled my streak in college for Oklahoma State, and while it established an NCAA record, The Yankee Clipper's record 56-game streak remains intact. *The Sporting News* named me College Player of the Year in both

1987 and 1988, and when I left Oklahoma State, I played for the United States Olympic team in Seoul. So by the time I stepped on the Major League diamond, I had accomplished a lot. I've been no slacker in the Bigs, either. Through 2000, I've had eight 20-home run seasons and seven 90-RBI seasons. I made it into the record books in 1995 when I became the eighth player in history to hit two grand slams in one game. I can throw some leather at you also — I've won a bundle of Gold Gloves for my defense at third base.

Who am I?

ANSWER

Robin Ventura

9. You heard about a thousand times during recent home run chases that Roger Maris hit 61 homers in 1961. But how did he fare in his career other than that season?

Did he hit 50 homers in a season before or after his record-breaking year? How about 40? Did he hit 400 home runs in his career? 300? What was Roger's second-highest season home run output and lifetime home run total?

A. 39 and 275   B. 41 and 341   C. 43 and 310   D. 48 and 402   E. 53 and 368

ANSWER: A

10. There are a few things we all know about Cal Ripken Jr.: He was a fixture in the Orioles infield from 1982–2001; he broke Lou Gehrig's consecutive games record in 1995; and he'll be elected to the Hall of Fame the first year that he's eligible. Here are four more facts about the Oriole superstar, along with one statement about Cal that's not true.

Which one is it?

A. He was named MVP of two All-Star Games.
B. He won the American League Rookie of the Year Award.
C. He holds the Major League record for fewest errors in a season by a shortstop.
D. He was named MVP of the American League twice.
E. He led the Major League in home runs one season.

ANSWER

E. Ripken was named MVP of the 1991 and 2001 All-Star Games; he was the American League's Rookie of the Year in 1982; he made just three errors in 1990; and he won the American League MVP in both the 1983 and 1991 seasons. He has never led the Major League — or the American League — in home runs; 34 is his top mark (1991).

Outrageous Episodes

BASEBALL: A STRANGE CAREER

In many ways baseball is one of the strangest of all careers, because a player has so short a period of time in which to earn his own place in the game.

Many potential professional ballplayers start learning the basic skills — running, throwing, hitting, fielding — when they're still of Little League age, in the primary grades at school. An early start and a fierce dedication to the game are absolutely essential. Let's say, roughly speaking, that a young man begins his pro career at the age of 18. Almost certainly he will be forced to retire 20 years later, at 38 or so. By that time he's lost his fleetness of foot, speed of reflexes, and, per-

haps, sharpness of eyes, among other things. At this age men in most other professions are just beginning to hit their stride.

Actually, a 20-year pro career is exceptional — the average length of a Major League career is only 5 years. Players who can perform effectively into their late thirties and early forties (a group including Pete Rose, Darrell Evans, Tony Perez, Carl Yastrzemski, Phil and Joe Niekro, Tommy John, Hoyt Wilhelm and Nolan Ryan) are the exception rather than the rule.

Frankie Frisch, the old Hall-of-Fame second baseman, may have said it best: "When you get to the point where you really know what you're supposed to do on the ball field, you're just too damned old to be able to execute."

A legion of players have experienced serious withdrawal symptoms and faced severe psychological problems when they were forced to retire because of age. Included in this group are such stars as Ty Cobb, Babe Ruth, Joe DiMaggio, Jimmie Foxx and Willie Mays.

"When you're forced to quit after playing for 20 and more years, it's like going cold turkey," Jimmie Foxx once said. It's like withdrawing from any longtime obsession.

In closing his 22-year big league career with the New York Mets in 1973, Willie Mays grumbled to a reporter: "It's really tough to be 42, hitting .210 and sitting on the bench half the time."

This book, filled with true stories of strange moments and events, strange plays and players, batters and pitchers and strange managers and owners, shows how they all fit into this strange game, one that forces players to try to compress their careers to "make it young," for only a few can even make it, much less make it a long career.

ON MOTHER'S DAY, FELLER'S MOTHER STRUCK BY A FOUL BALL

It was a warm Mother's Day, May 14, 1939, almost cloudless throughout much of the Midwest, and an ideal day for baseball. Bob Feller, the 20-year-old fireballing phenom for the Cleveland Indians, was scheduled to face the Chicago White Sox at Comiskey Park, and for the occasion Feller's family, including his father, mother and 8-year-old sister, Marguerite, decided to drive from the homestead in Van Meter, Iowa, to Chicago, a distance of some 250 miles, to see the game.

The Fellers found themselves comfortably ensconced in grandstand seats between home and first base just before game time, and they watched as the Indians scored 2 runs in the first inning and 4 more in the third to take a 6-0 lead. Rapid Robert Feller was in rare form as he blanked the White Sox for the first two innings, not allowing a hit.

In the bottom of the third, Chicago third baseman Marvin

"Mama, watch out!"

Owen, a pinch hitter, had trouble getting around on Feller's 99-mile-an-hour fastball as he sent three straight soft fouls into the stands between first and home. On the next pitch, Owen swung late again, but this time he got the barrel of the bat on the ball and sent a vicious foul liner to the first base stands again — and to the exact spot where the Feller party was seated. There was no time to duck, and, tragically, the ball struck Mrs. Feller in the face.

As Feller followed through with his pitching motion, he could see clearly that his mother was struck by the ball. In recalling the incident years later, Feller said, "I felt sick, but I saw that Mother was conscious . . . I saw the police and ushers leading her out and I had to put down the impulse to run to the stands. Instead, I kept on pitching. I felt giddy and I became wild and couldn't seem to find the plate. I know the Sox scored three runs, but I'm not sure how.

"They immediately told me the injury was painful but not serious. There wasn't anything I could do, so I went on and finished the game and won. Then I hurried to the hospital.

"Mother looked up from the hospital bed, her face bruised and both eyes blacked, and she was still able to smile reassuringly.

"'My head aches, Robert,' she said, 'but I'm all right. Now don't go blaming yourself . . . it wasn't your fault.'" Mrs. Feller spent a couple of days in the hospital and was released feeling no ill effects.

The Indians won that Mother's Day game 9-4 as Feller ran his record to 6-1. For the entire season he went 24-9 and struck out a Major League-leading 246 batters.

In his autobiography *Strikeout Story* (New York: A. S. Barnes &

Co., 1947), Feller emphasized that his mother was always a good soldier who helped to advance his baseball career in a thousand different ways.

Feller also said later: "It was a one-in-a-million shot that my own mother while sitting within a crowd of people at a ballpark, would be struck by a foul ball resulting from a pitch I made." And on Mother's Day!

STRANGE PINCH HITTER DRAWS ROARS WITH OUTRAGEOUS STUNT

It was Sunday, August 19, 1951, at Sportsman's Park, St. Louis, as the last place Browns tangled with the Detroit Tigers, who were also deep in the second division. The game was meaningless as far as standings were concerned.

During the season Bill Veeck, flamboyant owner of the Browns, had become a bit desperate because his rag-tag team floundered badly at the gate. (Total paid admissions for the year came to a sorry 294,000.)

As the late-summer game progressed before the usual sparse Sportsman's Park crowd, Browns' manager Zack Taylor sent in a pinch hitter named Eddie Gaedel, who had never appeared in a professional game before. Tigers right-hander Bob Cain walked Gaedel on four straight pitches, and after Eddie trotted down to first, he was replaced by pinch runner Jim Delsing.

By this time the crowd was in an uproar. Pinch hitters had walked before, but none of them were as small as Gaedel, who stood 3 feet 7 inches tall and weighed 65 pounds, the normal size for a genuine midget. As Gaedel, wearing the number $\frac{1}{8}$ on the back of his uniform shirt, swung his 17-inch bat menacingly at Pitcher Cain, he hollered, "Throw the ball right in here and I'll moider it!"

He had been told what to do. Bill Veeck wrote in his autobiography, "I spent many hours teaching him to stand straight up, hold his little bat high and keep his feet sprawled in a fair approximation of Joe DiMaggio's classic style. I told him I'll kill him if he swings the bat."

Plate umpire Ed Hurley had questioned Gaedel's credentials as a player, but under Veeck's able direction, the midget had produced a standard Major League contract from his hip pocket.

Bill Veeck, the "Barnum of Baseball," in all his years in the game had never gone this far, and he succeeded in pulling off the greatest single outrageous stunt in the history of the game.

On the next day American League President Will Harridge turned thumbs down on any future Tom Thumbs by outlawing any further such travesty of the game.

Bill Veeck may have gained an enormous amount of notoriety for sending a midget to the plate, but nothing he did could save his franchise. After the 1953 season he was forced to sell the Browns, who in 1954 were transformed into the Baltimore Orioles.

As for Eddie Gaedel, his place in the standard baseball record books is secure. He compiled a perfect record as a pinch hitter, getting on base in his only time at bat.

FOUR HUNDRED AND NINETY-NINE PITCHES IN ONE GAME!

In a so-called "normal," nine-inning Major League baseball game, an average of 250 pitches are thrown, or some 125 by each team. If the game is a high-scoring one, or goes a few extra innings, the count may reach the 300 mark, or in rare cases, 350.

In rarer cases, however, the pitch count may reach stratospheric heights. A case in point came in the September 14, 1998, game played between the Detroit Tigers and Chicago White Sox at Tiger Stadium. This clash turned out to be a 12-inning marathon as Chicago edged Detroit 17-16 in a wild and woolly affair.

The game was knotted at 12-12 at the end of the regulation 9 innings, and then both clubs scored three runs in the 10th to push the game to 15-15. The White Sox blasted back-to-back homers from Ray Durham and Craig Wilson in the top of the 12th, while the Tigers were able to score only once in their half of the inning, and thus they were nosed out 17-16 in what appears to be a football score.

The Tigers used ten pitchers and the White Sox used eight. Their total of eighteen tied the record for most pitchers in an extra-inning game. The White Sox corps of eight hurlers threw 229 pitches, while the Tigers corps of ten moundsmen threw 270 pitches, or 499 total — a fantastic amount! That comes to at least two games' worth of pitches. The game lasted for 5 hours and 12 minutes, about twice the length of an average game.

Tabulations of pitch counts were not made until recent years, but the Elias Sports Bureau of New York (official statisticians for Major League Baseball) believe that 499 pitches is the record for any game played through 12 innings. Records for pitch counts for games played to 20 innings or so are almost impossible to arrive at.

The number of hits and runs for the Chicago/Detroit donnybrook made the pitch counts run to those high levels. Chicago batters batted out 19 base hits, while the Detroit attack came through with 22 hits. Detroit pitchers walked 11 batters, while Chicago pitchers walked only a single batsman.

The Sox starting pitcher, John Snyder, threw the first 5 innings, gave up 5 runs (4 earned), and worked his pitch count up to 92 before he was relieved. The Tigers starter, Mark Thompson, got through 4 innings, giving up 6 runs (only 2 earned) before he was sent to the showers. Interestingly, he also threw 92 pitches.

Winning pitcher for Chicago was left-hander Scott Eyre, who threw the final two innings, while the losing pitcher for Detroit was Doug Bochtler, who gave up the winning run.

Chicago's Albert Belle and Craig Wilson were the hitting stars of the game as they drove in five runs apiece. Belle banged out three doubles to go with his two singles, and went 5 for 8. Wilson, a rookie, went 4 for 7 as he homered twice and singled twice. In that high-scoring game, Belle, a 10-year veteran, passed the 1000-RBI mark.

Jerry Holtzman, veteran Chicago sportswriter, commented, "You never know what's going to happen in a Major League baseball game. Depending upon the pitching, the score might wind up at 1-0, or a football-type score at 17-16. There's no use in making pregame predictions."

AUTOGRAPH HUNTERS ARE DANGEROUS TO A PLAYER'S HEALTH!

Running the gauntlet of autograph seekers can sometimes take its toll on a ballplayer. While many diamond stars try their best to accommodate fans, there are times when the clock says if you stop and sign, you'll pay a fine. In early August, 1987, New York Yankees outfielder Claudell Washington was running late for a night game in Kansas City. He tried valiantly to dodge the autograph seekers on his way into Royals Stadium and it cost him anyway. With a small army of

"Let me get away from those fans."

clutching fans serving as an obstacle course, the trotting Washington tripped over someone's leg!

He was holding a briefcase in his left hand, and he tried using that hand to break the fall. The unhappy result was that Claudell scraped two fingers on his left hand so badly that he was unable to grip the bat properly and required more than a week on the bench before he could resume play.

The moral of this tale might be: if you're going to beat the autograph hounds, come to the park early or work on your end-around move.

OWNER STEINBRENNER, BASEBALL'S DR. JEKYLL AND MR. HYDE

In 1886, Robert Louis Stevenson published one of his best-known stories, *The Strange Case of Dr. Jekyll and Mr. Hyde.* In this horror-fantasy, Stevenson spins a tale of a man with a dual personality: Dr. Jekyll, the brilliant physician, is able to periodically transform himself into the viciously criminal Mr. Hyde. Of all the major figures in baseball today, George M. Steinbrenner III stands as, perhaps, the most controversial because of his obvious dual personality.

On the one hand, Steinbrenner is able to perform extremely magnanimous deeds, and on the other he does many perfectly awful things, though in no way do we suggest that he gets nearly as nasty as Mr. Hyde.

Before Steinbrenner became principal owner of the New York Yankees in 1973, he owned the Cleveland Pipers professional basketball team, which nearly went bankrupt, and from that point he was anxious to gain control of a major sports franchise so that he could turn it into a success. His fortune is based on his ownership of the American Shipbuilding Co., now based in Tampa, Florida. Here we'll offer a brief representative list of five "Mr. Hydes" for Steinbrenner, and five "Dr. Jekylls."

Mr. Hyde:

1. Shortly after he gained control of the Yankees, Steinbrenner showed a definite lack of knowledge of many facets of baseball. In spring training in Florida, for example, he ordered one of his players to wear his cap properly. The player did have his cap on backwards, but he was a catcher!

2. Shows an extreme lack of tolerance for a player making an error. When Bobby Murcer once muffed an outfield ground ball in a spring exhibition game, Steinbrenner blurted: "I'm paying him more than $100,000 a year and he can't catch the ball."

3. Seems to take sadistic pleasure in squashing little people. Once he had the switchboard operator in a Boston hotel fired because she wouldn't allow him to place a long distance call from the telephone in a bar, as per regulations.

4. Constantly ridicules his top players in public. He has, for example, called Dave Winfield "Mr. May" for ostensibly not performing well in late-season stretch drives — and even criticized Don

Mattingly for being "selfish" after he hit a record-tying eight homers in eight straight games in 1987. Mattingly injured his wrist shortly after this record string, and Steinbrenner blamed it on Mattingly's "exaggerated home run swing."

5. Whenever the Yankees begin playing badly, Steinbrenner pushes the panic button and starts firing, or threatening to fire, his managers and pitching coaches. Steinbrenner changed managers at least 14 times since 1973, and has had an uncounted number of pitching coaches. In 1982, when the Yankees finished a dismal fifth in the Eastern Division, Steinbrenner employed three different managers during the season: Bob Lemon, Gene Michael and Clyde King. Before Steinbrenner fires a manager, he usually embarrasses him to no end in the public press.

Dr. Jekyll:

1. Steinbrenner may fire his managers as often as some people change their socks, but he ordinarily doesn't kick them out of the Yankees organization. They remain on the payroll either as general manager, super-scout, special assistant, or coach, if they so desire — and at handsome salaries. Ex-Yankee managers who've stayed on with the organization in one capacity or another, for at least a time, include: Lou Piniella, Bob Lemon, Gene Michael, Clyde King and, of course, Billy Martin.

2. In 1979, Steinbrenner led a delegation down to Curacao in the Caribbean in order to assist the Curacao Baseball Federation, both with special instruction and a generous donation of baseball equip-

ment. Yogi Berra and Billy Martin, among others, accompanied Steinbrenner on this little publicized goodwill tour.

3. Reggie Jackson helped Steinbrenner achieve some of his greatest successes during Reggie's five years with the Yankees (1977–81) — three pennants and two World Series victories — but was let go after 1981 because he was thought to be "over the hill." However, after Jackson hit his 500th Major League homer with the California Angels in 1984, Steinbrenner presented him with a very expensive sterling silver platter commemorating the event.

4. Steinbrenner made it a point to make a special trip to Cooperstown in July 1987 to witness Jim "Catfish" Hunter's induction into baseball's Hall of Fame. Steinbrenner signed Hunter as his first major free agent in 1975, and Catfish responded by playing a major role in helping the Yankees capture three American League pennants. No one appreciates true achievement more than George.

5. George M. Steinbrenner appreciates true achievement in any field. For example, he long admired the work of George E. Seedhouse, Supervisor of Community Centers and Playgrounds in Cleveland, Ohio, during the 1950s and 1960s. And in recognition of that work he named one of his American Shipbuilding Co. iron ore carriers (a 13,000-ton vessel) the *George E. Seedhouse.*

BILL VEECK: BASEBALL'S SHOWMAN EXTRAORDINAIRE

When Bill Veeck (as in "wreck") bought the Cleveland Indians in 1946, he took over a moribund baseball franchise that hadn't fielded a pennant winner since 1920. With an incredible flair for showmanship, he succeeded in boosting the season's attendance to over 1,050,000, shattering all previous Indians' records, though the team never managed to climb out of sixth place that year.

Veeck believed that when fans came to the ballpark they should be entertained totally. For starters, he hired several jazz combos to wander through the stands and perform at the end of each half-inning.

Next, he hired former minor-league pitcher Max Patkin, a contortionist, to coach occasional innings at third base. One of the strangest-looking characters ever to wear a baseball uniform, Patkin made it difficult for opposing pitchers to concentrate on the game as they couldn't help watching Max twist himself in and out of pretzel shapes along the coaching lines. Coaches rarely receive applause of any kind, but the fans howled with glee at the sight of "Coach" Patkin, and sometimes gave him standing ovations for his outlandish performances.

At about the time Patkin became an Indian, Veeck signed up 33-year-old minor-league infielder and stuntman Jackie Price as a player-coach. Price pulled off feats never seen before on a ball field. Among

Bill Veeck (center), player-manager Lou Boudreau (right) and coach Bill McKechnie
celebrate the Indians' World Series victory over the Boston Braves.

other things, he could throw two or three balls simultaneously and
make them all curve, he could catch balls dropped from blimps high
in the air, and even play an occasional game of shortstop for
Cleveland.

One of Jackie's most memorable stunts was to suspend himself upside down from a 12-foot-high horizontal bar, grab a bat and have balls pitched to him — which he hit distances of 150 feet and more. Fans jammed their way into the park to watch Patkin and Price go through their extraordinary acts.

Bill Veeck had operated the Milwaukee Brewers of the American Association with great success in the early 1940s, and in recognition of his achievements, he was named in 1942 by *The Sporting News* as Minor League Executive of the Year. He was only 28 then. Shortly after his Milwaukee Brewers' exploits, Veeck entered the U.S. Marine Corps, was shipped off to the South Pacific, and, while stationed at Bougainville during the height of World War II, sustained a severe injury to his right leg as the result of an artillery training exercise. Unfortunately, the leg never healed properly, but during that hectic summer of '46 Veeck hobbled around through the grandstands daily, talking to the fans and getting their views as to how the Indians could be improved. Numerous times after an arduous day promoting the team, Veeck would writhe in pain at night as his leg flared up.

Infection set in and on November 1, 1946, the leg was amputated nine inches below the knee. Shortly after the operation, Veeck, still under the influence of anesthesia and quite woozy, grabbed the telephone and called Franklin Lewis, sports editor of the *Cleveland Press*, to see how the Indians came out in the Major League draft. Baseball was always on his mind.

Veeck was fitted with an artificial leg, but the pain did not disappear, and there were other operations until finally, in 1961, he had to have an amputation above the knee. During all those years he never permitted physical pain to dim his enthusiasm for baseball. On frequent occasions he removed the artificial leg and amused friends by using it as an ashtray.

"Wild Bill" as he was called by the local writers, used every sort of promotion imaginable. One night, for example, he would give the ladies orchids specially flown in from Hawaii, and on other nights he would have former Olympic track champion Jesse Owens dress up in an Indians uniform and run a foot race against one of his players. Owens, then well into his thirties, generally won.

Unpredictable "Wild Bill" suddenly sold the team (at an enormous profit) and took a year's sabbatical from baseball before he bought the St. Louis Browns in 1951. Veeck used more promotional gimmicks to draw fans into Sportsman's Park to watch his inept Browns in action: He gave away a 200-pound block of ice one night, and another time live lobsters, and in desperation he sent a midget up to the plate to pinch-hit. (See *Strange Pinch Hitter Draws Roars With Outrageous Stunt.*)

Bill surfaced again when he bought the Chicago White Sox at the end of 1958. He reached his peak as a master showman when he introduced the exploding scoreboard at Chicago's Comiskey Park. Every time a White Sox player hit a homer the scoreboard would erupt into a crescendo of sound and shoot off a fireworks rocket display. Other Major League owners were shocked and called it an "outrage," but the fans loved it. Eventually other teams in both leagues installed their own exploding scoreboards.

Veeck was forced to sell the Sox after the 1961 season because of a severe illness. He re-emerged as a big league owner for the fourth and last time in 1975, when he headed a group that again bought the financially ailing White Sox. Next, "Wild Bill" had his team wear short pants during the hot days of summer in 1976. One sportswriter fumed, "The White Sox look like an amateur softball team." However, Veeck at no time allowed his critics to hamper his highly individualistic style of running baseball teams. He spent some of his last years rooting in the bleachers, sitting bare-chested and chatting with the other fans.

Bill Veeck was elected to the Hall of Fame by the Committee of Baseball Veterans in 1991. No one during the past half-century has made a greater impact on the baseball scene.

FASTEST PITCHER?
RYAN 100.9 MPH, DALKOWSKI 108

According to the "Guinness Book of World Records," the fastest recorded Major League pitcher is Nolan Ryan, who, on August 20, 1974, while with the California Angels, threw a pitch in Anaheim Stadium, California, measured at 100.9 miles per hour.

Steve Dalkowski, little-known left-hander (b. June 3, 1939), though not generally regarded as the fastest pitcher in baseball history, threw a pitch measured at 108 miles per hour while with Elmira in the Class A Eastern League in 1962.

Dalkowski spent nine years in the minor leagues (1957–65), mostly as a Baltimore Orioles farmhand, reaching as high as Rochester and Columbus of the International League, but his wildness prevented his promotion to the majors. He was invited to spring training several times by the Orioles, but never reached his true potential despite an enormous amount of raw talent.

In those nine years in the minors, Dalkowski put together one of the strangest pitching records in professional baseball history. Over the course of 236 games, he posted a 46-80 won-lost record (.366 percentage) and pitched 995 innings, allowing only 682 base hits. He walked the gargantuan total of 1,354 batters and struck out an equally gargantuan 1,396. His ERA was a rather bloated 5.59.

Thus, in a typical game Dalkowski gave up 6 hits, walked 12 and struck out 12 to 13. If he went the distance, his game almost always took more than three hours to complete, and no one who ever paid his way into a game pitched by Steve Dalkowski ever complained about not getting his money's worth. Every game he pitched was a dramatic event.

While with Stockton of the Class A California League in 1960, he pitched 170 innings in 32 games, won 7 games, lost 15, allowed only 105 hits, walked 262 and struck out 262! Obviously he was very hard to hit.

Dalkowski's great left arm began giving out before he was 27, and from that point on, his journey through life was not altogether happy. He worked for a time as a migratory laborer in California's vineyards and had long bouts with John Barleycorn.

In 1978, the Society for American Baseball Research (then based in Cooperstown, New York) honored Dalkowski by including him in a newly published biographical and statistical volume entitled *All-Time Minor League Baseball Stars.*

GEORGE BLAEHOLDER, FATHER OF THE SLIDER

George Blaeholder ran up a mediocre 104-125 record as a right-handed pitcher in the American League from 1925 to 1936, but he is credited with having been the first pitcher to throw the slider, one of the most difficult of all pitches to hit. He threw his first slider with the St. Louis Browns in 1928, and generously passed on his technique to other pitchers.

The slider takes off like a fastball, but then curves sharply just before it reaches the batter. Batters have scornfully referred to the slider as a "nickel curve." The pitch really didn't have a major impact upon baseball until the 1950s and 1960s.

Stan Musial, one of the greatest batters of all time (he banged out 3,630 base hits and averaged .331 in a 23-year career, 1941–63), once said, "I could have hit better in the latter years of my career and stayed around a while longer if it hadn't been for the slider."

IT DIDN'T PAY TO MESS WITH BURLY EARLY WYNN

Early Wynn, the Hall-of-Fame right-hander who piled up a 300-244 won-lost record over 23 big league seasons (1939–63, with time out for World War II service), looked as mean as a junkyard dog when he took the mound. He had his own special way of intimidating hitters. Most batters were afraid to dig in on "Burly Early" because they never knew when his brush-back pitch was coming.

One reporter commented that Early would knock down his own grandmother if she ever crowded the plate. Fortunately, she never had the opportunity of batting against her grandson. However, when Early was nearing the end of the trail with the Chicago White Sox in the early 1960s, he pitched against his 17-year-old son, Early, Jr., in batting practice. Well, Early, Jr., socked one of his dad's best pitches up against the bleacher wall. What do you suppose happened when the boy dug in for his father's next delivery? He was sent flying on his derriere, of course, in order to avoid the high, hard one.

One time Early was asked to name the toughest batter he ever faced. Wynn replied without a moment's hesitation, "There were two guys . . . one was named Hillerich and the other was Bradsby."

That meant Early's enemy was anyone with a bat in his hands.

PETE ROSE: SLUGGER BEGAN AT AGE 3, WASTED VALUABLE YEARS IN HIGH SCHOOL

Pete Rose's father Harry was anxious to get his first-born son started in baseball at the earliest possible age, so little Pete began at just 2 years to catch thrown balls. When Pete was 3 he started out as a slugger. The first time he remembers slugging he connected solidly with a pitch served up by his dad, and drove a hard rubber-coated ball to right-center field, over and out of the backyard ball field and against a glass windowpane that promptly cracked in the kitchen of the Rose home on Braddock Avenue in Cincinnati.

That long drive by the Cincinnati Red, who holds baseball's all-time career record of 4,256 hits, was swatted on a summer Saturday in 1944. The crack is still in the window. According to a July 7, 1987, *New York Times* report, LaVerne Noeth, Pete's mother, was standing in the kitchen that day more than four decades ago when she heard the glass crack.

"My husband said, 'Hon, come here, look where Pete hit the ball,'" Mrs. Noeth recalled recently. "He said, 'I don't want it fixed. I'm going to show people where he hit that ball.' Pete was so small then, he was always small."

Little has changed in the neighborhood. Braddock Avenue is still a clump of homes on a hill above the Ohio River, five miles west of downtown, and boys still play ball there. At the old Rose household, members of Pete's family have no trouble finding first base in the backyard although the ball field is now covered with honeysuckle shrubs and black locust trees.

After he hit that storied backyard liner at the age of 3, Pete Rose continued playing ball at a furious pace, and he became so involved in various sandlot leagues that it took him five years to get through high school in Cincinnati. By having to spend that extra year, Pete didn't start his pro career with Geneva, N.Y., of the New York-Penn League until he was 19 in 1960, when others began at 18.

If he had started in the minors a year earlier, he might have had an additional season in the big leagues and broken even more records. Pete didn't fail in high school because he was a bad student, mind you. His I.Q. had been measured as high as 150.

"What a boy, what a batter, that Pete."

BABE RUTH: BEATS WHOLE AMERICAN LEAGUE IN HOME RUN PRODUCTION

Home run hitting hit a peak in the Major Leagues in 1987 as 27 players hit for the circuit 30 or more times. Recent years have seen the single-season home run record shattered twice. Although there are many sluggers going for many homers, still there is no single slugger who dominates the long ball game as Babe Ruth did during the 1920s.

Ruth, in fact, on two separate occasions, in 1920 and 1927, personally hit more homers than each of the seven other teams in the American League. In 1920, the "Sultan of Swat" smacked out a record 54 homers and no team in the league matched that total. St. Louis came the closest with 50, followed by Philadelphia with 44; Chicago, 37; Washington, 36; Cleveland, 35; Detroit, 30; and Boston, 22.

In 1927, the Bambino reached the peak of his long ball power as he whacked a record 60 homers, and that year no single AL team managed to top that total. Philadelphia "threatened" Ruth with 56 four baggers, followed by St. Louis with 55; Detroit, 51; Chicago, 36; Washington, 29; Boston, 28; and Cleveland, 26.

No other Major League player has come close to matching this particular home run achievement of George Herman Ruth.

Most veteran baseball observers believe that no one could hit a baseball harder or farther than Babe Ruth when he was at his peak with the New York Yankees from 1920 to the early 1930s. Ruth's longest homer may well have been a 600-foot shot he belted in a spring exhibition game at Tampa in 1925.

No one ever measured the velocity of his drives, but pitcher Mel Harder, who came up with the Cleveland Indians in 1928, recalled the days when the Bambino batted against him at Cleveland's old League Park. This vintage-style ballpark (now torn down) had a concrete wall topped by a wire fence running from right field to right-center field. "Ruth's drives often hit that concrete right-field wall with such tremendous force that the ball would bounce all the way back to second base," Harder said. "Those balls would usually have to be thrown out of the game because they came back a bit flattened and carried a spot of green paint from the wall," he added.

JOB DIMAGGIO: ALWAYS ONE TOUGH HOMBRE TO STRIKE OUT

Most baseball experts feel that the greatest single achievement in baseball was Joe DiMaggio's hitting in 56 straight games in 1941. We beg to differ on this point — in our opinion, Joe D's most remarkable accomplishment was striking out only 369 times in his Major League career in approximately 8,000 total times at bat (including walks, sac flies, hit by pitcher, etc.).

Amazingly enough, Joltin' Joe hit 361 homers in his 13 years with the New York Yankees (1936–51, with three years out for World War II military service), a figure only 8 fewer than his total strikeouts! In his rookie year, DiMag fanned on 39 occasions, and he never again struck out that many times in a season.

From that point on, DiMaggio enjoyed six seasons in which he had more homers than K's. Here are the fantastic figures, with homers first and strikeouts second: 1937 — 46, 37; 1938 — 32, 21; 1939 — 30, 20; 1940 — 31, 30; 1941 — 30, 13; 1946 — 25, 24; and 1948 — 39, 30. The "Yankee Clipper" almost made it again in 1950 when he slammed 32 homers against 33 strikeouts.

Even Bob Feller, baseball's unrivaled strikeout king from the mid-1930s through the 1940s, had a tough time fanning DiMaggio. Joe D, who had a career batting average of better than .320 against Feller, once told us:

"Feller is best known for his great fastball, of course, but he also had a wicked curve which made him extremely effective. At the same time, he was a proud man and never tried too many curves against me . . . He almost always tried to blow the fastball by me — and since I pretty much knew what to expect I never had too much trouble with him."

We should emphasize here that DiMaggio never struck out much against anybody because he had extremely quick reflexes, perfect coordination and keen eyesight.

MIZE AND TED WILLIAMS VERY TOUGH TO STRIKE OUT

Three times in his career Johnny Mize posted records where his homers topped the totals of his whiffs. While with the New York Giants in 1947, the big left-handed-hitting first baseman bashed a career-high 51 homers and fanned only 42 times — and in the following year he hit for the circuit 40 times against only 37 strikeouts.

In 1950, as a member of the New York Yankees, Mize homered 25 times against 24 strikeouts. Overall, in a 15-year big league career (1936–53, with three years out for World War II military service), Mize rang up 359 homers against 524 strikeouts, an excellent ratio.

"I never swung crazy," Mize told us recently. "If the pitch was out of the strike zone, I just didn't go for it . . . I always tried to wait for my pitch," he disclosed.

Ted Williams, who possessed extraordinary vision, and who knew how to control a bat as well as anyone in baseball, had four seasons in which his homers outnumbered his strikeouts. In this listing the homers are given first: 1941 — 37, 27; 1950 — 28, 21; 1953 — 13, 10; and 1958 — 28, 24. Overall, in a 19-year career (1939–60,with three years out for World War II military service),Williams hit 524 homers as opposed to 709 strikeouts, a superb ratio.

BILL DICKEY: DIDN'T TAKE MANY THIRD STRIKES EITHER

Bill Dickey, the Hall-of-Fame New York Yankees catcher, is another throwback to an earlier era when some of the game's top power hitters were hard to fan. Though he didn't hit as many homers as

DiMaggio, Mize or Williams, he still managed to have five seasons when his homers exceeded his strikeouts, and once when they were even (in 1933 he had 14 homers and 14 strikeouts).

Those five sterling Dickey seasons are (homers first): 1932 — 15, 13; 1935 — 14, 11; 1936 — 22, 16; 1937 — 29, 22; and 1938 — 27, 22. In 17 seasons with the Yankees (1928–46, with two years out for World War II military service), Bill Dickey rapped out 202 homers against only 289 strikeouts.

Said Dickey, years after his playing days: "In many ways baseball today is strange to me because so many big-leaguers — or supposed big-leaguers — are lunging at the ball in trying to get distance, and they're striking out 3, 4 and even 5 times a game in the process."

"SHOELESS" JOE JACKSON: MORE TRIPLES THAN STRIKEOUTS

While with the Chicago White Sox in 1920, Joe Jackson accomplished a feat that would be virtually impossible for a modern player to match — he actually had more triples than strikeouts, 20 to 14. While with the Cleveland Indians in 1912, "Shoeless" Joe lined out 26 triples, but we don't know if his three-baggers outnumbered his whiffs because strike-out records were not kept until 1913.

Compared to Joe Jackson, Dale Mitchell, who was active from 1946 to 1956, was a "modern" player in the strict sense. In any event, Mitchell was the last Major Leaguer, according to our best calculations, to triple more times than strike out in a single season. While with the Cleveland Indians in 1949, Mitchell, a left-handed slap hitter, tripled 23 times against only 11 strikeouts, a better than a 2-1 ratio. Fantastic!

Sam Crawford, the all-time triples leader with 312, had one season we know about where his three-baggers exceeded his strikeouts: 1916 — 13, 10. ("Wahoo Sam" was with the Detroit Tigers at the time). Crawford may have had other triples-over-whiffs seasons, but Crawford's strikeout totals while he was with Cincinnati and Detroit from 1899 through 1912 were not kept.

Ty Cobb may have had at least one triples-over-whiffs season, but his 1907–1912 strikeout figures also are shrouded in mystery.

FIRST (ILLEGAL) USE OF A DESIGNATED HITTER

There were mutterings for a DH rule as far back as the 1930s. Hitting was the dominant factor in baseball in the 1930s and 8 batters out of 9 got the job done, so the DH idea failed to take hold. Then much later, pitchers began to rule the game and scores were low, so the pitcher's turn at bat became more important.

Interestingly, several informal and abortive attempts at using a DH were made many years before the rule was officially adopted by the American League in 1973. For example, a little known exception was made in 1939 when Chicago White Sox pitcher Bill "Bullfrog"

Dietrich found himself struggling during the course of a hot mid-summer afternoon against the Cleveland Indians at Comiskey Park, Chicago. Sox manager Jimmy Dykes went over to Cleveland manager Oscar Vitt and asked him if it was all right with Vitt if Dykes used a pinch hitter for Dietrich but allowed Bullfrog to remain in the game. "It's okay with me if it's okay with the umpires," said the gentlemanly Vitt.

The pinch hitter was used and Dietrich remained in the game!

STILL A REGULAR AT 44—
YAZ SETS MARK FOR LONG CAREER

Carl Yastrzemski starred for the Boston Red Sox for 23 years, and in 1983, at the age of 44, he became the oldest player in modern big league history to play regularly. Though "Yaz" was an outfielder for most of his career, he saw service mostly as a designated hitter in 1983 — his final season — as he played in 119 games, collecting 101 base hits and batting a respectable .266.

In sporting the Red Sox uniform for nearly a quarter century, Yastrzemski set an American League record by playing in the most games — 3,308 — and registering the most times at bat — 11,988 — while slamming out 3,419 base hits, good for a solid .285 lifetime batting average. He also won three batting championships (including a "Triple Crown' in 1967 when he swatted .326, bashed 44 homers and drove in 121 runs). He also tied a Major League record by playing in

100 or more games for 22 seasons, and led the American League in intentional walks — 190.

He was elected into baseball's Hall of Fame at Cooperstown in 1989, his first year of eligibility.

Carl Yastrzemski's endurance records were subsequently tied and/or broken by Pete Rose of the Cincinnati Reds. In 1985, the 44-year-old Rose, by then the Reds manager, played in 119 games (mostly at first base), tying Yaz, and in 1986, at the age of 45, he played semi-regularly (72 games) at first before he benched himself permanently (as it turned out) in mid-August.

SCOTT SETS CONSECUTIVE GAME RECORD BEFORE BEING BENCHED FOR WEAK HITTING

Everett "Deacon" Scott, a native of Bluffton, Indiana, broke into the Major Leagues in 1914 with the Boston Red Sox as a 21-year-old short-stop, and just over two years later, on June 20, 1916, began one of the most remarkable streaks in baseball history. From that day through the 1921 season, he never missed a game with the Red Sox — over 800 of them.

After the 1921 campaign, Scott went to the New York Yankees in a multi-player trade, and from that point continued his "Iron Man" role. A fine fielder, he went more than three additional seasons, never missing being in the lineup through May 5, 1925. This ran his streak of consecutive games played to 1,307. Scott, a runt of a man standing 5 feet 8 inches and weighing 150 pounds, but an extremely durable athlete, became the first man in professional baseball to play more than 1,000 games in a row.

Scott could have gone on to extend his streak even further but Yankees manager Miller Huggins had to bench him for weak hitting! The Yankees in those years with Babe Ruth were called "Murderers' Row" and Scott batted around .250.

Interestingly, Scott's teammate, the hard-hitting, 22-year-old first baseman named Lou Gehrig, began his own record-breaking streak of 2,130 straight games on June 1, 1925, less than a month after the Little Deacon was benched.

In early August 1925, Scott was sent to the Washington Senators on waivers and finished his big league career with the Chicago White Sox and Cincinnati Reds in 1926. Everett Scott ended with a career batting average of a modest .249 in 1,654 Major League games, but had remained in the lineup on a daily basis so long because of his sure-handed fielding. He led American League shortstops in fielding percentage for a record eight years, all in succession, 1916 through 1923.

BATTING AVERAGES HIT BOTTOM— ONLY ONE .300 HITTER IN AL

By the middle 1960s hitting in the majors, especially in the American League, had declined so much that the lords of baseball decided something had to be done. The low point for hitting came in 1968 when the ten American League teams posted a combined batting average of .230. The Minnesota Twins took the team batting crown with a "robust" .240, while the New York Yankees finished last with an anemic .214 mark. Carl Yastrzemski of the Boston Red Sox had the distinction of being the AL's only .300 hitter, taking the batting crown with a .301 average, the lowest average for a batting leader in Major League history.

The National League did a bit better as their ten teams combined for a .243 batting mark.

By contrast, in 1930, considered to be a peak year for Major League hitting, the eight American League teams posted a combined .288 mark, while the eight National League clubs swatted .303. The New York Giants led the parade with a very substantial .319 team average.

STRANGE DEMISE OF THE METS . . . A LITTLE BIRD DID THEM IN

The New York Mets in 1986 dominated baseball as they posted a glittering 108-54 won-lost mark in, finishing first in the National League's Eastern Division 21½ games ahead of the second-place Philadelphia Phillies. The Mets went on to defeat the Houston Astros, the NL's Western Division Champs, four games to two in the League Championship Series, and climaxed their amazing season by whipping the Boston Red Sox four games to three in a dramatic World Series. The Mets reigned supreme as baseball's world champions.

The 1987 New York Mets never seemed to get off on the right foot as they went on to disappoint their fans by finishing second in the NL East, five games behind the St. Louis Cardinals. All sorts of strange happenings prevented the Mets from reaching the top for a second straight season.

For starters, Ray Knight, their star third baseman and World Series MVP, defected to the Baltimore Orioles after a contract dispute, and Dwight Gooden, their top pitcher, spent the first two months in a drug rehab clinic. Several other key pitchers, including Bob Ojeda and Rick Aguilera, were out for long spells with injuries.

However, the strangest incident of all, and one that typified the Mets' ill luck in 1987, occurred at the Sunday, April 12 game at Shea Stadium, when the '86 champs faced the Atlanta Braves. Dion James, Braves outfielder, hit a fly ball toward left-center field, but before any

Met could catch up to it, the ball struck and killed a pigeon in full flight. Both the ball and pigeon dropped down onto the field in a thud and James was awarded a ground-rule double. The Mets went on to lose that game 11-4.

When Rafael Santana, Mets shortstop, picked up the dead bird in his hand, he muttered, "We're not getting any breaks at all."

BLUE JAYS SET NEW RECORD, HAMMER 10 HOMERS IN ONE GAME

"I don't think anyone threw well. It was an embarrassing baseball game . . . I'm not the only one embarrassed. Everybody in the club-house is embarrassed," moaned Baltimore Orioles' manager Cal Ripken, Sr., after his team was devastated 18-3 by the Toronto Blue Jays at Toronto's Exhibition Stadium on Monday, September 14, 1987.

What made the game particularly embarrassing for the Orioles was Toronto's awesome display of home run power. The Blue Jays hammered out 10 "dingers," breaking the Major League record of 8 in one game. (The New York Yankees of 1939 set that mark the first time when they blasted 8 roundtrippers against the Philadelphia A's. A number of other teams have since hit that figure.)

Blue Jays' catcher Ernie Whitt began the home run parade when he led off the second inning with a shot into the right-field bleachers. Whitt, a 6-foot-1-inch, 200-pound left-handed pull hitter, belted another solo homer in the fifth inning, and added a 3-run poke in the seventh. (A number of renowned home run hitters, including Hank Greenberg, never hit 3 in a single game.)

Left fielder George Bell and third baseman Rance Mulliniks each contributed two homers to the onslaught. Center fielder Lloyd Moseby hit one out of the park and his late-inning replacement, rookie Rob Ducey, also got into the act with a drive into the right-field seats. Designated hitter Fred McGriff, also a rookie, made it an even 10.

Baltimore Mike Hart, a rookie center fielder, saved face for the Orioles slightly when he hit for the circuit in the third inning, making it 11 homers for the two teams, tying the all-time single game record set by the Yankees with six, and the Detroit Tigers, five, in 1950.

SUPER FAN MISSED ONLY ONE WORLD SERIES GAME IN 42 YEARS

C. E. "Pat" Olsen, a 6-foot-2-inch right-handed power pitcher, signed a contract with the New York Yankees in 1923 as a 20-year-old and was fully expected by the Yankees to become a star.

For the next five years Olsen labored in the minor-league vine-yards with stops at Des Moines, Pittsfield and Springfield, Massachusetts, St. Joseph, Missouri, Atlanta, and Amarillo, Texas.

"In 1924, I roomed with Lou Gehrig at the Yankees spring train-ing complex at St. Petersburg, Florida, and thought I was ready at that time to make the big leagues, but I was sent back down to the minors just before the season began," Olsen reminisced. "After my last stop with Amarillo of the Western League in 1927, I decided to call it quits as a ballplayer because by that time I knew I wouldn't make it to the majors. . . . Then I got into the oil business in Texas," Olsen added.

Over the years Olsen became an oil millionaire, but his passion for baseball continued unabated. In 1933 he attended the Major League's first All-Star Game played at Chicago's Comiskey Park, and from then through 1987 he never missed seeing any of the 58 midsummer classics. Olsen died in May, 2000, but he reported in 1987 that he'd attended nearly 300 World Series games — in fact, from 1938 until 1980, Pat witnessed 255 consecutive World Series contests, missing the final game of the Kansas City–Philadelphia Series (in Philadelphia) because of a vital business commitment. That's the only Series game he failed to see in nearly 50 years. In 1987, he had been to every Hall of Fame Induction Ceremony at Cooperstown since 1939.

"I doubt very much if any other fan has compiled an attendance record of this magnitude," observed Bob Fishel, Executive Vice President of the American League and a baseball executive with more than 40 years experience.

"I never made more than $300 a month as a minor league player, but once I established myself in business and had the time and resources to travel, I made up my mind not to miss a single one of baseball's premier events," said Pat Olsen. The Aggies of Texas A&M University in College Station, Texas, honored him by naming their baseball park Olsen Field.

BABE'S SIGNATURE WORTH $500, BUT BEWARE! SOME PHONY

It is estimated that Babe Ruth signed at least two million autographs during his lifetime. With only a small fraction of those autographs being extant, values of genuine Ruth signatures are climbing steadily. A Ruth signature on a baseball generally sells for $500 and more.

Collectors should beware, though, because Ruth autographs have been widely counterfeited.

Mel Ott, the Hall-of-Fame New York Giants home run hitter, didn't mind autographing for fans since his name consists of only six letters. "Master Melvin" got to a point where he could sign 500 autographs per hour.

LUKE APPLING FIELDS A COFFEE POT AT CHICAGO'S COMISKEY PARK!

Luke Appling, the Hall-of-Fame shortstop, had a big league playing career spanning 20 seasons (1930–1950, with a year out, 1944, for military service) and was known as a great raconteur. He was a baseball "lifer": he managed and coached a long series of major and minor-league teams until his passing at the age of 84 in 1991.

Appling made sports headlines in the summer of 1985, when, at the age of 78, he slammed a home run into the left field stands at Washington D.C.'s Robert F. Kennedy Stadium during an old-timer's

game. Who threw the gopher ball? Why, it was none other than Hall-of-Famer Warren Spahn, who was a sprightly 64 at the time. After the game, Spahn said, "Appling hit the homer on a hanging curve."

About a year after Appling blasted that "senior home run," we had a chance to interview him at length at a major card show staged in Los Angeles. We asked Luke what was the strangest experience he ever had on a big league baseball diamond.

With only a moment's hesitation Appling replied, "The old Comiskey Park in Chicago was built over a rubbish dump. That means the entire baseball diamond consisted of landfill. In my first full season as a White Sox regular in 1931, we were playing the Detroit Tigers and I think it was the Tigers second baseman, Charlie Gehringer, who hit a hot ground ball down to short and I dug deep into the ground in trying to pick up the ball. I didn't come up with the ball, but I did bring up a rusty old coffee pot that had been buried years before the park was completed!

"The next day the team's ground crew laid down a thick layer of fresh topsoil over the infield so that players at Comiskey could concentrate on picking up baseballs rather than rusty old trash."

LARRY LAJOIE'S 1901 BATTING AVERAGE ZOOMS FROM .401 TO .422

Larry Lajoie, the great-fielding, hard-hitting second baseman who played in the majors for 21 years (from 1896 through 1916), won the American League batting crown in 1901 with a purported .401 average while with the Philadelphia Athletics.

Of course, a .401 average for a full season is super, but in reality Lajoie did even better. Some 50-odd years later statisticians, led by the eagle-eyed Cliff Kachline, discovered that through mistakes in addition, Lajoie was short-changed by nine hits. He actually piled up 229 base hits, including 48 doubles, 13 triples, and a league-leading 14 homers, and that boosted his average by 21 points, from .401 to .422. That .422 still stands as the highest seasonal average by an American Leaguer. (Ty Cobb's .420 in 1911 and George Sisler's .420 in 1922 now rank second.)

After the conclusion of the 1901 season, league statisticians just didn't add up Lajoie's hit total correctly — his at-bats remained the same at 543, and the nine additional base hits raised his lifetime big league average by one point, from .338 to .339.

EDD ROUSH'S 48-OUNCE BAT

Edd Roush, whose career spanned the 1913–1931 period and who was one of the greatest all-around players in the National League, was such a ferocious competitor that he became known as "The Ty Cobb of the National League." Roush entered the Hall of Fame in 1962, with many baseball historians maintaining that he should have been given his bronze plaque at Cooperstown much earlier.

Roush's brilliant career was marked by one peculiarity: he used a 48-ounce bat, the heaviest bat ever used by a Major League player. Contemporary players generally use bats weighing from 32 to 34 ounces, while a number even use 31-ouncers, even sluggers. The ballplayer of today feels he can gain greater bat speed with a lighter piece of lumber, enabling him to drive the baseball a greater distance.

As Roush approached his 80th birthday, he said, "I hit very different from the way they hit today. I don't believe anyone used a bat heavier than the 48-ounce type I had. It was a shorter bat, with a big handle, and I tried to hit to all fields. Didn't swing my head off, just used a snap swing to make contact and drive the ball."

Roush retained his batting style and his 48-ounce wooden bat even though the lively ball came into being in 1919–1920 and other players went for much lighter clubs to generate more bat speed in order to hit for distance.

His tactics obviously paid off, because Edd Roush won two National League batting championships while with the Cincinnati Reds in 1917 and 1919, averaging .341 and .321, respectively. In 1967 big league games he averaged .323 and piled up 2376 base hits. While he managed only 67 home runs, he hit 339 doubles and 183 triples, the latter being a very lofty stat.

DAVE KINGMAN—
FOUR TEAMS IN ONE SEASON!

David Arthur Kingman, a 6-foot-6-inch, 220-pound home run slugger, slammed out 442 circuit blasts during his checkered 16-year big league career (1971–1986), and that gives him the distinction of having the most homers for a player not in baseball's Hall of Fame.

Throughout his tenure in the big leagues, Kingman was noted for not speaking with reporters and being generally hostile to the press as a whole. Early on, after he reached the majors with the San Francisco Giants in 1971, he claimed he was badly misquoted after giving out a series of interviews. And because of his generally ornery personality, Kingman went from one team to another, playing for a total of seven teams in both Major Leagues.

He was signed out of the University of Southern California by the San Francisco Giants and he debuted with the parent club late in the 1971 season. Just before the start of the 1975 campaign, Kingman was sold to the New York Mets. By that time he had worn out his welcome with the Giants.

Big Dave remained with the Mets for the entire 1976 season, and then in '77 he really hit the jackpot for changing teams. In that year he played for exactly four of them. He went to the San Diego Padres in a June 15 trade, then on September 6 he was sold on waivers to the California Angels. His tenure with the Angels lasted for exactly 9 days because on September 15 he was sold to the New York Yankees. Yes, he did remain with the Yanks for the remainder of the season: 2 whole weeks. Baseball historians found that seeing service with four big league teams within a single season at least ties a record.

The Yankees had no interest in signing Dave for 1978, and so the big slugger signed with the Chicago Cubs, where he remained, remarkably enough, for three full seasons.

Though he was on the disabled list for nearly a month in '78, Dave still managed to hit 28 homers in 119 games. In '79, when many baseball experts said that Dave was nearing the end of the road, he surprised everybody by having a "career year" as he led the league with 48 homers and 115 runs batted in while averaging a solid .288 — all career highs for him. Dave's fortune declined in 1980 as he went on the disabled list three times, but when he was on the diamond he did play well, batting .278 in 81 games with 18 homers.

The Cubs soured on Kingman for a variety of reasons, particularly because of one grisly incident. He took a strong dislike to one female Chicago baseball reporter and expressed his displeasure with her writing by placing an expired rodent in her handbag.

Dave went over to the New York Mets at the beginning of 1981, and though he was happy about getting back to his old club, he again spent a bit of time on the DL, and was also benched at various times for striking out too much. Though he averaged .221 in 100 games, he did manage to slam 22 homers. The Mets knew that Kingman was a big gate attraction, a real threat at the plate. Moreover, fans liked to see his 450- to 500-foot "homers" into the stands during batting practice.

"King Kong" Kingman tried mightily to mend his ways in '82, and he kept himself off the bench by showing sporadic and game-winning bursts of power. While he averaged a skinny .204 (going 109 for 535 in 149 games), he led the league with 37 circuit blasts and drove in 99 runs. No other player has led the league in homers with that low an average. A free and sometimes wild swinger, Dave struck out a league-leading 156 times. Dick Young, then a baseball writer for the *New York Daily News,* and long one of Dave's severest critics, called him "King Kong Kingman, The Strikeout King."

Kingman went on to have a career-worst season in '83 as he "rode the pines" for long periods. He batted less than his weight, 198 in 100 games, and homered only 13 times.

He certainly wasn't ready to quit baseball at that point. After his release by the New York Mets, he signed with the Oakland Athletics in

1984, and remained with the A's for three full seasons, retaining his reputation as an authentic home run threat. In those 3 years he hit exactly 100 homers — 35, 30 and 35, respectively. His 1984 stats were particularly good: he averaged a strong .268 and knocked in 118 runs. Kingman was miffed that he didn't make the American League All-Star team in 1984, although he did play in the 1976 and 1980 All-Star games.

After being released by the A's following the '86 season, Kingman still had visions of reaching the magic 500 home run mark, and tried making a comeback in July '87 by signing with Phoenix of the Triple A Pacific Coast League. But after 20 games, with a sub-standard .203 average and only 2 homers, Dave hung up his uniform for good.

There are still those baseball writers who are long ball aficiona-dos and feel Kingman is Hall-of-Fame material, despite his .236 life-time batting average in the majors. They also point to his 1210 runs batted in and his home run ratio of 6.6% (measured against official times at bat) — a stat good enough to give him a fifth-place spot on the all-time list among retired players. Dave's detractors point to his 1816 strikeouts — another fifth-place all-time rating.

We had the opportunity to interview Dave Kingman in October 1998. Frankly, we've never encountered a more affable and approach-able interviewee. Said Kingman, "I may not have liked sportswriters when I was playing, and though I may have been a bit tough to get along with, I've always felt I was a decent person. Maybe I got a less-than-excellent reputation early in my career, but I was young, maybe a bit immature, but I have grown up. Remember, there are real pressures in playing big league baseball. Some basically excellent players fold because they cannot handle the pressure and play at their best before big and noisy crowds. I've felt that most baseball fans are fair and decent to the players, but the noisy boo-birds can get under your skin and warp your personality. By the same token, baseball writers in general are decent guys, but there are those who rip you all the time, and that kind of stuff can affect you. In general, I had a good career and have no regrets. Playing big league baseball is a rough and tumble profession."

AVERAGE LIFE OF A MAJOR LEAGUE BASEBALL IS ONLY SIX PITCHES!

During Major League baseball's so-called "Stone Age," the late 1870s up to the turn of the century, a ball stayed in the game until it became so discolored, or even misshapen, that it had to be thrown out for a replacement. There are even confirmed reports that a single baseball was used for an entire game back in those days! In fact, the use of beat-up balls continued to be a practice in the big leagues up to around the World War I period.

Edd Roush, a National League outfielder, heavy hitter, and Hall of Famer, often spoke of mashed-up baseballs being used in championship games. He spoke of this in great detail in an interview that appeared in Lawrence S. Ritter's landmark book *The Glory of Their Times,* published in 1966.

Roush, who played in the majors from 1913 to 1931, mostly with the Cincinnati Reds and New York Giants, recalled, "Until 1919, they had a dead ball. Well, the only way you could get a home run was if the outfielder tripped and fell down. The ball wasn't wrapped tight and lots of times it'd get mashed on one side.

"I've caught many a ball in the outfield that was mashed flat on one side. Come bouncing out there like a jumping bean. They wouldn't throw it out of the game, though. Only used about three or four balls in a whole game. Now they use 60 or 70. "

Roush had that just about right. A recent study by Major League Baseball indicates that the average ball has a life of only about six pitches in a game. Rawlings Sporting Goods, Inc., based in Saint Louis, supplies all the baseballs used by the thirty teams making up the American and National Leagues. Those thirty teams gobble up 720,000 baseballs every season, according to Rawlings. A baseball retails for $6, but the Major Leagues buy them up at wholesale prices.

Mark McGwire, the St. Louis Cardinals slugger, hit a lot of homers out of the park, but even when he connected 60 or 70 times in a season, that amounted to only a fraction of the baseballs lost in action. And that says nothing of the many baseballs McGwire hits out of the park in batting practice. McGwire, in fact, draws crowds of fans who want to see him blast baseballs into the bleachers and over the stands in batting practice.

Rawlings Sporting Goods also supplies baseballs to most of the minor league teams, as well as to thousands of amateur teams scattered across the United States. Virtually all of the Rawlings baseballs are made overseas, particularly in Haiti, where the company takes advantage of low-priced labor. Baseball manufacture is labor intensive because the balls must be hand-stitched. Neither Rawlings nor any other company has been able to develop machinery to stitch baseballs on an assembly-line basis. The work must be done with human hands.

WHEN IS A RECORD NOT REALLY A RECORD?

When George Edward "Rube" Waddell, the brilliant but eccentric Philadelphia Athletics left-hander, struck out a supposed total of 343 batters in 1904 (Rube went 25-19 in 384 innings of work), that posting stood as a Major League record for decades.

Fast-forward to the 1946 season when Bob Feller, fireballing right-hander of the Cleveland Indians, went on a strikeout binge and wound up with 348 Ks in 371 innings of work as he went 26-15.

Did Feller set a new record? Apparently he did, but *whoa!* Researchers at the weekly *Sporting News,* led by editor Cliff Kachline, checked through all Philadelphia Athletics box scores of 1904 when Waddell pitched, and discovered that Rube actually fanned 349 batters. The 349 figure was duly recognized, relegating Feller's strikeout total to second place. (Subsequently, of course, Waddell's record was broken, first by Sandy Koufax with 382 Ks in 1965, and then by Nolan Ryan with 383 Ks in 1973.)

Kachline commented on this strange statistical phenomenon: "Official scorers over the years turned in scoresheets with mistakes in them, often simple mistakes like addition. Researchers have gone over these erroneous scoresheets and made the necessary corrections. Thus, the stat has to be changed. Scorers erred because they were usually under deadline pressure. For example, newspapers wanted them in a hurry so they could be printed in a particular edition."

Kachline also mused, "Sometimes, the official scorers, who were working sportswriters, did not always show up to the game in any kind of condition to do accurate work. No wonder so many mistakes were made."

GREAT PITCHERS

THE QUESTION OF WALTER JOHNSON'S VICTORY TOTAL

When fireballing right-hander Walter Johnson retired following the 1927 season after spending 21 years with the Washington Senators, his victory total was given at 413 against 279 losses. Only Cy Young, who won 511 games, has a higher big league victory total than Johnson.

Strangely enough, however, Walter "Big Train" Johnson hadn't finished winning ballgames. Several years after his death in 1946, a number of researchers checked all of the box scores of games in which Johnson pitched and discovered that the scorers did not give him credit for three additional victories. Now all the standard references give Johnson 416 total wins.

Johnson's grandson, Henry W. Thomas, wrote an excellent and well-received biography on the "Big Train" in 1996, appropriately titled *Walter Johnson: Baseball's Big Train,* and said with great family pride, "My granddad was such a great pitcher that he won three Major Leagues games after he died."

Thomas added that the "Big Train" also struck out 11 batters after his passing since his K total was revised from 3497 to 3508.

Walter Johnson was reputed to have thrown a baseball as fast or faster than any other pitcher in baseball history. He was called "Big Train" because it was said that his best pitch traveled faster than any locomotive in existence. Radar guns were not invented during Johnson's era, but most baseball experts who saw "Big Train" in action said they've never seen a pitcher who could match his speed. In today's terms, his fastball traveled a tad over 100 miles per hour. No human could match that kind of speed.

In his 458-page tome on his grandfather, Henry Thomas repeatedly emphasized again that Walter Johnson made it a practice never to throw close inside to a batter. With his speed, Johnson, one of the true gentlemen of the game, never wanted to hit a batter with his blazing fastball.

Henry Thomas wrote, "If Granddad had pitched tight like so many pitchers of today — including Don Drysdale, who pitched in tight continuously — he could have become a 500-game winner. He never wanted to take a chance of hitting a batter with all that speed. If Walter Johnson threw inside as a matter of strategy, batters would be afraid to dig in. He gave the batters an even chance by not intimidating them, and he still established himself as one of the greatest pitchers of all time."

Two other stats reflect the true greatness of Johnson as a moundsman: his ERA stands at a very skinny 2.17 (good for seventh best on the all-time list), and he threw 110 shutouts, and that is *the record*. He threw only one no-hitter on July 1, 1920, against the Boston Red Sox.

EXTRAORDINARY MOUND FEATS BY EXTRAORDINARY PITCHERS

Nowadays most big league pitchers "baby" their arms. In the old days, most Major League teams utilized a four-man rotation; now it's a five-man rotation. That is, hurlers today work every fifth day instead of every fourth day. And these five starters are backed up by a "relief crew" of seven additional pitchers.

The seven relievers are classed into categories: "long men," "set-up men," and "closers." Oftentimes, a reliever will be thrown into the fracas with the purpose of blowing out only a single batter. That "specialist" may be a left-hander whose job it is to get out a left-hand-ed batter in a critical situation late in the game.

Today, moundsmen are taken out of a game if their "pitch count" reaches a certain number of pitches. Some starters are limited to as few as 100 pitches before they're taken out of a game. Very seldom is a starter allowed to hurl as many as 130 pitches per game. A relief pitcher, who often is called upon to "put out fires" two or three times a week, is limited to 30 or perhaps 40 pitches at most. The closer usually comes in to shut down the other side for a single inning. That is true of famous closers like Dennis Eckersley and John Franco. When they go past one inning in a closer situation they make news.

Strangely, there are now cases where a moundsman appears in about as many games as innings pitched. Take the case of Eckersley, one of the premier relievers of the 1990s: In 1993 with the Oakland Athletics, he appeared in 64 games and chalked up only 67 innings pitched; he did have 36 saves — a very good performance. Then with Oakland in 1995, he appeared in 52 games and hurled only 53 innings. He recorded 36 saves, and though his won-lost record was a less-than-mediocre 1-5, that stat doesn't mean all that much. Relievers are paid according to games saved.

John Franco's stats in respect to games played and innings pitched are similar to Eckersley's. While with the New York Mets in 1991, he appeared in 52 games and threw in 55⅓ innings to go with 30 saves; in 1996 with the Mets, he got into 51 games and threw 54 innings, with 28 saves. Franco is the prototypical closer who rarely goes beyond a one-inning stint. Thus, complete games have become a relative rarity in the big leagues.

Greg Maddux, the star Atlanta Braves right-hander, led the National League in complete games in 1993, 1994 and 1995 with 8, 10, and 10, respectively — low numbers for the leader in that category.

Back in the old days, a reliever was often brought in with the idea that he would finish the game for the starter who was knocked out of the box. In general, lengthy relief appearances have almost gone the way of the carrier pigeon.

Eddie Rommel, the old Philadelphia Athletics star right-hander, spent the last couple seasons in his 13-year Major League career (1920-32) as a reliever, and he chalked up what is generally thought to be the longest relief assignment in big league history.

That came in a July 10, 1932 game against the Cleveland Indians. Athletics starter Lew Krausse was taken out of the game in the first inning when he gave up 3 runs and 4 hits. With two outs, Rommel came in to put out the fire. What finally happened was that this turned out to be one of the most unusual and highest-scoring games in Major League history. This wild and woolly games lasted for 18 innings before the Athletics won by a fat 18-17 score!

Strangely, Rommel was allowed to "go the distance," and he gained the victory with his "tight" relief pitching. In 17⅓ innings of work, he allowed 14 runs and 29 base hits. Clint Brown, the Indians' starting pitcher, was relieved in the late innings by Willis Hudlin and Wesley Ferrell. In this 18-inning marathon, the Indians stroked 33 base hits while the A's hit safely 25 times for the astounding total of 58.

John Burnett, the Indians' second baseman, established a record that still stands after 70 years: 9 base hits in a single game in 11 at bats. Indians' second baseman Billy Cissell had 4 hits, while first baseman Eddie Morgan hit safely 5 times.

For the A's, first baseman Jimmie Foxx picked up 6 hits in 9 at bats, while left fielder Al Simmons went 5 for 9. No doubt about it, the Indians and the A's had their hitting clothes on during that hot July day in 1932.

The Indians and Athletics were tied 15-15 after 15 innings, but both teams scored a brace of runs in the 16th to knot the score at 17-17. Then the A's scored a single run in the top of the 18th to put the game away at 18-17, a football-type score. Nowadays, a game of that length would require about six or so pitchers on each side, but in this monumental clash only five moundsmen saw action.

Rommel had a reputation for being a workhorse, since he had a string of games to his credit where he pitched well beyond nine innings. In an April 13, 1926, game against Washington, for example, he hooked up in a pitching duel with the great Walter Johnson. The Senators squeaked out a 1-0 victory over the Athletics in fifteen innings. Both pitchers went the distance, of course. That wouldn't happen today, because pitchers are rarely allowed to go beyond nine innings. Later on in his career, Rommel became an American League umpire and served for 23 seasons (1938–1960) as an AL arbiter.

We had the chance to speak with Eddie Rommel on several occasions. He was an imposing figure, standing about 6 foot 2 inches and weighing an athletic 200 pounds.

We asked Rommel why pitchers of his era were often able to work so many innings at a single stretch. He answered, "When I broke into pro baseball back in 1918 with the Newark Bears of the International League, we were just coming out of the 'dead ball' era and getting a new, juiced-up, lively ball that made it easier to hit homers. Even after the lively ball came into being in about 1919–20, a lot of hitters liked to continuing to 'slap' the ball and tried more than anything to 'place' relatively short hits. Ty Cobb was basically a slap hitter — I pitched to him many times, and he rarely tried to go for homers.

"Remember, Cobb became a little jealous of Babe Ruth hitting all those homers, and in 1925 Ty said, in effect, 'There's no real trick to hitting homers.' Then he set out to prove his point. In back-to-back games against the St. Louis Browns at Sportsman's Park early in May that year, Ty changed his batting style by taking a full swing. He hit three home runs in the first game, and two more on the following day, giving him five for the two games."

Historians indicated that Cobb was unlucky to hit seven homers in 2 days. Two of his shots missed the roof at Sportsmen's Park and dropped for doubles. Rommel went on to say that after that spectacular 2-day performance, Cobb went back to his old batting style, consisting of a snap swing and a quick chop so that he did not have to set himself. That made him able to shift quickly so he could meet any kind of pitch — high, low, inside, outside. The snap swing enabled him to meet the ball squarely even while he was shifting.

Rommel concluded his observations by saying that since pitchers in his era didn't have to worry all that much about game-breaking home runs, they didn't have to absolutely "bear down" on every pitch. He said, "We could pace ourselves." Rommel also emphasized that back in his playing days, pitchers objected to being relieved and strove to remain in the game as long as possible. Thus, starters of that era rolled up more innings per season generally than today's mounds-men. And by the same token, relievers didn't like being relieved, and that's one of the reasons he threw that famed 17⅓-inning, 29-hit relief performance on the afternoon of July 10, 1932.

BOB FELLER DIDN'T COUNT HIS PITCHES

From the time Bob "Rapid Robert" Feller broke in with the Indians in mid-season in 1936 as a 17-year-old who could heave the baseball 100 miles per hour, he was hailed as the Tribe's best pitcher since old Cy himself. When Feller enlisted in the navy on December 9, 1941 (2 days after Pearl Harbor), he had already won 107 games for Cleveland (against 54 losses). No pitcher in baseball history had piled up that many victories that quickly — not even Cy Young himself. Before Feller joined the U.S. Navy, many baseball historians thought that the fireballing right-hander had an even chance of at least approaching Cy Young's monu-mental victory total. However, Feller's navy duty took him away from baseball for 3½ years. He was discharged from the navy toward the end of July 1945. In his first game back, he defeated the Detroit Tigers 4-2 and struck out 12. He obviously regained his old form.

Feller went 5-3 for the last couple of months in the '45 season, and then in 1946 he turned in an almost unbelievable iron-man performance as he rolled up a 26-15 record for the sixth-place Indians. The Indians posted a mediocre 68-86 record that season; thus, Feller won nearly 40% of the team's games.

In 48 games, he pitched an almost incredible 371 innings, gave up a sparing 277 base hits, and came up with a skinny ERA of 2.18. He made 42 starts and led the league in complete games with an amazing 36. He struck out 348 batters, a figure that was thought to be a record, but later Rube Waddell's strikeout total with the 1904 Philadelphia Athletics was raised to 349.

Feller was thrown into relief situations six times so that he could pitch extra innings in order to have a better chance at breaking Rube Waddell's one-season strikeout record. No starting pitcher in the current era of baseball was ever called upon to go into a game as a reliever.

Still, Feller's regular season stats give only a part of his over strenuous pitching activities in 1946. Feller wanted to recover the lost baseball income during the nearly four years he served in the U.S. Navy. He organized a 30-day nationwide barnstorming tour composed of two teams consisting of Major Leaguers, plus top players from the Negro professional leagues. During that barnstorming tour, Feller pitched at least 60-70 innings in competition, and thus for the whole of 1946, he threw something like 450 innings. And that's not to say how many innings he threw in spring training in 1946. Nowadays no pitcher would follow a schedule that outrageously arduous.

Bob Feller would have piled up even more impressive lifetime pitching stats had it not been for a strange accident that occurred in a game he was pitching against the Philadelphia Athletics in June 1947. He fell off the mound — it was a bit slippery since it had been raining that day — and injured his right pitching shoulder.

From that point on, Rapid Robert was never quite the same again. He would never be able to throw those 100-plus mile-per-hour fastballs. But, despite the injury, Bob had a lot of baseball savvy and retained enough good stuff to remain in the majors for another decade. He finished the '47 season at 20-11, and then struggled through the Indians' 1948 pennant with a 19-15 record. While he led the league in strikeouts with 164 in 280 innings, that was well under par for Rapid Robert.

Feller's great ambition was to win a World Series game, but he failed in that quest because of one of the strangest plays in the history of the "Fall Classic." Bob started Game 1 against the Boston Braves at

Boston. The game was scoreless through the first 7 innings. Then, in the bottom of the eighth, Bill Salkeld singled to open the inning and Braves manager Billy Southworth sent Phil Masi in to run for him. Mike McCormick sacrificed and Eddie Stanky drew an intentional walk. Feller then attempted to pick off Masi, who had taken a big lead off second. Feller whirled around and fired a bullet to shortstop-manager Lou Boudreau, who cut in behind the runner. Masi slid back and was called safe by base umpire Bill Stewart, although Boudreau protested vehemently that he had made the tag well before the runner had reached the bag. Pitcher Johnny Sain then flied out, but Tommy Holmes came through with a single, driving in Masi. That was the only run of the game as Boston won the 1-0 squeaker. Films of the play revealed that Boudreau had tagged Masi out before the latter had gotten within 2 or 3 feet of second base.

Feller told us in a 1997 interview, "That was a strange call, all right. Stewart made a mistake because he was not in position to see the tag out. That's the breaks of the game." Feller can be very philosophical about misadventures in baseball. In going the distance, Feller allowed only two hits, walked only three, and struck out two.

After Bill Stewart retired from the National League umpiring crew several years later, he began a new career as a Major League scout. And who hired him to that post? Why, none other than the Cleveland Indians. Strange.

In the '48 World Series, Feller got a second chance to win a Series game. In Game 5 at Cleveland Stadium, a clash that drew a standing-room-only crowd of 86,288 (then a record crowd for any big league game), Bob was sent to the showers in the same inning with only one man out. He gave up 7 runs on 10 hits, as the Tribe took an 11-5 drubbing. The Indians did take the Series 4 games to 2, with Rapid Robert being the team's only losing pitcher against the Braves.

Feller went 15-14 and 16-11 in the 1949 and 1950 season, respectively — not bad, but not approaching Rapid Robert's past greatness. In 1951, he enjoyed an extraordinary season as he posted a glittering 22-8 record. Many sportswriters were ready to write off Feller as a front-line pitcher at this point in his career, and though Feller's fastball was no longer in the 100-mile-per-hour zone, he made up for it in craftiness. He struck out only 111 batters in 250 innings of work, but he led the American League in wins and in winning percentage with a .733 posting. Even at that fairly late point in his career, Bob threw 16 complete games in 34 starts (more CGs than most league leaders achieve today), including a no-hitter against Detroit on July (the third no-hitter in his career).

Toward mid-season, Feller was involved in just about the strangest of all games in his 18 years as an Indian — a game against the Philadelphia Athletics. The Indians had their hitting clothes on in that clash, and they whomped A's pitchers for 21 runs. The Athletics were no pushovers in the hitting department that day either, as they scored 9 runs. Did Feller get any relief in that slugfest? Absolutely not! He went the distance in picking up the victory. Today, if Feller had been pitching, he would have been yanked after 5 or 6 innings, just enough to get credit for a win, and the members of the relief corps would have been called in to mop up.

In our 1997 interview with Bob, we asked him why he was permitted to remain on the mound for the entire game when he was getting shelled. He answered, "I asked our manager, Al Lopez, to keep me in the game for a solid purpose. I was experimenting with a couple of new pitches, and I wanted to throw them in game conditions, so it didn't make any difference if I allowed Philadelphia to score a few additional runs, for we had the game wrapped up from the get-go. I know that you can't get away with stuff like that today, but I was glad to work out those pitches in competition and that did help me a lot down the road. And I've got to give credit to Al Lopez who allowed me to work on those new pitches. And I'm glad to see that Al made it into the Hall of Fame as a manager." Bob concluded, "I must have thrown at least 175 pitches in that game, but then nobody was counting."

Feller dropped to a 9-13 record in 1952, went 10-7 in 1953, and then roared back in 1954 where he posted a 13-3 winning season as a "spot starter." In 19 starts, he threw 9 CGs — not bad. That was the year when the Indians established a Major League record for most victories in a season — 111 wins against 43 losses.

Feller thought he had another shot at winning his first World Series game against the New York Giants, who finished the season at a comparatively modest 98-59. Unfortunately, the Giants swept the Indians in four straight games with Bob Lemon, Early Wynn and Mike Garcia taking the losses (Lemon two of them). Manager Lopez had scheduled Feller to pitch the fifth game, but since there was no necessity for a fifth game, Bob never got to pitch in the Series. Feller, philosophical as ever, said, "Stranger and worser things have happened to me before and since. I'm not going to worry about things that I have little or no control over."

Feller wound up his career in the 1955 and 1956 seasons as a spot starter and reliever, and in his 18 years in the majors he came up with a lifetime record of 266 victories and 162 defeats. Through the late 1960s, his strikeout total of 2581 ranked fourth on the all-time list.

While Feller may not have won a World Series game, he did participate in five All-Star games and went 1-0, having been the winning pitcher in the 1946 clash at Fenway Park when the American League clobbered the Nationals 12-0.

Bob Feller certainly wasn't through with baseball after he threw his last pitch for the Cleveland Indians. He continued to appear at old-timers' games and special exhibitions and kept hurling those balls toward the plate into the early 1990s, when he was past 70 years old — or "70 years young," to use our choice of words. Moreover, he still does his own yard work at his large home in Gates Mills, Ohio, near Cleveland.

DAVID WELLS— A SUPER BABE RUTH FAN

New York Yankees left-handed pitcher David Wells, who helped the Bronx Bombers take the 1998 American League pennant and the World Series crown with an 18-4 regular season record (including throwing a perfect game), has long been noted as a super Babe Ruth fan.

When Wells joined the Yankees in 1997, he asked to wear Babe's retired number 3. When that request was denied, he settled for number 33. From that point, he purchased one of Ruth's game-worn caps at auction for $35,000, and wore it in a 1998 game against the Cleveland Indians. Wells is known in baseball circles as a free spirit.

HALL OF FAMERS' SALARIES BEFORE THE AGE OF TELEVISION

Back in the so-called "good old days," most big league baseball players, even the biggest stars, hustled around to find temporary jobs in the off-season. During the 1940s and 1950s, many of the game's biggest stars, Hall of Famers, held everyday jobs. Duke Snider, Brooklyn Dodgers outfielder, carried mail from the Brooklyn post office during the holiday period; Stan Musial, St. Louis Cardinals outfielder/first baseman, worked as a clerk in his father-in-law's grocery store in Donora, Pennsylvania; Phil Rizzuto, New York Yankees shortstop, worked as a salesman in a New York men's clothing store; Mike Garcia, Cleveland Indians, worked in a Cleveland dry cleaning shop and then bought the business; Bob Feller, Cleveland Indians, sold insurance and then opened his own insurance company (which eventually went bankrupt); Early Wynn, Washington Senators, Chicago White Sox, and Cleveland Indians, was a construction laborer and then head of his own construction company in Alabama; and Carl Furillo, Brooklyn Dodgers, elevator repairman, Manhattan. We could list countless other stars who had to take on a variety of jobs following their playing careers, and those who had to work at odd jobs in the off-season in order to provide for their families.

It's been only within the past generation or so that baseball salaries have skyrocketed. Nowadays a player who signs a big multi-year contract is usually financially set for life.

We can state the reason for the almost geometric increase in baseball in one single word: television. Back when baseball games were first televised in the late 1940 and early 1950s, there were many baseball experts who maintained that TV would "kill" attendance at games. These so-called "experts" said, "Why would anyone go to a game if he could see it for free on TV?" It so happened that TV got many millions of new fans interested in the game, with box office receipts zooming as a result.

Back during the 1920s and 1930s when ballgames were broadcast on radio, revenues from that source were almost inconsequential. In many cases, Major League teams waived potential broadcast fees because they were happy just to get the free publicity.

The Cleveland Indians received their first "big" TV contract from station WXEL in 1951. That contract called for WXEL to broadcast all of the Indians' 77 home games, plus 6 games on the road. For those 83 games, the Indians received $250,000 — a lot of money in those days; in fact, enough money to cover more than half the player salaries.

Minimum salaries were not agreed upon until the late 1940s. When Jackie Robinson, the first African-American player in the Major Leagues, was promoted from the Montreal Royals of the International League in 1947 to the Brooklyn Dodgers under general manager Branch Rickey, he was given a $5,000 contract, the big-league minimum at the time. Player salaries before that time were generally paltry.

Then there's Jeff Heath, a Cleveland Indians outfielder from 1936 to 1945. He continuously complained about having to play for "peanuts." After he hit .343 and drove in 112 runs for Cleveland in 1938, he was given a contract for the 1939 campaign for about $3,000 — the equivalent of a Cleveland public school teacher's salary at the time.

After Heath finished his big league career with the Boston Braves in 1949, he signed a contract with the Pacific Coast League's Seattle Rainiers in 1950 worth $25,000 — the highest salary by far he had ever received in baseball. In fact, no minor-league player up to that point was given that type of generous contract.

Baseball salaries during the Depression era of the 1930s were generally very low, even for the biggest stars. Frank "Lefty" O'Doul led the National League in batting in 1932 while with the Brooklyn Dodgers. He averaged a fat .368. Did he get a raise for that performance? No. He was cut $1,000, down from $8,000 to $7,000, but he still ranked among the top-paid big leaguers.

Lou Boudreau, star shortstop of the Cleveland Indians, who as a brilliant sophomore in 1940 played in every one of the team's 155 games, averaged a solid .295, drove in 101 runs, and led American league shortstops with a .986 fielding percentage. For that grand effort Boudreau played under a contract calling for the munificent sum of $5,000, which amounted to little more than $30 per game.

Indians' owner Alva Bradley, a business tycoon with interests in myriad industries, felt guilty about that contract, so he gave Boudreau a $2,000 bonus at season's close. Then Bradley doubled Boudreau's salary to $10,000 — making him one of the higher-paid players in the big leagues.

MIKE PIAZZA AND THE TERMINAL TOWER

Sometimes the cost of player salaries becomes a little too steep, even for a multi-billionaire like Rupert Murdoch. Early in 1998, Mike Piazza, the Dodgers star catcher, demanded a 6-year contract, calling for a cool $100 million. Murdoch declined to offer such an obscene contract, and Piazza eventually wound up with the New York Mets before the '98 season got too far along. The Mets offered Piazza $85 million for six seasons, which added up to just over $14 million per year and would have been the richest baseball contract in history. Piazza felt he was justified in asking for a nine-figure contract because with the 1997 Dodgers he had perhaps the greatest hitting year of any catcher in the history of the game. In 152 games, he averaged a lofty .362, swatted 201 base hits, including 40 homers, and drove in 124.

However, the Dodger organization felt that Piazza, at age 30, would be vulnerable to injury as an everyday catcher, and that he might have a hard time fulfilling the extent of any overblown contract. Piazza was booed throughout the 1998 season by fans in most of the National League for his outrageous salary demands, but he took the jeering in stride as he rolled up another good year, batting .329 in 151 games, with 184 hits, 32 homers, and 111 runs batted in.

$100,000,000 is an enormous amount of money, especially when the sum is considered as a long-term contractual commitment to a baseball player. Consider Cleveland, Ohio, in connection with a massive downtown building project completed in 1930-31. The project featured the Terminal Tower (52 stories and 708 feet high, the second-tallest building in the U.S. outside of New York City), plus four other solid 20 plus-story structures, including the Midland Building. It cost a total of $ 100,000,000 — a massive amount of money in those days. Sure, the dollar is different today than it was two generations ago, but Mike Piazza demanding Terminal Tower money is zany!

GEORGE "SHOTGUN" SHUBA: "I'D SETTLE FOR THE LICENSING FEE"

George "Shotgun" Shuba, who played for the Brooklyn Dodgers from 1948 to 1955 and who was the first National Leaguer to hit a pinch-hit homer in the World Series (in the '53 Series against the New York Yankees), discussed baseball salaries at length at a New York City card show. He said, "When I played, there were very few fringe benefits. Sure, some of the big stars, like Stan Musial, Yogi Berra, Ted Williams, Joe DiMaggio, and Bob Feller, made pretty fair money from commercial endorsements, but for the average player there weren't all that many opportunities to make money on the side. If I had the chance, I'd like to get a coaching job for a big league team, and I'd work for free. I'd just settle for the licensing fee."

The Major League Players' Association has an agreement with Major League Baseball to share all licensing fees for the use of the MLB logo as well as individual team logos on commercial products. The royalty fee is currently pegged at about 8%. Thus, if a manufacturer retails a jacket bearing the MLB logo, or a team logo, for $50, the MLB Players' pool will receive $4. Tens of millions of dollars of income are generated this way.

Currently, each Major League player, manager, and coach receives well over $100,000 in licensing fees annually. No wonder Shotgun Shuba would be willing to coach for zero salary!

DIMAGGIO'S BIG BUCKS FOR SIGNING BASEBALL BATS

While Joseph Paul DiMaggio refused to sign baseball bats at card shows, he did autograph lumber under special circumstances — and if the price was right. And DiMag's rates for bat signings were not cheap. There's something special about having a big star of the game sign a bat, especially one in the rare upper echelons in the Hall of Fame like Joe DiMaggio.

Of all of his deeds on the diamond, DiMaggio is perhaps best known for his 56-game hitting streak in 1941. Most baseball historians feel that this is one of the records that will not be broken. (Standing - ted safely in 44 straight games while with Cincinnati in 1978 — that's the National League record.)

DiMaggio signed bats for free for fans earlier in his playing days, but he stopped that altogether when the autograph craze started taking off in early 1980s. Sometime toward the end of 1990, an ambitious promoter asked DiMaggio if he would sign 1,941 bats to commemorate the 50th anniversary of his 1941 hitting streak. The promoter made DiMaggio an offer he could not refuse. He would pay the old Yankee Clipper exactly $2,000 for each signed bat. The promoter then proceeded to advertise the bats at $3,995 each!

DiMaggio, working in a private office, spent nearly 3 full days signing those 1,941 bats. For those labors, his check came out to a little under $3.9 million. No sports person in the history of this planet has made more than $3.9 million for less than 3 days work.

For a weekend card show, DiMaggio often cleared more than $100,000. In some cases, the promoter would take not a penny from that amount. He'd use DiMaggio as a "loss leader." The number of fans jamming into the place because of Joltin' Joe's presence would attract more business.

In the few years before his death, Joe was bringing in his own attorney to monitor these shows because he didn't want to miscount the number of autographs he signed. Remember, there was big money involved. Whenever there was a Joe D signing session, there was a big business atmosphere that breathed the "Fortune 500."

DiMaggio was also a stickler for "expenses" incurred while starring as an autograph guest at card shows. In a late 1990s card show appearance, he tacked on a $6.00 charge for taxi fare. We've got to watch those nickels!

Please don't misunderstand us — we fully appreciate Joe DiMaggio's contribution to the game of baseball and to American folklore. We interviewed this baseball great on numerous occasions and he was always a gentleman. In fact, we consider ourselves lucky because Joe didn't ordinarily grant interviews to reporters. And he was always more than happy to give us a free autograph, which we gave out to friends. Thus, we established a personal relationship with him and stand in awe of his accomplishments.

DiMaggio's strange hold upon the American sporting public was dramatically illustrated at a mid 1990s card show appearance he made at Hofstra University. The show was staged at Hofstra's cavernous

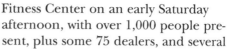

Fitness Center on an early Saturday afternoon, with over 1,000 people present, plus some 75 dealers, and several ex-star players' autograph guests. As Joe entered the room, a sudden hush fell over the crowd as all eyes strained to get a glimpse of the former Yankee great, then past 80 with a shock of pure white hair. DiMaggio, slightly stooped and with a history of medical problems, still maintained the majestic stride of a super athlete. Fathers lifted their small sons onto their shoulders so they could get a quick look at a true baseball icon, a legend in every sense of the word. This scene was of such magnitude that it could never be forgotten.

DiMaggio always took his autograph appearance very seriously. He dressed impeccably — a tailored suit, tailored shirt and silk tie. And even as he passed his 80th birthday, his signature remained clear and bold. He always took his time and signed carefully. Many big-time athletes just scrawl their signature at card shows.

At earlier card shows, DiMaggio would personalize any autograph, but starting in the early 1990s, he would sign his name only. At a full-fledged card show, he'd do 1,000 autographs on a Saturday, and then another 1,000 on Sunday; he just couldn't take the time to write out personalizations.

MARK MCGWIRE'S 70TH HOME RUN BALL SELLS FOR $3,005,000 AT AUCTION

The baseball hammered out by Mark McGwire on September 27, 1998, at Busch Stadium in St. Louis for his record-breaking 70th home run, brought an incredible $3,005,000 at a public auction staged a New York City's Madison Square Garden on January 12, 1999. The hammer price came to $2,700,000. With the auction house's commission, the total realization added up to $3,005,000.

It goes almost without saying that this marks the highest realization for any single item of baseball memorabilia sold at public auction. The winning bid was cast by Todd McFarlane, 37, a native of Calgary, Alberta, and now a resident of Tempe, Arizona. McFarlane, who claimed he spent his life's savings on this historic baseball, heads his own company, Todd McFarlane Productions, which produces a wide variety of comic books and related products. McFarlane, who is also a part-owner of the Edmonton Oilers in the National Hockey League, calls himself of "psycho baseball fan."

New official Major League baseballs, produced in a factory in Costa Rica, retail for about $6.

CATCHING BASEBALLS
THROWN OFF OF TALL BUILDINGS

Charles "Gabby" Street, who gained fame first as Walter Johnson's "personal catcher" with the Washington Senators and later as a pennant-winning manager of the St. Louis Cardinals in 1930-31, is destined to be best remembered for an offbeat stunt performed in the nation's capital on the morning of August 21, 1908.

Prompted by a bet between two local sportsmen, Street won a $500 prize and worldwide publicity by catching a baseball thrown by Johnson from the top of the 555-foot high Washington Monument. Though considerably jarred by the impact of the ball as it landed in his glove, it wasn't enough to keep him from catching Walter Johnson's 3-1 victory over the Detroit Tigers that afternoon. It was said that Street's experience on the receiving end of Johnson's "cannon-balls" had uniquely prepared him to accomplish the feat at the

Washington Monument.

Several years later, Brooklyn Dodgers manager and former catcher Wilbert Robinson was supposed to catch a baseball thrown from the top of a newly-built New York City skyscraper. Prankster Casey Stengel, a young Brooklyn outfielder, substituted a large grapefruit for a baseball. Robinson made the catch but he was furious when he found himself covered with grapefruit pulp.

In mid-season 1938, Cleveland Indians back-up catcher Hank Helf caught a ball thrown from near the top of the 708-foot Terminal Tower (then America's tallest skyscraper outside New York City). Helf made the catch, and today his name is still remembered for that performance.

Baseballs dropped from the height of skyscrapers travel more than 150 miles an hour when they reach the ground. That type of stunt has, for all intents and purposes, been banned by Major League Baseball as being too dangerous.

"SPLASHY" NEW BALLPARK INNOVATIONS

The Arizona Diamondbacks, based in Phoenix, became the National League's newest franchise in 1998 by going all out in making their new Diamondbacks Stadium one of the most innovative ballparks ever.

Chief among the innovations is a swimming pool, together with an adjacent hot tub, beyond the outfield barriers. The pool area is housed in a special section of Diamondbacks Stadium. For a half-dozen seats or so, plus access to the pool and its accessories, fans pay more than $4,000 for season reservations. The fans can also catch some rays on a suntanning deck and, if they want, watch a little baseball.

The Tampa Bay Devil Rays, the American League's newest franchise, which also debuted in 1998, took second place to no one in ballpark innovations when they opened Tropicana Field. This way, fans who get bored with baseball can go down to a stadium super-mall underneath the outfield stands and shop for everything from shoes and shirts to new cars.

In the *Wall Street Journal* Sam Walker commented on the new era ballpark phenomena: Critics contend that all the sideshows won't build a true fan base and once the novelties wear off, some operators will lose money. Nevertheless, team owners see it differently; they say the added attraction will lure new groups to the stadiums and prompt them to stay, spend all day, and spend a little money.

ZANY BASEBALL CARDS: GLENN HUBBARD AND HIS PET PYTHON

In a 1998 survey, the weekly *Sports Collectors Digest* named the 1984 Fleer specimen showing Atlanta Braves second baseman Glenn Hubbard with his favorite pet, a 9-foot python, draped around his neck and shoulders, as the zaniest/wackiest baseball card. Hubbard seems to be enjoying the friendship of his reptilian friend, for he has a broad smile on his face. The python, a healthy-looking specimen, obviously has been well fed.

Baseball's Funniest People

STEER CRAZY

Home run slugger Ken Griffey of the Seattle Mariners and Team Manager Lou Piniella made a tasty little bet during batting practice in April of 1995. Griffey bet Piniella he could club a certain number of balls out of the stadium in practice. The loser of the home run wager would have to buy the winner an expensive steak dinner. Lou accepted the bet and the contest was on. Unfortunately for Griffey, he lost and had to pay up. Equally unfortunate for Piniella, superstar Griffey's unique sense of humor played a part in paying off the debt. Three days later, manager Lou Piniella walked into his office in the Mariners' clubhouse and discovered a 1,200-pound Hereford cow waiting for him. "There's your steak," Ken Griffey said to Lou Piniella.

HERE'S YOUR STEAK, LOU!

OLD JOKE

Sometimes baseball players make honest replies to questions without realizing the humor in their responses. Take Hall-of-Famer Mel Ott, one of the game's greatest hitters. Young Mel was only sixteen years old when he was brought up to the Majors to play for the New York Giants. At the time, Ott was a catcher. New York's manager looked at the sixteen-year-old and asked him a question. "Son, did you ever play the outfield?" asked Manager John McGraw. Very seriously, Mel Ott replied, "Yes sir, when I was a kid."

HARE-BRAINED

Hall-of-Fame baseball star Walter James Vincent Maranville is better known by his funny nickname, "Rabbit." Rabbit Maranville played for the Boston Braves in the mid-1900s. Maranville was one of baseball's earliest pranksters. Once when it was his turn to bat, he crawled through umpire Hank O'Day's legs on his way to home plate — much to the delight of the hometown crowd!

HOMEWARD BOUND

Pitcher Pat Caraway of the Chicago White Sox pulled off a zany stunt in his rookie season in the Major Leagues. Caraway, who was a native Texan, found it tough to endure the bitter cold of early-season games played in blustery Chicago. He complained and complained and complained. Finally, the manager of the team, tired of hearing Pat grumble about the chilly weather, asked, "What do you want me to do about the weather?"

"Well," replied Caraway, "can I at least go home and get an overcoat?"

"Fine! Go get an overcoat," the manager shouted. And so Pat Caraway exited the stadium, left Chicago, and flew home to Texas to get an overcoat.

NAME GAME

After Mickey Rivers retired as a player, he got a job working with the New York Yankees and manager Billy Martin as a special assistant. One day during spring training, Rivers went into Martin's office and told him he wanted to be known from that day on as "Miguel Rivera" instead of Mickey Rivers.

"What's wrong with the name Mickey Rivers?" manager Martin wanted to know.

"Too many people are looking for me," zany Mickey Rivers replied very seriously.

THE HOLE STORY

In 1993, ex-Phillies infielder Dave Sveum was talking about his former team and said he missed playing in the City of Brotherly Love about as much as he missed having a hole in his head. When Philadelphia General Manager Lee Thomas heard about Sveum's comment, he fired off a fast retort that rates as one of baseball's funniest replies. "Dave Sveum is a real classy guy," he said. "We did give him an opportunity — a big opportunity. He says he misses playing here like a hole in the head. Well, what about the hole in his bat?"

SHORT STORY

Albie Pearson stood tall at the plate when it came to hitting, but he took a lot of kidding about his size. Someone once said of Albie, "If he walked around with a lit cigar in his mouth he'd burn everyone in the knee."

Another teammate of Albie's had this to say: "Having a catch with Albie Pearson is very relaxing. It's like throwing downhill."

NUTTY NEWS

Sportswriter Edward T. Murphy was a baseball fan with an ironic sense of humor. Trying to think positive during the 1930s, when the Brooklyn Dodgers fielded some mighty weak squads, Murphy wrote, "Overconfidence may cost the Dodgers sixth place."

PIE-EYED

Larry Anderson was the team clown of the 1993 Philadelphia Phillies. Anderson, who liked to pester his teammates with wacky questions like "Why do people sing 'Take Me Out to the Ballgame' at the stadium when they're already there?" and "Why do people drive on the parkway and park in the driveway?" got a bitter taste of his own nutty medicine in April of 1993. While Anderson was taping an important television interview, teammates Curt

Schilling and Pete Incaviglia sneaked up behind him and smacked him in the face with a shaving-cream pie. Larry Anderson's pie-in-the-eye television interview turned into an instant smash hit thanks to the practical joke.

INSIGHT

Paul Casanova, a catcher for the old Washington Senators during the 1960s, had a bad habit of dropping pop-ups. When someone asked him if he planned to make improvements in that area, he was ready with a witty reply. "This year I have a new strategy," Casanova said. "I am not going to close my eyes when I try to catch pop-ups."

LARRY "YOGI" BERRA

Hall-of-Famer Larry "Yogi" Berra, who played for the New York Yankees and managed the Yankees and the New York Mets, was not only one of the game's greatest hitting catchers, but also one of baseball's funniest guys. His wacky remarks, side-splitting stories, and nutty exploits are definitely of funny Hall-of-Fame caliber.

Food For Thought

When one of Yogi's favorite restaurants started to attract too many customers, Berra stopped patronizing it. When someone asked him about the restaurant, Yogi said, "Nobody goes there anymore. It's too crowded."

Eye Sore

Yogi was at spring training in Florida one summer when something weird happened during a rain delay. Two streakers jumped over the center-field fence and ran buck naked across the infield. When Berra went home that night, his wife asked him about the incident. "Were the streakers boys or girls?" she asked Yogi. "I don't know," he replied. "They had bags over their heads."

Home Boy

When Yogi Berra was the manager of the New York Yankees, he was interviewed at the start of the season. "I love home openers," Yogi said, "whether they're at home or on the road."

A Swinging Guy

In 1982, the New York Yankees managed by Yogi Berra had difficulty hitting home runs. In fact, during one stretch of 28 games the Yankee club clouted a total of only 14 home runs. Explaining his team's lack of power at the plate to the press, Yogi Berra said, "We're swinging at too many bad balls; that's why we're not hitting home runs." When a reporter on hand mentioned that Yogi himself was notorious for swinging at bad balls during his playing career, Yogi was quick to respond. "Yeah," snapped Berra, "but I hit 'em!"

YO! BROTHER

In 1934, Dizzy's brother Paul "Daffy" Dean was also a member of the St. Louis Cardinals pitching staff. In September of that year, the Dean brothers were scheduled to appear on the mound in a doubleheader against the Brooklyn Dodgers. Dizzy Dean pitched the first game of the doubleheader. Going into the eighth inning, Dizzy was hurling a no-hitter. However, in the last two innings Dizzy gave up three hits but still easily won the game.

Daffy Dean took the mound for the second game and turned in a dazzling pitching performance. He bested his brother's three-hitter by hurling a no-hitter for the win. After the second game ended, Dizzy ran out to congratulate Daffy. As the brothers shook hands, Dizzy asked, "Why didn't you tell me you were going to pitch a no-hitter? Then I would have pitched one too!"

A Bit Hit

One day the St. Louis Gas House Gang took on an opposing team that had a weak pitching staff. After four straight St. Louis players were issued walks, the starting pitcher was yanked from the game. The next pitcher walked two more Cardinals players and hit the next two batters with pitched balls. The ninth batter in the order, pitcher Dizzy

Dean, then stepped up to the plate. Dean swung at the first pitch and dribbled the ball back to the mound. The opposing hurler had trouble fielding the ball and Diz was safe at first. "A fine team I'm playing on," said Dizzy to the first-base coach. "It isn't enough that I do the pitching, I have to do the hitting, too."

Weather Vain

While broadcasting on the radio a baseball game that was held up by a thunderstorm, Dizzy had this to say to his listeners: "If you don't know why the game is being delayed," said Dean, "stick your head out of an open window."

COLORFUL

Baseballs have always been white. If Charlie Finley had gotten his way, that would not be so. Charlie once tried to have the game of baseball played with orange balls. He even started a company that produced orange baseballs.

THOUGHTLESS—
THE LEGENDARY BABE HERMAN

Babe Herman was a great hitter for the old Brooklyn Dodgers. However, Babe resented the fact that he was sometimes referred to as a talented, but goofy, player. "I'm a smart fella," Babe once told a reporter. "I read a lot of books. Go ahead. Ask me a question about anything."

The reporter thought for a minute. Finally, he said to Babe, "What do you think of the Napoleonic Era?"

"Ha!" scoffed Babe Herman. "It should have been scored a hit!"

Ah, Skip It

Babe Herman's wacky ways are legendary. Babe didn't like to report to spring training, so he seldom signed his yearly contract until the season was about to begin. Everyone thought Babe "held out" each year just to squeeze more money out of the Dodgers team, which might not have been the whole truth. A teammate once asked Babe, "Is it worth skipping spring training every year just to get a few more dollars?"

Wacky Babe Herman, the worst fielder in baseball, replied, "I don't do it for the money. The longer I stay out of training camp the less chance I have of getting hit by a fly ball."

All Hail Babe Herman

The stories about Babe Herman's blunders in the outfield are endless. Babe was a terrible fielder, but such a terrific hitter that he was one of manager Wilbert Robinson's favorite players. In fact, in Wilbert's eyes Babe could do no wrong. That sometimes irked other Dodger players, including pitcher Hollis Thurston and backup catcher Paul Richards.

One afternoon, the Dodgers were beating the Chicago Cubs when Chicago pitcher Kiki Cuyler stepped to the plate. As Thurston and Richards watched from the Dodgers bullpen in right field, Cuyler swung and lofted an easy fly ball down the right-field foul line. The right fielder should have caught it . . . but the right fielder was Babe Herman! Babe never saw the ball. In fact, he never moved until the ball hit the turf just inside the foul line. By the time Babe threw the ball in, Cuyler was standing on third base with a lucky triple.

When the inning ended, Hollis Thurston said to Paul Richards, "Let's walk to the bench and hear what Robinson says to Herman about the fly ball." The men were sure Babe was going to get bawled out.

When manager Wilbert Robinson saw Thurston and Richards approaching, he stepped out of the dugout and scowled at them. "Hey, you two!" he hollered. "What were you doing in the bullpen, sleeping? Why didn't you yell to Babe that Cuyler's hit was going to be a fair ball?"

Triple Trouble

Could Babe Herman hit! However, he didn't always think straight. One day the daffy outfielder came to the plate with the bases loaded and no outs. He quickly walloped a triple. Unfortunately for Babe and the Dodgers, the triple turned into a double play when Herman raced past two of his Brooklyn teammates on the base paths in his rush to reach third base. The runners he passed were declared out.

Bonk

Babe Herman was a terrible fielder who muffed countless catches of fly balls in the outfield. Still, he always tried to convince reporters he wasn't that bad a fielder. "If a fly ball ever hits me on the head, I'll quit the game of baseball forever," Babe promised.

"What if one hits you on the shoulder?" a reporter asked Babe.

"The shoulder?" replied Babe Herman. "That doesn't count."

Bogus Babe

During his heyday, Babe Herman was a well-known celebrity. However, for a short period of time an imposter made the rounds of New York restaurants and nightclubs claiming to be Babe. "Look," Babe Herman said to the press when asked about the imposter. "Showing up that fake is easy. Just take the guy out and hit him a fly ball. If the bum catches it, you know it ain't the real Babe Herman!"

HERMAN "GERMANY" OR "DUTCH" SCHAEFER

Herman "Germany" Schaefer played Major League baseball from 1901 to 1918. He was a member of the Washington Senators, the Chicago Cubs, the Detroit Tigers and the Cleveland Indians. At the time of World War I, when Germany as a country wasn't too popular, Herman Schaefer dropped his original nickname and called himself "Dutch" instead. No matter what name you call him, Germany Schaefer was one of the game's craziest clowns.

Hit or Be Missed

When Schaefer was playing second base for the Detroit Tigers, he entered the game as a pinch hitter. Since Germany wasn't known for his skill as a batter, the crowd booed. Schaefer turned toward the crowd and doffed his cap. "Ladies and gentlemen," he announced, "permit me to present Herman Schaefer, the world's greatest batsman. I will now demonstrate my hitting prowess."

Amazingly, Germany stepped up to the plate and clouted the next pitch for a home run. Germany raced down the line and slid into first base. He stood up and yelled, "At the quarter Schaefer leads by a head!" He then dashed toward second and slid into the base. He got up and shouted, "At the half, the great Herman Schaefer leads by a length." He ran and slid into third base. Germany jumped up. "Schaefer leads by a mile!" he yelled out as he ran for home. He slid into the plate and stood up. Germany Schaefer turned toward the crowd and made an announcement. "This concludes Herman Schaefer's afternoon performance," he bellowed. "The world's greatest batsman thanks you, one and all." He then trotted off the field.

FAMILY FUN

Someone asked catcher Joe Garagiola what Hall-of-Famer Stan Musial was really like. "Stan was a nice guy," Garagiola said. "Whenever I caught against him he'd step up to the plate and ask me about my family," Joe smiled and then continued, "But before I could answer he'd be on third base!"

Swan Song

Quick-witted commentator Joe Garagiola talks about a baseball team that was so bad that they had five runs scored against them during the National Anthem.

SAY, WHAT?

Frankie Frisch, the manager of the St. Louis Cardinals' famous Gas House Gang, knew how to have fun on the field. One day during a close contest, Frisch began to bug the home-plate umpire. Frankie complained to, yelled at, and badgered the ump inning after inning. However, the Cardinal skipper had enough sense not to do or say anything serious enough to get himself thrown out of the game. Finally, late in the game, Frisch shouted something to the ump from the St. Louis dugout. The umpire couldn't make out Frankie's remark. "What did you say, Frisch?" he yelled to the leader of the Gas House Gang.

"Hey," called Frankie Frisch, "you guessed at everything else today. See if you can guess what I just said." Frisch and his players roared in laughter.

"Okay, I will," shouted back the ump. "And for saying it you're out of the game, Frisch!" On the way to the locker room, Frankie Frisch didn't find anything humorous about the umpire's funny reply.

BUTT OUT

Umpire Frank Umont also had some hot exchanges with Earl Weaver. In 1969, Umont ejected the Baltimore skipper for smoking a cigar in the dugout before a game. The next day, Earl Weaver brought the team's lineup card to Frank Umont at home plate — with a candy cigarette dangling from his lips!

POOR GUYS

Texas Rangers outfielder Pete Incaviglia tried to make people believe Major League baseball players were not overpaid when he made this funny remark in 1990: "People think we make three or four million dollars a year," said Incaviglia. "They don't realize most of us make only $500,000!"

STOP IT

Baseball funny man Bob Uecker owns up to the fact that he wasn't much of a hitter during his playing days. Uecker claims manager Gene Mauch once said to him, "Get a bat and stop this rally!"

CLOUDING THE ISSUE

Outfield slugger Jackie Jensen of the Boston Red Sox launched base-balls into the clouds in the 1950s, but liked to keep his feet on the ground. Jensen was so afraid of airplane travel that he refused to fly to his team's away games. In fact, Jackie was so afraid of flying that he retired from baseball. He returned to the big leagues only after a year of therapeutic hypnosis, which cured his problem.

SHAME ON YOU!

Shortstop Johnny Logan, of the old Milwaukee Braves, was asked to pick his number-one Major League ballplayer of all time. Logan, who had a habit of mangling the English language, replied, "Well, I guess I'd have to go with the immoral Babe Ruth."

SEE YA

Major League baseball umpires have been the target of many wise-cracks over the years. Players argue with them. Managers and coaches complain about their calls. Even the fans criticize the men in blue. Way back in 1942, Gladys Gooding, the stadium organist at Ebbets Field, the home of the Brooklyn Dodgers, got into the act. As the umpires walked out on the field one day, Gladys played "Three Blind Mice."

THE PUPPET MASTER

In 1995, outfielder Andy Van Slyke, then a member of the Philadelphia Phillies, had a slight disagreement with a team mascot. In the heat of the moment, Van Slyke hit the mascot Bert from the children's television show "Sesame Street." Van Slyke thought the incident was forgotten until he stepped to the plate for a game in Pittsburgh a few days later. As soon as he appeared, the stadium organist began to play the popular "Sesame Street" theme as a gag.

DIFFERENT, BUT THE SAME

Casey Stengel was asked to compare second baseman Billy Martin of the New York Yankees to second baseman Nellie Fox of the Chicago White Sox. In his best Stengelese, Casey replied, "They're very much alike in a lot of similarities."

Mental Problem

Duke Snider, the great Dodger center fielder, loved to listen to Casey spout Stengelese. However, at one point it did cause him some concern. "I got to where I could understand Casey real well," said Snider. "That sort of worried me."

Three Tries

When Casey was the manager of the New York Mets, one of his players was Marvelous Marv Throneberry, a fan favorite who never became a great Major League player. However, the hapless Marv was almost as zany as Ol' Casey.

During the 1962 season, Throneberry came to the plate late in a game against the Chicago Cubs. There were two outs and the bases were loaded. When Marvelous Marv hit what appeared to be a game-winning triple, no one was more surprised or happier than Casey Stengel. Casey jumped up and down, and clapped and cheered. He was so busy celebrating that he never noticed that Marvelous Marv missed first base in his haste to get to third. However, almost everyone else in the ballpark noticed Marv's mistake, including the Cubs.

When the Cubs' pitcher tossed the ball to first base, Throneberry was called out. Stengel shot out of the dugout in a rage. He stalked up to the umpire and began to dispute the call.

"Calm down, Casey," said the ump. "Not only did he miss first, he missed second, too."

Casey, who was never at a loss for words, quickly fired back, "Well, I know damn well he didn't miss third. He's standing on it!"

Fired Up

Casey Stengel wasn't the type of guy to take complaints lying down. When the New York Yankees traded hurler Mickey McDermott, McDermott complained that manager Stengel never gave him enough chances to pitch. When Stengel heard about Mickey's remark, he was quick to reply in kind. "I noticed whenever anyone gave Mickey McDermott enough chances to pitch," said Casey, "a lot of managers got fired."

Wild Pitch

The "old perfessor" once said this about fastball pitcher Rex Barney of the Dodgers, who had difficulty throwing strikes: "He has the power to throw the ball through a wall," said Casey, "but you couldn't be quite sure which building."

KNOCKED OUT

Leo Durocher was famous for staging lengthy disputes with umpires. However, umpire George Magerkurth once got the best of Lippy Leo. During the course of an important game, manager Durocher was constantly complaining about Magerkurth's calls. Finally, the ump had enough. "One more word out of you, Durocher, and you're out of the game," the umpire threatened. Since Leo didn't want to get thrown out, he shut up.

A short time later, one of Durocher's players was called out by Magerkurth on a close play at first. Leo raced out of the dugout. Without saying a word, he grabbed his chnd shouted, "The runner is still out. And you, Durocher, whether you're dead or alive, you're out of the game, too!"

BILL VEECK

Bill Veeck was the P.T. Barnum of Major League baseball. As the owner of the old St. Louis Browns and the president of the Chicago White Sox, Veeck pulled off some of the wildest and funniest stunts in baseball history.

Veeck's Files And UFOs

In 1959, the UFO craze was sweeping the country. People everywhere were concerned about alien spacecraft and invaders from Mars. In Chicago, Bill Veeck was running the Chicago White Sox and used the lure of space aliens to stage a wild publicity stunt. On the 1959 roster of the White Sox were Nellie Fox and Luis Aparicio, two of the smallest players in the Major Leagues at the time. Bill Veeck arranged for "Martians" to land at the ballpark to kidnap Fox and Aparicio before the start of a game.

BATTY

Lefty Gomez was always a weak hitter at best. Nevertheless, he couldn't pass over a chance to talk about his prowess at the plate. He once said, "I tried to knock dirt out of my spikes with a bat the way the big hitters do, and I cracked myself in the ankle and broke a bone!"

Throwing The Bull

Late in his career, Lefty Gomez was traded to the Boston Braves, who were managed by Casey Stengel. "The trouble with you," Casey told Lefty, "is you're not throwing as hard as you used to."

"You're wrong," Gomez answered. "I'm throwing twice as hard, but the ball is only going half as fast."

MAD MAN

Al Hrabosky, who pitched for the Atlanta Braves in the 1980s, was often called the "Mad Hungarian"! Hrabosky earned his nickname by talking to himself during games and by stomping around the pitching mound like a man possessed.

HOT JOKE

One of former Major Leaguer Al Schacht's diamond tales deals with a conversation about baseball between Saint Peter and the Devil himself. The talk turned to who could field a better baseball team, and the two got into a heated debate. "Just remember," said St. Peter. "We've got guys like Babe Ruth, Lou Gehrig, and Roger Hornsby playing on our side."

The Devil nodded slyly. "True," he admitted. "But we've got all the umpires on our side."

ROYAL TREATMENT

When Dan Quisenberry was pitching for the Kansas City Royals, he watched in terror as his outfielders made a series of bad plays game after game. Finally, Quisenberry came up with a humorous suggestion for improving the Royals' outfield play. "Our fielders have to catch a lot of balls," said Quisenberry, "or at least deflect them so someone else can."

○ **329** ○

CAR SICK HUMOR

Satchel Paige never shied away from compliments or publicity, but a newspaper story about him once got him angry. The story appeared when Paige arrived in the Major Leagues in 1948. The article claimed that Satchel Paige owned a big, red car with the words "Satchel Paige, World's Greatest Pitcher" printed on its side.

"Now, that story isn't true," Satchel complained to his teammates. "I don't own a red car, it's maroon!"

MEAL TICKET

Cletus "Boots" Poffenberger spent most of his professional baseball career in the minor leagues. Nevertheless, Boots was one of the game's craziest characters. Once after he'd been called up from the minors to play for the Detroit Tigers, he checked into a fancy hotel. Poffenberger quickly dialed room service. "Send up the breakfast of champions," Boots said . . . and then clarified his statement by ordering six cold beers and a steak sandwich.

A STAR IS BORN

When Wes Ferrell was pitching for the Houston Astros in the Major

Leagues, he was a student of the stars. Ferrell believed in astrology and always tried to get his starting assignments on the mound to coincide with his astrological "lucky days."

WRITE THIS DOWN

Pitcher Larry Anderson of the San Diego Padres provided lots of comic relief for his team. He was on the bench one day when he turned to a teammate and asked, "How do you know when your pen runs out of invisible ink?"

FUNNY FOLLOWING

Max Patkin played in the minor leagues as a pitcher, but is best known in baseball circles for his zany clowning on the diamond. He once served as a "clown" coach for Bill Veeck's Cleveland Indians team.

Max's career as a diamond clown began by accident. Patkin was pitching in a service game in Honolulu against an Armed Forces team that included future Hall-of-Famer Joe DiMaggio. When DiMaggio

IF YOU LIKE MY PITCHING, YOU'LL LOVE MY CLOWN ACT!

clouted a homer, Max went crazy. He threw his glove down in disgust and stomped around the mound. Next, he twisted his cap so the brim faced sideways and contorted his face into wild expressions. As DiMaggio rounded the bases, Max Patkin took off after him. He followed Joe all the way home as the crowd laughed and applauded. And that's how Max Patkin's baseball clown act was born.

HEROIC FEET

Frank "Ping" Bodie was best known as the lonely roommate of New York Yankees star Babe Ruth. Babe spent so many nights out on the town that Ping once commented he "roomed with Babe Ruth's suitcase."

During a game in 1917, Bodie was thrown out by a wide margin while trying to steal a base. This prompted sports reporter Art Baer to write, "His heart was full of larceny, but his feet were honest."

You Make the Call

WALKS FROM THE PAST

The bases-loaded intentional walk is a rare case, but one such incident occured on July 23, 1944, when the Giants player-manager, Mel Ott, faced the Cubs and Bill Nicholson. The Cubs strongman had homered three times in the first game of the twinbill, and wound up with six homers in the series by the time Ott made his unusual move. Nicholson's hot streak pushed him by Ott for the league leadership for homers. All this set the stage, and in the second game of a doubleheader at the Polo Grounds, Ott, with a 10-7 lead in the eighth inning, gave Nicholson (who represented the go-abead run) a free pass with the bases loaded and two outs. Ott's logic was it's better to give up one run than four on a grand slam. For the record, the move worked, as the Giants held on to win, 12-10.

Legend has it that Hub Pruett walked Babe Ruth on purpose with the bases jammed on June 14, 1923, but reliable sources say this isn't true.

Nap Lajoie was actually the very first man to draw a bases loaded intentional walk. On May 23, 1901, the White Sox led the Athletics 11-7 in the ninth, but with the bases loaded and nobody out, player-manager Clark Griffith left the bench and became the relief pitcher.

At that point he decided to give the walk to Lajoie, who represented the tying run. Lajoie would hit over .400 that year, but had the bat taken out of his hands on that occasion. The decision to walk him paid off when Griffith got the next three batters. So, while the move is extremely rare, it has been done. Still, don't hold your breath waiting for the next time a manager pulls this tactic out of his cobwebbed bag of tricks.

BACK TO OTT

Ott, by the way, was no stranger to drawing walks. He drew five walks in a game four times during his career — a record that still stands. He also shares a record for coaxing seven straight walks over a three-day period in 1943. Additionally, from 1936 through 1942, he compiled 100-plus bases on balls, also an all-time big league record.

Then there was the time he drew six walks in a doubleheader. He was playing against the Phillies on October 5, 1929, and, as the season was winding down, he was shooting for the home run title. Chuck Klein of the Phillies was also trying to win that crown. So, Klein's manager, Burt Shooton, instructed his pitchers to pitch around Ott. Klein, in part thanks to the Shooton strategy, went on to lead the league in homers.

OTHER FACTORS

Will Clark, the right-handed first baseman, was 6 feet, 2 inches tall and weighed 205 pounds. Dodger manager Tommy Lasorda knew he could walk Clark since first base was open. That would set up a force play at every base and allow the bullpen to face the number-five hitter instead of Clark.

Lasorda had already decided he was sticking with his reliever Tom Niedenfuer. The big (6 feet, 5 inches; 225 pounds) righty had entered the game when starter Orel Hershiser got in a tough spot after recording just one out in a 3-run 7th inning for the Cards. Niedenfuer was 7-9 out of the bullpen. He had 19 saves and an earned run average of 2.71 on the season.

Lasorda's dilemma was to issue a walk to Clark or to have Niedenfuer go right at Clark to secure the final out.

Keep in mind three final bits of information: First, Niedenfuer had absorbed the loss in the fifth game of the NLCS just two days earlier. In that game, he had surrendered a 9th-inning game-winning home run to Ozzie Smith, of all people. Smith was just starting to shed his "good glove, no stick" label in 1985, but even then he had hit just six regular-season homers.

Second, the Dodger reliever had already whiffed Clark to help calm down a St. Louis uprising in the 7th inning. If he had Clark's number, it might be best to defy common strategic practice and pitch to Clark.

Third, if the Dodgers gave Clark a walk, the next batter they'd have to face would be a lefty, the 24-year-old outfielder Andy Van Slyke, coming off a .259, 13 home run, 55 RBI season.

In such a situation, what would your call be?

The Actual Call And Results

Lasorda felt they could get Clark out. If your call was to walk Clark, you can gloat since Clark teed off on the very first pitch, jacking it out of the park for a pennant-winning home run. The Dodgers did have three outs left, but they were dead, going out one-two-three in the bottom of the ninth.

Incidentally, according to one version of this story, Lasorda instructed his reliever to pitch carefully to Clark, giving him an "unintentional-intentional walk." Still, a straightforward order for an intentional pass seems to have been the proper call.

While Lasorda's call took a lot of nerve, it also certainly went against the book. When you make such a call and things work out, you look like a genius. However, you wear the goat's horns when the call backfires.

TO HOLD OR NOT TO HOLD

Assume a runner is taking a lead off first base in a situation that seems to call for a stolen base. Also assume the runner does not possess the blazing speed of Brian Hunter, but he is a pretty good runner, definitely a threat to run, considering the game situation.

If your team is on defense, you might consider calling for a pitchout. You'd have the pitcher blister a high fastball way out of the strike zone, giving the catcher a ball he can handle easily. This strategy allows the catcher a great shot at gunning down the potential base burglar, especially since the pitchout gets the catcher out of his deep crouch.

Now, here's the question. Do you instruct your pitcher to hold the runner just a bit looser in such a situation? In other words, does the pitcher try not to tip off the runner that a play is on? In effect, does he encourage the man on first to run, almost enticing him, since you feel the catcher will fire the runner out. Is this wise?

Answer: Most managers would say you don't do anything special in this case. Rick Sutcliffe, winner of the Cy Young Award, once said, "You throw a normal pitch [a fastball with your normal delivery] to the plate. You glance at the runner with peripheral vision, but you do not hold him less closely."

According to Sutcliffe, the only thing that is different is that you don't throw over to the first baseman in an obvious attempt to hold the runner. So, you allow the runner his normal lead, but you make absolutely no pick-off moves when the pitchout is on. Pretty basic stuff, actually.

RUTH'S WORLD SERIES LARCENY

It's the 9th inning of the seventh game of the 1926 World Series. Today's winner will be the new world champion. The St. Louis Cardinals are leading the New York Yankees by a score of 3-2. You are the Yanks skipper, Miller Huggins, winner of 91 regular-season games.

Despite all that success, you are down to your last out. But all is not lost yet — Babe Ruth is on first base after drawing a walk. The game is still alive. If the "Bambino" could reach second base, he'd be in scoring position. A single could tie it up. Not only that, the batter now in the box is your cleanup hitter, Bob Meusel, and Lou Gehrig is on deck.

Meusel missed part of the season with a broken foot, but he still drove in 81 runs. Gehrig, meanwhile, had 83 extra base hits in 1926, his second full season in the majors. As for Ruth, he had swiped 11 bases during the season and was considered a pretty good base runner in his day.

Final Factors

The St. Louis pitcher was Grover Cleveland Alexander. Although he would come back in 1927 to post a stellar 21-10 record, the 39-year-old Alexander was on the downside of his career. He had pitched a complete-game victory just the day before our classic situation unfolded. Baseball lore states he had celebrated the win by going out on the town that evening . . . and into the morning. They say he didn't even witness the events prior to being called into the game because he was by then sleeping soundly in the bullpen.

Now, having worked flawlessly for 2 innings prior to the walk to Ruth, the game was on the line. He peered in to get the signal from his catcher, Bob O'Farrell, who had a .976 career fielding percentage.

Armed with all the data, what would you have done if you were in charge? Call for a hit-and-run play? Do nothing and let Meusel swing away? Have Meusel take a strike (not swing at a pitch until Alexander throws a strike)? This last would show whether Alexander was getting wild and/or tired; after all, he had just walked Ruth. Would you have Ruth steal to get into scoring position? Any other ideas?

What Happened

Ruth took his lead. Alexander fired a pitch, and Ruth, who had stolen a base the day before, took off for second. O'Farrell's throw beat Babe easily as St. Louis player-manager Roger Hornsby applied the tag. The Series was over with the Yankees losing on a daring play that most experts felt was also a very foolish play.

Accounts of the game indicate that Huggins actually had Meusel hitting away and did not have Ruth running. The story goes that Ruth was running on his own, a terrible blunder. Few, if any, managers would have had Ruth running — it was way too risky.

DISTRACTION

At the Major League level, do managers and players employ tactics that work at the level of American Legion ball? Specifically, if you were a catcher, could you distract an opposing batter by pounding your mitt in an effort to trick him? The batter, hearing the sound coming from the mitt, can tell where the catcher is holding the glove. Presumably, he is telling the pitcher where he wants the pitch thrown.

The reality is that managers don't spend time teaching such tactics, but some players say you can distract or play mind games with your opponent. The story goes that one catcher used to toss dirt and pebbles into a batter's spikes to annoy him. Similarly, Yogi Berra was infamous for making small talk with a hitter in an effort to ruin his concentration. Remember when Hank Aaron responded to Berra's ploys by saying he was in the batter's box to hit, not chatter?

Mark Grace, an All-Star first baseman with the Chicago Cubs said, "Pounding the glove can work. It can distract you. It puts a thought in your mind. For example, the pitcher went inside with the last pitch, and the catcher is pounding the glove inside again. It can make you think. It's a mind game, but it doesn't stay in the mind too long." With a good hitter like Grace, once the pitch is on the way, such annoyances disappear, and the batter is set to hit.

Grace added that one thing that works for sure and is quite distracting is sheer intimidation. "It works for a pitcher," he stated. "That's what chin music is all about. A Nolan Ryan or a Dwight Gooden throws tight and sends a message: 'Don't dig in!'"

WHERE DO YOU BAT HIM?

Imagine you're at the helm of a pennant-winning team, and you're about to play the fourth game of the World Series. Would you consider batting your starting pitcher somewhere other than the traditional number-nine slot in the lineup?

Answer: You might, if the pitcher were George Herman Ruth. Babe Ruth left the ranks of pitchers after 1919, although he did pitch in five scattered contests after that. He became a pretty fair hitter, with a .342 lifetime batting average and 714 homers.

Actually, he was a fine hitter even while pitching — why do you suppose his manager moved him to the outfield full-time? In the last two seasons in which he spent a significant time on the mound (1918 and 1919) he was used as an outfielder in 59 and 111 games respectively. He hit 11 homers in 1918, then 29 the following year. Both totals were good enough to lead the American League. He also drove in 66 runs, followed by 114 runs.

So, with all that in mind, it's not so shocking to learn that in 1918 (his 11-homer year), in his final Series outing as a pitcher, he hit in the sixth spot for the Boston Red Sox. This marked the only time in World Series history that a starting hurler appeared any place but ninth in the batting order.

The Outcome

The Sox skipper, Ed Barrow, made a good call. Although Ruth grounded out early in the game, he tripled-in two of Boston's three runs. In his final at bat, he sacrificed. Meanwhile, the man who did hit in the ninth spot was a catcher by the name of Sam Agnew. He went 0 for 2 after hitting .166 on the year.

On the mound, Ruth worked 8 innings, got in trouble in the ninth, was relieved, then moved to the outfield as the Sox held on to win, 3-2. Boston also went on to win the Series 4 games to 2. By the way, during this game, Ruth's streak of 29⅔ consecutive scoreless innings (a record at the time) came to an end.

QUICK QUIZ

Do managers normally try to steal home in a situation like this? The runner on third can be anyone you choose. If you'd like, select Ty Cobb, who stole home an all-time record 50 times during his illustrious career. (Who wouldn't like that prospect?)

Now, does it matter if the batter is a lefty or righty as long as you have the fiery Cobb barreling down the line as soon as the pitcher commits to throwing the ball to the plate?

Answer: Yes, it matters. Most managers feel they'd definitely prefer a right-handed batter in the box when they attempt a steal of home. Back in the 1940s, Jackie Robinson was known to have done it with a lefty in the batter's box, but he was special.

Incidentally, stealing home was rather common in the Cobb era, a dead-ball era in which you'd scratch for runs any way you could come by them.

Lately, swiping home is a rarity. Wade Boggs, a sure future Hall of Famer, says that nowadays you just don't see it done. "It's probably a lost art. Mostly it's done now with first and third. The guy on first takes off, then the guy on third takes off."

Nevertheless, when an attempt to steal home does occur, you still don't want a lefty at bat. A left-hander stands in the batter's box to the right of the catcher. Conversely, a right-handed hitter stands on the left side of the catcher.

What's the logic involved here? Kevin Stocker of the Tampa Bay Devil Rays explained, "If you're on the right side of the plate, and you're straight stealing, the catcher can see the runner coming and has no one to go around." In other words, there's nothing obstructing his tag.

Or, as Atlanta Braves manager Bobby Cox, perennial winner of division titles, put it, "You want the batter in the right hander's box to help block out the catcher." A righty obstructs the catcher's view of the runner dashing down the line. The catcher may not realize a play is on until it is too late to do anything about it.

There was once a runner who stole home standing up. This happened because the pitcher threw a pitch that was so wild, the catcher was only able to grab it after lunging out of the line of action. Thus, he couldn't even come close to tagging the runner.

WHEN A CATCH IS OR ISN'T A CATCH

In 1991, Triple-A minor leaguer Rodney McCray was roaming the outfield for Louisville. On a long smash, McCray actually ran through a panel of the right-field fence near the 369-foot marker. David Justice called this the most amazing thing he had ever seen on a diamond. Justice was in awe of McCray's courage. "At some point he had to know that he had been running for quite a long time." Bone-jarring impact was inevitable.

Clearly McCray made a spectacular catch, hauling the ball in on the dead run under those circumstances. Or did he make the catch?

What's the ruling on this play? Is it illegal because he caught the ball but left the field of play because of his momentum?

The rule book states that, in order for a play to be a catch, the fielder has to have complete possession of the ball. In addition, the release of the ball must be voluntary, as opposed to, say, dropping the ball. Had McCray dropped the ball as a result of his impact with the fence, it would not have been a catch. As it was, the catch counted, and McCray became an instant hit on highlight films.

GREAT CATCH

A similar play took place on May 3, 1998, in Three Rivers Stadium in Pittsburgh. Turner Ward of the Pirates puffed a "McCray" when he crashed through the right-field wall after making his superb catch. Ward, who hurt his arm on the play, came back through the wall like a pro wrestler dramatically entering the ring. Then he short-armed the ball to a teammate.

SACRIFICIAL PLAYERS

Imagine that Bernie Williams of the Yankees is at the plate with a runner on third and nobody out. Williams powers the ball to deep left field where Barry Bonds races for the catch. Realizing the runner from third will easily score on the sacrifice fly, Bonds lets the ball hit his glove, but instead of securing the catch, he begins to bobble the ball. In a weird sort of juggling act, he continues to bounce the ball in and out of his glove while running towards the plate.

When he finally gets to very shallow left field, nearing the short-stop position, he lets the ball settle into his glove. The runner from third knows he can't tag up now, and he stays at third.

Is the Bonds trick legal?

What Bonds did will count as a legal catch. The runner from third, though, was foolish. The rules say you can tag up the moment the ball touches the fielder's glove, not when it is actually caught. If this play really had happened, both the runner and third-base coach would have been ripped by the manager and the media as well.

QUICK QUIZ

Here are umpiring situations that come up from time to time. You make the quick calls on these relatively simple situations.

1. A ball is rolling in foul territory between home plate and first base. Before a fielder touches it, the ball hits a pebble and rolls back into fair ground where it comes to a stop.

Fair or foul?

2. Roberto Alomar hits a Baltimore chop; the ball hits home plate before it takes its first high hop. He beats the play out at first.

Is this a single or a foul ball for hitting the plate?

3. A grounder trickles through the right side of the infield, just inside the first base line. It barely eludes Will Clark of the Texas Rangers. In frustration Clark turns, takes off his mitt, and fires the glove at the ball. The mitt strikes the glove, causing it to roll foul near the right-field stands.

Make your call.

ANSWERS:

1. The ball is fair. The decision depends on where the ball comes to a halt. On slow-moving balls in foul territory, fielders always hustle to touch the ball before it can roll back into fair territory. This kills the play, avoiding a cheap single.

2. Contrary to what many fans believe, the plate is in fair territory. Give Alomar a hit.

3. The penalty for hitting a fair ball with a thrown glove is three bases for the batter. Any runners on board at the time also are awarded three bases. If Clark's mitt had struck a thrown ball, the punishment would have been two bases.

FOLLOW THE BOUNCING BALL

On May 26, 1993, as Texas was playing the Cleveland Indians, a long fly ball off the bat of Carlos Martinez headed towards Jose Canseco. The not-so-hot-with-the-glove Canseco caught up to the ball, but he didn't catch it. In fact, the ball actually hit him on the head before soaring over the right-field fence.

Was it a ground-rule double or a homer?

The umpires that day ruled correctly that it was a (highly embarrassing) home run.

MORE BOUNCES

Back in 1993, Damon Buford was in the Orioles batter's box facing pitcher Matt Young. A pitch to Buford hit the ground and bounced up towards the plate. Buford didn't care that it one-hopped its way to the strike zone; he swung and hit a comebacker to Young. When Young lobbed the ball to first, Buford was ruled out.

Did the umpire blow this call? Should it have been a dead ball and no pitch?

Answer: The call was correct. Herb Score, a 20-game winner in 1956, said he once "threw one up to the plate that bounced, and the batter swung and hit a home run." Even if a batter is hit by a pitch that hits the dirt first, it counts. Such a runner would be given first base.

LITTLE LEAGUE CALL

Kids and even some Little League umpires seem to foul up the next situation. Let's say a batter hits a grounder to shortstop. The hitter beats the play out by a half step. His momentum carries him several strides down the right-field line. He then makes a slow turn to his left, towards second base. The first baseman is still holding the ball. Seeing the runner make his little turn, the first baseman tags the runner, claiming that if you veer at all towards second base you are in effect running there, giving up your right to saunter safely back to first base.

Is the defensive player correct in his logic?

No. This is a common fallacy of baseball. It doesn't matter which way the runner turns when coming back to first base as described. The only time you can tag out the runner is when he turns to his left and makes an actual attempt to go to second.

THE WAITING GAME

With no runners on base, Angels fireballing reliever Troy Percival came into a game to face the Baltimore Orioles. Percival, in a less dramatic version of Al "The Mad Hungarian" Hrabosky, went behind the mound to gather his thoughts. The home-plate umpire timed Percival, said he violated a delay of game rule, and called an automatic ball on him.

Can this happen?

Yes. The rule states that with no men on base, a pitcher has just 20 seconds to deliver a pitch. Thus, the relief pitcher was behind in the count, 1 and 0, before even throwing a pitch.

The umpires probably invoked this little-known rule because Percival is notorious for such tactics. The Orioles manager, Ray Miller, said of the relief pitcher, "This guy warms up, nervous as hell, walks around the mound, says prayers, bows behind the mound, looks over the center-field fence, and everything else. They got tired of it and called ball one."

MORE DELAYS

Albert Belle, Baltimore's volatile former slugger is at the plate. Let's say he gets irate over a strike call you, the umpire, just made. He starts to jaw with you. After a few moments, you get fed up with the delay and tell Belle to get in the box and quit squawking.

What do you do if Belle refuses to obey your orders?

In this case, you would order the man on the mound to pitch the ball. As a punishment, you would call that pitch a strike even if it isn't in the strike zone. In addition, if the batter still refuses to step in and face the pitcher, every subsequent pitch is ruled a strike until the recalcitrant batter whiffs.

In real life, this happened to Frank Robinson after he argued about a called strike two. Moments later, the umpire called strike three, and the future Hall of Famer had lost the battle and the war.

WHEN A NON-PITCHER COMMITTED A BALK

In May of 1984, Jerry Remy was playing second base for the Boston Red Sox when he caused a balk. Not only that, he did it without even touching the ball!

Here is how it happened: Marty Castillo of the Detroit Tigers had just doubled. The Sox felt he had missed first base and were about to make an appeal play. Remy thought there was a chance that the Boston pitcher, lefty Bruce Hurst, would overthrow the ball. Since it never hurts to back up a play, Remy positioned himself behind first base in foul ground.

Although the appeal was denied, a strange play resulted. The Tigers requested a balk call because Remy's actions, they argued, violated Rule 4.02, which states that all players other than the catcher must be in fair territory when a ball is in play. The umpires agreed with the Tigers' contention and charged Hurst with a bizarre balk. That's a clear case of an almost innocent bystander being victimized. Ultimately though, according to the rules, Hurst must take the responsibility.

AN EASY HOMER

On July 1, 1997, the Astrodome was the site of yet another crazy play. The Houston Astros were playing the Cleveland Indians. Traditionally, these two teams wouldn't meet during the regular season because they are in different leagues. However, due to interleague play, they were squaring off.

Each park has its own ground rules, so players need to know the quirks of the ballpark. Not knowing such rules cost the Indians a home run. Manny Ramirez, often accused of having a short attention span, was in right field when a Tim Bogar bouncer rolled down the first base line. Ramirez saw the ball come to rest under the Houston bullpen bench, and he waved to an umpire that the ball was out of play.

The only problem was that the bench was, in fact, in play. First base umpire Charlie Reliford gestured that the ball was still alive. Ramirez's hesitation and lack of knowledge gave Bogar time to circle the bases with an easy inside-the-park home run.

The Last Pitch

SCREEN PLAY

Some tricky third basemen run their own version of a screen-play when a runner is at third in a sacrifice-fly situation. Knowing the runner must wait until he sees the outfielder snag the ball before he can tag up, a wily third baseman might purposely get his body in such a position as to block the view of the runner. If the runner can't see the exact moment of the catch, he'll be a second or so slower at leaving the base and, thus, a step or two slower reaching home.

RED HOT CHILI

In 1995, Sandy Alomar's backup catcher, Tony Pena, and Dennis Martinez recreated one of the most famous trick plays ever. The first time this bit of deception took place was during the 1972 World Series. The Oakland A's were in a situation in which an intentional walk to Johnny Bench made sense. They went through the motions, but at the last second they fired strike three past the befuddled Bench.

Actually, World Series-bound Cleveland did the A's one better — they got away with it on two occasions. Pena and Martinez cooked up the play on their own. Alomar recalled: "Dennis was struggling, and he needed a play to get out of an inning. He had thrown a lot of pitches, and it was a perfect situation to do it. It was a smart play. It worked on Chili Davis who was very upset about it. They did it one time to John Olerud."

It seems incredible that this play could work twice in a season in this day and age when highlights are constantly played and replayed on television. Alomar concurred, "If I'm a player for a different team, I guarantee you I see that on ESPN, and they wouldn't get me."

JETER APPROVES

The 1996 American League Rookie of the Year, Derek Jeter, was asked what trick plays he's seen that were interesting or unusual. Without skipping a beat, the Yankee shortstop responded, "Tony LaRussa batting the pitcher eighth over there in St. Louis — that's a little different!"

Arguments aside about whether or not this is actually a trick play, he's right. On July 9, 1998, when he penciled his starter in at the number-eight spot, LaRussa made Todd Stottlemyre the first big league pitcher in twenty years to bat anywhere but last in the order. Although Stottlemyre did hit .236 the previous season, there was another reason for the strategy. At first, some fans thought LaRussa was doing this because the man who did bat ninth, Placido Polanco, might be a weak hitter. Also, Polanco was making just his second major league start.

Fans and writers recalled that the last pitcher to hit higher than ninth was Philadelphia's Steve Carlton on June 1, 1979. In that case, it was true that Carlton was often a bigger threat with the bat than, say, Bud Harrelson, who hit ninth when Carlton was in the number-eight spot.

After much speculation, the truth came out. LaRussa revealed that his motive for the move was to get more men on base ahead of the heart of the lineup. Not a bad thought, especially when the aorta of that heart is big Mark McGwire, who was in the midst of chasing Roger Maris and the single-season home run record of 61.

Said the St. Louis manager, "I don't see how it doesn't make sense for the ninth-place hitter to be a legitimate hitter. This gives us a better shot to score runs. It's an extra guy on base in front of Ray Lankford, Mark McGwire, and Brian Jordan. The more guys who are on base, the less they'll be able to pitch around Mark."

LaRussa said he first conceived of the scheme at the All-Star break and that it "doesn't have anything to do with the pitcher." Nothing, that is, except get his weak bat out of the way and allow a real hitter in the ninth spot to become, in effect, an additional leadoff hitter in front of McGwire and Company.

A logical question for LaRussa, then, was why not just drop McGwire to the cleanup position so he could always have three bona fide hitters preceding him. However, LaRussa said that because McGwire hits third, he come to the plate in the 1st inning of every game, a big advantage in LaRussa's book.

LAME TRICK

Many baseball fans feel the trick play in which the pitcher fakes a throw towards the runner off third base, then swivels, fire and tries to pick off the runner from first is lame. Somehow, though, it succeeded in 1998.

On the last day in June, the Oakland A's were hosting the San Diego Padres. Entering the top of the ninth, Oakland was clinging to a 12-8 lead. Two outs later, the Padres were rallying. They had scored two runs. Now they had a runner at third with the tying run on first.

With a 2-and-2 count on Mark Sweeney, A's catcher Mike Macfarlane gave reliever Mike Fetters the sign to put on a special pick-off move. Fetters, however, was confused — he had spent the last six years with the Milwaukee Brewers and momentarily mixed up their signals with those of the A's.

So Macfarlane waved his hand in the direction of first, then third to indicate what he wanted. Even after all of that blatant gesturing, Padres runner Ruben Rivera was caught snoozing. Eventually, the rookie Rivera was tagged out trying to make it to second base.

A's manager Art Howe was thinking along the lines of Tony Pena when he called his trick play. "It just didn't seem like anybody was going to make an out, so I said, 'Let's manufacture one,'" commented Howe.

The play was especially mortifying for several reasons. For example, it's foolish to do anything risky (or not pay attention) on the bases in such a situation. After all, this play ended the game and gave the A's a win. Not only that, Rivera was in the game for his running skills — the Padres had just put him in moments earlier as a pinch runner.

Oakland's Jason Giambi observed, "You know the old theory about that play never working? Well, it did today."

THE 300 CLUB

Certain numbers have a magical quality in baseball. For example, as a rule, if a hitter connects for 500 homers, he's headed for the Hall of Fame. For pitchers, making it into the 300-Win Club — a highly exclusive circle of stars — is a coveted goal. Has a pitcher ever managed to lose 300 games?

Answer: Yes, and ironically the man to lose the most games in big league history (313 to be precise) is the same man whose name graces the trophy that personifies pitching excellence — Cy Young. So the award given for pitching excellence actually has its origin with the game's biggest loser. Of course, to be fair, Young also won a staggering 511 games, the most ever in the annals of the game. The next highest win total is nearly 100 less than that — Walter Johnson's 416 victories.

By the way, the only other man to drop 300 decisions was an obscure pitcher from the late nineteenth century named Pud Galvin. This right-hander made it to the Hall of Fame, as did Young. Galvin pitched only 14 years, yet he won 361 games and had such unusual numbers as a 46-29 won-lost record in 1883 and 46-22 the next season.

Imagine, he won 92 games in just two years — that's four and a half to five years' worth of toil for a good pitcher today. Of course, his 51 losses over that two-year span would also take quite a few years for a good pitcher to reach today.

BETTER THAN PERFECT

This question involves a very famous game that took place in the 1950s. Did a pitcher ever throw a perfect game that went beyond 9 innings?

Answer: Even though the above question seems to give away the answer, this question, like a Gaylord Perry pitch, is loaded. While it's true Harvey Haddix threw a perfect game that went into the 13th inning back in 1959, a bizarre ruling by baseball officials in 1991 took away his perfect game status. The rule states that in order for a pitcher to get credit for a no-hitter, he must pitch 9 innings and pitch the whole game (including the innings beyond the ninth) without surrendering a hit. Therefore, what most experts agree was the most perfect game ever is not recognized as such.

Here's what happened on that historic night. Haddix, a diminutive lefty for the Pirates, was perfect through 12 innings against the Milwaukee Braves. Felix Mantilla led off the 13th and reached base on a throwing error by Pirates third baseman Don Hoak. Eddie Mathews then sacrificed the runner to scoring position. That prompted

Pittsburgh manager Danny Murtaugh to issue an intentional walk to the dangerous Hank Aaron, setting up a double play.

Pandemonium ensued when Joe Adcock homered. But, due to yet another baseball rule, he only received credit for a double. The reason he was robbed of a home run isn't quite as bizarre as the ruling that hurt Haddix, however. Aaron saw the ball soaring deep and figured it would drop near the fence, so he touched second base, but he never bothered to go to third. As Adcock rounded the bags and touched third base, he was technically guilty of passing a runner and, therefore, received credit for two bases, not four. Adcock also received just one run batted-in instead of three.

MARTINEZ ALSO ROBBED

In 1995, Montreal Expos pitcher Pedro Martinez also got ripped off by the new no-hitter rule. Facing the Padres, he was perfect through 9 innings. Shortly thereafter, when Bip Roberts doubled to lead off the tenth, the perfect game was gone. Martinez then gave way to closer Mel Rojas, who retired the last three batters. The expos went on to win a 1-0 classic.

ROSTER

Aaron, Hank, 95–96, 130, 182, 186, 215, 223–224, 297, 340, 359
Abbott, Glenn, 102
Adcock, Joe, 359
Agee, Tommie, 184
Agnew, Sam, 108, 342
Aguilera, Rick, 262
Akin, Roy, 22
Alexander, Grover Cleveland, 107–108, 338-339
Allen, Dick, 59, 167
Alomar, Roberto, 346-347, 353-354
Alou, Moises, 224
Altrock, Nick, 77
Anderson, Bob, 16
Anderson, Larry, 311-312, 331
Anderson, Sparky, 77–78, 119, 169, 207
Aparicio, Luis, 327
Appling, Luke, 29–30, 184, 266–268
Ashburn, Richie, 45, 194
Assenmacher, Paul, 223
Ausmus, Brad, 202
Averill, Earl, 17–19

Baer, Art, 332
Baker, Dusty, 103–104

Banks, Ernie, 43
Barker, Len, 186
Barney, Rex, 326
P.T. Barnum, 327
Barrett, Marty, 117
Barrow, Ed, 108, 341
Bavasi, Buzzi, 171
Baylor, Don, 116, 166, 207
Beck, Walter "Boom-Boom", 33–34, 82
Bench, Johnny, 118, 213, 353
Bell, George, 264
Bell, Jay, 160
Belle, Albert, 128, 236, 350
Bench, Johnny, 213, 355
Bentley, Jack, 193
Berra, Yogi, 28–29, 65–67, 170, 186, 211, 241, 296, 312-314, 340
Bevington, Terry, 168
Bichette, Dante, 170, 171
Biittner, Larry, 210–211
Blaeholder, George, 248
Blowers, Mike, 226
Blue, Vida, 72, 102
Blyleven, Bert, 171
Bochtler, Doug, 236
Bodie, Frank "Ping", 332
Bogar, Tim, 352
Boggs, Wade, 109, 343
Boisclair, Bruce, 210–211

Bonds, Barry, 103, 150, 185, 224, 345
Boudreau, Lou, 243, 287, 294
Boyer, Clete, 127–128
Bradley, Alva, 294
Bradley, Scott, 153
Brede, Brent, 103
Brenley, Bob, 9
Brett, George, 168, 185
Briscoe, Robert, 211
Bristol, Dave, 31–32
Brock, Lou, 183, 203
Brown, Bobby, 145
Brown, Clint, 281
Browning, Tom, 186
Bruton, Bill, 137, 191
Buckner, Bill, 204
Buford, Damon, 348
Buhl, Bob, 44
Buhner, Jay, 63–64
Burnett, John, 282
Burrell, Stanley, see Hammer, M. C.
Busch, August, 172
Byrne, Tommy "Wild Man", 123

Cain, Bob, 233
Calderon, Ivan, 158
Campaneris, Bert, 198
Candiotti, Tom, 200–201

Roster

Canseco, Jose, 132, 152, 185, 347

Cantillon, Joe, 46

Caraway, Pat, 309

Carbo, Bernie, 77–78

Carlisle, Walter, 22–23

Carlton, Steve, 169, 355

Carson, Al, 22

Carson, Johnny, 180

Carter, Gary, 158, 206

Cartwright, Alexander Joy, 96–98, 302–304

Casanova, Paul, 312

Casey, Hugh, 155

Castillo, Frank, 209

Castillo, Marty, 351

Cavarretta, Phil, 99

Cedeno, Cesar, 204

Chambliss, Chris, 119

Chance, Dean, 58

Chapman, Ray, 37

Charlton, Norm, 90

Chozen, Harry, 21—22

Cissell, Billy, 282

Clark, Jack, 106

Clark, Peter P., 48–49

Clark, Will, 162–163, 335-336, 346-347

Clemens, Roger, 213, 225

Clemente, Roberto, 200

Cobb, Ty, 34–36, 39–40, 87, 109, 183, 230, 257, 268-269, 283, 342

Cockrell, Alan, 87

Coleman, Choo-Choo, 197

Coleman, Jerry, 123

Coleman, Vince, 14–15, 154, 186, 203

Concepcion, Dave, 118

Cone, David, 159, 186

Conigliaro, Tony, 172

Cooper, Cecil, 125

Corrales, Pat, 202

Correll, Vic, 31

Cosgrove, Mike, 101

Cotto, Henry, 151

Cox, Bobby, 110, 207, 343

Craig, Roger, 19–20

Cramer, Doc, 23–24

Crawford, Sam, 257

Cromartie, Warren, 132

Cruz, Victor, 134

Cuyler, Kiki, 317

Dalkowski, Steve, 246–248

Darling, Gary, 154

Darling, Ron, 226

Dark, Alvin, 16, 102

Davis, Gerry, 202

Davis, Chili, 212-213, 22, 354

Davis, Mike, 127–128

Dawson, Andre, 190–191

Dean, Jay Hanna "Dizzy", 68–69, 149, 152, 167, 173, 314-315

Dean, Paul "Daffy", 314-315

Delsing, Jim, 234

Daulton, Darren, 150, 164

Deer, Rob, 121–122

Delmore, Vic, 15–16

Delsing, Jim, 84

DeMuth, Dana, 154

Dent, Bucky, 57–58

DeShields, Delino, 103

Dickey, Bill, 155, 174, 255–256

Didier, Bob, 10

Dietrich, Bill "Bullfrog", 257–258

Dietz, Dick, 133

DiMaggio, Joe, 42, 155, 161, 174, 226, 230, 234, 255256, 296, 297–300, 331

Dorish, Harry, 111

Doubleday, Abner, 96–98, 302–304

Drabek, Doug, 163

Drabowsky, Moe, 60

Dressen, Charlie, 166

Drysdale, Don, 50–51, 133, 186, 279

Ducey, Rob, 264

Durante, Sal, 93

Durham, Ray, 202, 235

Durocher, Leo "The Lip", 68, 88, 149, 166, 326-327

Dykes, Jimmy, 258

Dykstra, Lenny, 163

Eckersley, Dennis, 280

Eichhorn, Mark, 41

Elway, John, 216

Erickson, Scott, 121–122

Ennis, Del, 45, 58

Evans, Billy, 21

Evans, Darrell, 230

Eyre, Scott, 236

Roster

Franco, John, 280
Feeney, Charles S., 32
Feeney, Chub, 118
Felder, Mike, 125–126
Feller, Bob, 85, 231–233, 254, 276, 284–290, 291, 296
Ferrell, Wesley, 281, 330-331
Fetters, Mike, 356
Fidrych, Mark, 64
Fields, Mrs. Debbie, 70
Fingers, Rollie, 102, 213–214
Finley, Charlie, 70–72, 89, 154, 315
Finley, Steve, 90
Fishel, Bob, 265
Fisk, Carlton, 157–158
Flannagan, Mike, 172
Foiles, Hank, 58
Foster, George, 151
Fox, Nelson, 49, 184, 327, 329
Foxx, Jimmie, 17, 40–41, 105, 230, 282
Freese, Gene, 137
Fregosi, Jim, 90–91, 184
Frey, Jim, 169
Frisch, Frankie, 68, 230, 321
Fryman, Travis, 207
Furillo, Carl, 292

Gaedel, Eddie, 83–84, 233–235

Gaetti, Gary, 167
Gagne, Greg, 122–123
Galvin, Pud, 357
Gant, Ron, 103
Gantner, Jim, 121–122
Garagiola, Joe, 7, 74–75, 320-321
Garcia, Mike, 289, 291
Garciaparra, Nomar, 219
Garvin, Jerry, 157
Gehrig, Lou, 17–18, 39, 52–53, 54, 107, 174, 214–215, 224, 228, 260, 264, 329, 338
Gehringer, Charley, 17, 267
Gentile, Jim, 43
Geronimo, Cesar, 142–143
Giamatti, A. Bartlett, 20
Giambi, Jason, 357
Gibson, Bob, 169, 176
Giles, Warren, 16
Goetz, Larry, 138
Gomez, Preston, 100–102
Gomez, Vernon "Lefty", 17, 27–28, 84–86, 172, 328
Gonzalez, Juan, 182, 224
Gooden, Dwight, 185, 206, 262, 340
Gooding, Gladys, 323-324
Goosen, Greg, 170
Gordon, Joe, 155
Goryl, Johnny, 207
Gowdy, Hank, 193
Grace, Mark, 340
Graffanino, Tony, 204

Gray, Pete, 25—26
Greenberg, Hank, 224, 264
Griffey, Jr., Ken, 64, 91–92, 117, 129, 219–220, 224, 307
Griffith, Clark, 333-334
Grimes, Burleigh, 131–132
Grimm, Charlie, 60–61, 63
Groat, Dick, 137
Groom, Bob, 46
Grote, Jim, 142
Grove, Lefty, 38
Gruber, Kelly, 161
Guerrero, Pedro, 121
Guidry, Ron, 114
Guillen, Jose, 199–200

Haas, Eddie, 31
Haddix, Harvey, 358-359
Haig, Alexander, 180
Halper, Barry, 98, 303
Hammer, M. C., 72
Harder, Mel, 253
Harmon, Chuck, 58
Harper, Terry, 130–131, 162
Harrah, Toby, 170
Harrelson, Bud, 355
Harridge, Will, 234
Hart, Mike, 264
Harwell, Ernie, 201
Hayes, Charlie, 154
Heath, Jeff, 293
Helf, Hank, 302
Henderson, Rickey, 183
Henrich, Tommy, 155–156

Roster

Henry, Doug, 202
Herman, Babe, 59, 72–74, 316-319
Herman, Billy, 53
Hernandez, Keith, 9
Hershiser, Orel, 104, 133, 178, 335
Herzog, Whitey, 168, 169, 172
Hoak, Don, 11, 358
Hodges, Gil, 115–116, 123
Hoiles, Chris, 144
Holloman, Alva "Bobo", 175
Holmes, Tommy, 287
Holtzman, Jerry, 237
Horlen, Joe, 172
Horner, Bob, 173
Hornsby, Roger, 87, 108, 151, 329, 339
Howard, Frank, 208
Howe, Art, 356
Hrabosky, Al, 328, 349
Hubbard, Glenn, 305
Hudlin, Willis, 281
Huggins, Miller, 76, 106, 108, 260, 338-339
Hundley, Todd, 78
Hunter, Brian, 337
Hunter, Jim "Catfish", 71, 241
Hurley, Ed, 234
Hurst, Bruce, 43, 351

Incaviglia, Pete, 312, 322
Jackson, "Shoeless" Joe, 256

Jackson, Reggie, 88–89, 146–147, 170, 171, 182, 186, 224, 241
James, Dion, 262–263
Jensen, Jackie, 323
Jeter, Derek, 354
John, Tommy, 203-204, 230
Johnson, Howard, 19–20
Johnson, Walter, 38, 46, 217, 277–279, 282, 301-302, 357
Jolley, Smead, 75, 322
Jones, Andruw, 204–205
Jones, Willie "Puddin' Head", 45
Jordan, Brian, 355
Jose, Felix, 121
Justice, David, 344

Kachline, Clifford, 39–40, 268, 276–277
Kay, Michael, 92, 96–98, 302–304
Keller, Charlie, 155
Kelly, Tom, 121–123
Kemp, Steve, 116
Kessinger, Don, 124
Kiner, Ralph, 78, 152–153
King, Clyde, 240
Kingman, David Arthur, 270–274
Kirby, Clay, 100–101
Klein, Chuck, 224, 334
Kluszewski, Ted, 61–62
Knight, Ray, 166, 262
Knowles, Darold, 88–89,

171
Koufax, Sandy, 178, 276
Kranepool, Ed, 170
krausse, Lew, 281
Kruk, John, 160, 163–164, 171
Kuhn, Bowie, 32

Lacy, Lee, 118
LaJoie, Larry, 268
Lajoie, Nap, 333-334
Lankford, Ray, 104, 355
Lansford, Carney, 161
Larkin, Barry, 150–151
LaRussa, Tony, 354-355
Lasorda, Tommy, 335, 336
Law, Ruth, 79–80
Lazzeri, Tony, 174
Leach, Rick, 216
Leary, Tim, 144–145
Lefebvre, Jim, 204
LeFlore, Ron, 135
Lemon, Bob, 240, 289
Lewis, Franklin, 244
Lind, Jose, 160
Lindblad, Paul, 102
Lindtrom, Freddie, 193
Linz, Phil, 66
Lofton, Kenny, 182
Logan, Johnny, 323
Long, Dale, 43
Lopez, Al, 289
Lowrey, Harold "Peanuts", 127
Luciano, Ron, 75
Lutz, Joe, 92–93
Lyons, Ted, 184

Roster

Macfarlane, Mike, 356
Mack, Ray, 23–24
Maddux, Greg, 217, 223, 225, 281
Magerkurth, George, 326-327
Maglie, Sal "The Barber", 149–150
Mantilla, Felix, 358
Mantle, Mickey, 40–42, 140, 182, 186, 201
Manwaring, Kirt, 199
Maranville, Rabbit, 195, 308
Marino, Dan, 216
Maris, Roger, 54, 93, 227, 357
Martin, Billy, 41, 123–124, 126, 145–146, 240–241, 309, 324
Martin, J. C., 140–141
Martin, John "Pepper", 68–69
Martinez, Carlos, 347
Martinez, Dennis, 186, 204, 212–213, 353-354
Martinez, Pedro, 360
Masi, Phil, 287
Mathews, Eddie, 215, 358
Mattingly, Don, 42–43, 114, 160, 216, 239–240
Mauch, Gene, 169, 322
May, Derrick, 223
Mayne, Brent, 103
Mays, Carl, 37
Mays, Willie, 149–150, 159,

214, 224, 230
McCarthy, Joe, 60, 84, 86
McCarver, Tim, 170
McCatty, Steve, 89
McClendon, Lloyd, 206
McCormick, Mike, 287
McCovey, Willie, 105
McCray, Rodney, 344
McDermott, Mickey, 326
McFarlane, Todd, 300-301
McGee, Willie, 104, 162–163, 203
McGraw, John, 308
McGraw, Tug, 170
McGriff, Fred, 264
McGwire, Mark, 54–56, 93–94, 103–104, 171, 185, 219, 275, 300-301, 355
McKechnie, Bill, 243
McLain, Denny, 176
McNeely, Earl, 193
McRae, Brian, 209–210
Medwick, Joe "Ducky", 60
Merced, Orlando, 164
Metzger, George, 22–23
Meusel, Bob, 107–108, 338-339
Michael, Gene, 240
Milan, Clyde, 12
Miller, Bing, 17
Miller, Eddie, 148
Miller, Ray, 350
Miller, Stu, 216
Mitchell, Dale, 256–257
Mitchell, Kevin, 64
Mize, Johnny, 49, 88,

254–255
Molitor, Paul, 121, 125, 186
Monday, Rick, 132, 190-191
Moon, Wally, 58
Moore, Charles, -22–23, 134
Moran, Charlie, 63
Moreno, Omar, 118
Morgan, Eddie, 282
Morgan, Joe, 186
Morris, Hal, 156–157
Moseby, Lloyd, 264
Mulholland, Terry, 9, 150
Mulliniks, Rance, 264
Mungo, Van Lingle, 195
Munson, Thurman, 140
Murcer, Bobby, 127, 239
Murdoch, Rupert, 294
Murphy, Edward T., 312–313
Murray, Eddie, 120, 121, 160, 186
Murtaugh, Danny, 359
Musial, Stan, 16, 40, 177, 248, 291, 296, 320

Nettles, Graig, 86, 89–90, 112–113, 127–128
Newhouser, Hal, 145–146
Nicholson, Bill, 333
Niedenfuer, Tom, 335
Niekro, Joe, 214, 230
Niekro, Phil, 114, 214, 230
Nilsson, Dave, 226
Noeth, LaVerne, 250

Roster

Norman, Fred, 118

Oates, Johnny, 144
O'Day, Hank, 308
O'Doul, Frank "Lefty", 294
O'Farrell, Bob, 107–108, 339
Ojeda, Bob, 262
Olerud, John, 213, 354
Olsen, C. E. "Pat", 264–265
Olson, Greg, 154
Ott, Mel, 186, 266, 308, 333-334
Owen, Marvin, 231–232
Owen, Mickey, 155
Owen, Spike, 158
Owens, Jesse, 245
Ozersky, Philip, 94

Paige, Satchel, 71, 165, 330
Palmeiro, Rafael, 206
Park, Chan Ho, 86
Pasquats, Dan, 157
Patkin, Max, 242, 244, 331-332
Pearson, Albie, 61–62, 310
Pelekoudas, Chris, 130
Pena, Tony, 212–213, 353-354, 356
Pendleton, Terry, 154
Percival, Troy, 349-350
Perez, Tony, 101, 230
Perry, Gaylord, 358
Pfirman, Charles, 147
Piazza, Mike, 186, 200, 219, 294–295
Pierce, Billy, 111

Piersall, Jimmy, 25, 330
Piniella, Lou, 119, 139, 156–157, 178, 240, 307
Plimpton, George, 189
Poffenberger, Cletus, 330
Polanco, Placido, 354
Polonia, Luis, 155
Poole, Jim, 104
Power, Vic, 215
Price, Jackie, 242–244
Pruett, Hub, 333

Quirk, Jamie, 77
Quisenberry, Dan, 77, 329

Ramirez, Manny, 182, 352
Ramos, Pedro, 41
Randolph, Willie, 121
Raschi, Vic, 123–124
Ready, Randy, 125
Reagan, President Ronald, 40
Reichler, Joe, 41
Reliford, Charlie, 352
Remy, Jerry, 351
Richards, Gene, 131, 162
Richards, Paul, 111, 317
Richert, Pete, 142
Rickey, Branch, 68, 293
Ridzik, Steve, 138
Righetti, Dave, 125
Rigney, Bill, 61
Ripken, Jr., Cal, 39, 182, 186, 228
Ripken, Sr., Cal, 39, 263
Ritter, Lawrence S., 274
Rivera, Ruben, 356-357

Rivers, Mickey, 309
Rizzuto, Phil, 95, 145–146, 161, 291
Roberts, Bip, 360
Robinson, Brooks, 182, 186
Robinson, Frank, 138, 214, 351
Robinson, Jackie, 109, 293, 342
Robinson, Wilbert, 79, 302, 317
Rodgers, Buck, 205–206
Roenicke, Gary, 151
Rogers, Kenny, 186
Rojas, Mel, 360
Rolen, Scott, 218–219
Rommel, Eddie, 281–284
Root, Charlie, 52–54
Rose, Pete, 40, 116, 184, 230, 250–251, 259, 298
Roth, Mark, 76
Rothschild, Larry, 207
Roush, Edd, 269–270, 274–275
Ruel, Muddy, 193
Ruth, Babe, 17–19, 36, 40, 52–56, 76, 89, 94–95, 107–109, 147, 151, 167, 180–181, 215, 230, 252–253, 260, 266, 283, 290-291, 323, 329, 332, 333, 338-339, 341-342
Ryan, Nolan, 230, 246, 276, 340

Sain, Johnny, 287

Roster

Salazar, Luis, 223
Salkeld, Bill, 287
Salmon, Tim, 219
Sanders, Deion, 170, 186
Santana, Rafael, 263
Sasser, Mackay, 150, 159–160
Schacht, Al, 329
Schaefer, Herman "Germany", 12–13, 319-320
Schilling, Curt, 226, 311-312
Schiraldi, Calvin, 223
Schofield, Dick, 121
Schroeder, Jay, 216
Score, Herb, 348
Scott, Everett, 39, 259–260
Scott, George, 86
Seedhouse, George E., 241
Selkirk, George, 174
Sewell, Joe, 34–36, 37–40, 175
Sewell, Truett "Rip", 147–148
Sheaffer, Danny, 217
Sheeby, Phil, 67
Sherdel, Bill, 147
Shooton, Burt, 334
Showalter, Buck, 103
Shuba, George "Shotgun", 296
Simmons, Al, 224, 282
Simmons, Curt, 130
Sisler, George, 268
Slaught, Don, 160, 164, 203

Slaughter, Enos, 191
Smalley, Roy, 112–113
Smith, Dave, 163
Smith, Lonnie, 180
Smith, Ozzie, 121, 186, 335
Smoltz, John, 154
Snider, Duke, 291, 324-325
Snyder, John, 236
Sosa, Sammy, 54, 56, 93, 184, 224
Southworth, Billy, 287
Spahn, Warren, 267
Speaker, Tris, 23, 39
Spiers, Bill, 212
Springstead, Marty, 173
Stack, Edward W., 50
Stanky, Eddie, 287
Steinbrenner, George, 89–90, 94, 179, 238–241
Stengel, Casey, 33, 79–82, 123–124, 145, 166, 170, 305, 324-326, 328
Stephens, Vern, 161
Sterling, John, 91, 96, 302
Stewart, Bill, 287
Stewart, Harry, 22
Stieb, Dave, 114
Stocker, Kevin, 110, 343
Stottlemeyre, Todd, 354
Street, Charles "Gabby", 301-302
Stuart, Dick, 88
Sutcliffe, Rick, 337
Sveum, Dave, 310
Sweeney, Mark, 356

Tanner, Chuck, 118
Taylor, Sammy, 16
Taylor, Tony, 13
Taylor, Zack, 83, 233
Tenace, Gene, 214
Terry, Bill, 59, 68
Tettleton, Mickey, 119
Thomas, Darrell, 201
Thomas, Henry W., 278
Thomas, Lee, 310
Thomassie, Pete, 21
Thompson, Fresco, 59
Thomson, Bobby, 137
Thomson, Mark, 236
Throneberry, Marv, 197, 325
Thurston, Hollis, 317
Tolan, Bobby, 213
Torberg, Jeff, 134, 184
Torre, Frank, 137, 168
Torre, Joe, 221
Trachel, Steve, 218
Trebelhorn, Tom, 168
Trillo, Manny, 206
Turner, Ted, 30–32, 169

Uecker, Bob, 167, 322
Umont, Frank, 322

Van Slyke, Andy, 156, 324, 336
Vargo, Ed, 131, 162
Veeck, Bill, 12, 82–84, 175, 233–235, 242–246, 327-328, 331
Velarde, Randy, 157–158
Ventura, Robin, 158, 227

Roster

Vitt, Oscar, 258

Waddell, George Edward "Rube", 276, 285
Wagner, Leon, 13—14
Waitkus, Eddie, 45
Walker, Harry "The Hat", 152
Wallach, Tim, 158
Ward, Turner, 204–205, 344-345
Washington, Claudell, 237–238
Weaver, Earl, 75–76, 166, 173, 322
Weiss, George, 95
Wells, David, 186, 290–291
West, Max, 10
Whitehill, Earl, 17
Whitt, Ernie, 263

Wilhelm, Hoyt, 230
Williams, Bernie, 345
Williams, Dick, 213
Williams, Matt, 163
Williams, Mitch, 177, 223
Williams, Ted, 23–24, 111, 148, 254-5, 296
Wills, Maury, 186, 197
Wilson, Craig, 235–236
Wilson, Don, 101
Wilson, Glenn, 170
Wilson, Hack, 34, 45, 174, 224
Wilson, Willie, 186
Windelstedt, Harry, 133
Winfield, Dave, 117, 186, 195-196, 200–201, 203, 239
Witt, Mike, 186
Womack, Tony, 179, 182

Wright, Clyde, 220
Wright, Jaret, 220
Wrigley, Phil, 99
Wynn, Early, 249, 289, 291
Wynn, Jimmy, 157

Yastrzemski, Carl, 176, 186, 230, 258–259, 261
Yeager, Steve, 22
Young, Cy, 48–49, 277, 284, 357
Young, Dick, 272
Young, Matt, 348
Yount, Robin, 121, 177

Zeile, Todd, 121
Zimmer, Don, 57, 112–113, 206–207